STORM OF STEEL

A worldwide bestseller published shortly after the end of World War I, *Storm of Steel* is a memoir of astonishing power, savagery, and ashen lyricism. It illuminates not only the horrors but also the fascination of total war, as seen through the eyes of an ordinary German soldier.

Young, tough, patriotic, but also disturbingly self-aware, Ernst Jünger exulted in the Great War, which he saw not just as a great national conflict but also—more importantly—as a unique personal struggle. Leading raiding parties, defending trenches against murderous British incursions, simply enduring as shells tore his comrades apart, Jünger keeps testing himself, braced for the death that will mark his failure.

"An articulate, often beautifully so, introduction to the world view of a different breed of man: the born warrior."
—Karl Marlantes, from the Foreword

"The definitive World War I account from the German point of view." —Margaret Atwood, *Entertainment Weekly*

"*Storm of Steel* is what so many books claim to be but are not: a classic account of war." —*London Evening Standard*

"Extraordinary . . . Michael Hofmann's superlative translation retains all the coruscating vitality of the original."
—Niall Ferguson, author of
Civilization, Colossus, and *The Ascent of Money*

PENGUIN CLASSICS (Ⓟ) DELUXE EDITION

STORM OF STEEL

ERNST JÜNGER (1895–1998) was born in Heidelberg, Germany. He ran away from school to enlist in the Foreign Legion and in 1914 volunteered to join the German army. He fought throughout the war and recorded his experiences in several books, most famously in *In Stahlgewittern* (*Storm of Steel*). While admired by the Nazis, he remained critical of them and through novels such as *On the Marble Cliffs* (1939) sought to understand the impasse into which Germany was heading. Throughout the Nazi period he was a controversial "inner emigrant," distanced from the regime yet only obliquely in opposition. His most famous later books include *Heliopolis* (1949), *The Glass Bees* (1957), *Eumeswil* (1977), *Aladdin's Problem* (1983), and *A Dangerous Encounter* (1985).

MICHAEL HOFMANN has translated Joseph Roth, Hans Fallada, Herta Müller, Zoë Jenny, Wim Wenders, Wolfgang Koeppen, Durs Grünbein, and Franz Kafka. He is a professor of English at the University of Florida.

KARL MARLANTES is the *New York Times* bestselling author of *Matterhorn* and *What It Is Like to Go to War*. He served as a Marine in the Vietnam War, where he was awarded the Navy Cross, the Bronze Star, two Navy Commendation Medals for valor, two Purple Hearts, and ten air medals. He lives near Duvall, Washington.

ERNST JÜNGER

Storm of Steel

Translated with an Introduction by
MICHAEL HOFMANN

Foreword by
KARL MARLANTES

PENGUIN BOOKS

PENGUIN BOOKS

An imprint of Penguin Random House LLC
375 Hudson Street
New York, New York 10014
penguin.com

In Stahlgewittern first published in Germany 1920
This final revised edition first published 1961
This translation made from the edition prepared from the *Saemtliche Werke,
vol. I: Der Erste Weltkrieg*. Klett-Cotta, Stuttgart, 1978
This translation first published in Great Britain by Allen Lane, an imprint of
Penguin Books, 2003
Published in Penguin Books 2004
This edition with a foreword by Karl Marlantes published 2016

Copyright © 1920, 1961 by J.G. Cotta'sche Buchhandlung Nachfolger
GmbH, Stuttgart
Introduction and translation copyright © 2003 by Michael Hofmann
Foreword © 2016 by Karl Marlantes

LIBRARY OF CONGRESS CATALOGING-IN-PUBLICATION DATA

Names: Jèunger, Ernst, 1895–1998 author. | Hofmann, Michael,
1957 August 25–translator.
Title: Storm of steel / Ernst Jèunger ; translated with an introduction by
Michael Hofmann ; foreword by Karl Marlantes.
Other titles: In Stahlgewittern. English
Description: New York City : Penguin Books, 2016. | "First published in
Germany 1920"—Introduction. | Includes bibliographical references.
Identifiers: LCCN 2015046875 | ISBN 9780143108252
Subjects: LCSH: Jèunger, Ernst, 1895–1998. | World War, 1914–1918—Personal
narratives, German. | Jèunger, Ernst, 1895–1998—Diaries. |
Soldiers—Germany—Diaries.
Classification: LCC D640 .J69313 2016 | DDC 940.4/144092—dc23

Printed in the United States of America
3   5   7   9   10   8   6   4

Set in Sabon

Contents

Foreword by KARL MARLANTES   vii
Introduction by MICHAEL HOFMANN   xiii
Bibliography   xxix

STORM OF STEEL

In the Chalk Trenches of Champagne   5
From Bazancourt to Hattonchâtel   16
Les Eparges   23
Douchy and Monchy   34
Daily Life in the Trenches   51
The Beginning of the Battle of the Somme   67
Guillemont   91
The Woods of St-Pierre-Vaast   111
Retreat from the Somme   121
In the Village of Fresnoy   131
Against Indian Opposition   141
Langemarck   156
Regniéville   180
Flanders Again   192
The Double Battle of Cambrai   204
At the Cojeul River   219
The Great Battle   224
British Gains   257
My Last Assault   274
We Fight Our Way Through   283

Foreword

Storm of Steel was constructed from the wartime diary of a very young man. Ernst Jünger experienced combat for the first time at the age of nineteen, in late December of 1914; he was twenty-three when the war ended. This is common: when I was a Marine infantry officer serving during the Vietnam War, the vast majority of Marines in my company were under twenty. What is uncommon is to write the raw material of a classic memoir at this age and then have it published at the age of twenty-five, just two years after the war's end.

It should surprise no one that Jünger's book contains almost no political, moral, or philosophical commentary: Young men generally don't think deeply or philosophize about most things. But the lack of such commentary is not just because of the author's age; it is also because *Storm of Steel* was written by the type of person I call a "born warrior." Born warriors are interested in war and fighting, not philosophy or politics.

During my own war, I had the privilege of living in close proximity to born warriors. The Marine Corps has a lot of them. I am not one of them. I would consider myself a citizen soldier, and most of the young men I served with were citizen soldiers as well. We became warriors, through either volunteering or being drafted, for the time that we were needed by our country. As soon as we could, we left the military and returned home. Born warriors are different. For them, war *is* home. They like to fight.

It is too often assumed that if someone is at home in war and likes to fight, then that makes him somehow cruel or lacking in compassion or even sociopathic. The born warriors I lived with wept when their friends died, were often frightened, struggled with issues of when to kill and when not to kill, missed their girlfriends, and appreciated the song of a bird or a beautiful jungle stream just like the rest of us. They, however, experienced war not as something to endure but as something meaningful to them, something they wanted to engage in more than anything else. Think about a born musician who gets clinically depressed if she is unable to play her instrument, or how differently she experiences a string quartet from the rest of us.

One of the many born warriors I knew was George Jmaeff, a young Canadian who came south and joined the U.S. Marines to fight in Vietnam. He was about six foot three, looked like Errol Flynn, and carried a sawed-off M-60 machine gun—normally a crew-served weapon, but he had modified it so he could wield it alone. He always walked point. He always volunteered for the dangerous jobs. "Canada," as everyone called him, was iconic, known and talked about all over the regiment. Yet he wasn't crazy or stupidly aggressive. He was levelheaded, cool under fire, and a born leader who did not expose his fellow Marines to unnecessary risk. In short, he was good at war.

One night I asked him what he was going to do when the war was over. He said, "Sir, I'd go crazy in the peacetime Marine Corps, but I don't think I'll go home. I was just born in the wrong country at the wrong time. I think I'll probably go to Biafra. I hear they're looking for mercenaries there." I didn't ask him which side he wanted to fight on, and I strongly suspect that he didn't particularly care, knowing as well as I did that both sides thought they were right and that it's exceedingly rare when one side has clear claim to any moral high ground. If Canada had been born in China, he would have come south to join the North Vietnamese Army (NVA).

Warriors choose sides. This is why they are very different from police, who must be on the side of the law. I am quite sure that Jünger was on Germany's side for no other reason than that he was German, much as Robert E. Lee chose to fight for Virginia, without regard for Virginia's position on slavery, because he was a Virginian. Had I been born in Germany in 1920, I would have joined the Wehrmacht. Samurai—archetypal warriors—commit ritual suicide when they disagree with their lord rather than desert him or switch sides. We don't choose, as Heidegger puts it, how we are "thrown into the world." We choose how we conduct ourselves.

My fellow Marine Canada was badly wounded in an assault. He was honorably out of the fight, in the care of a U.S. Navy corpsman, lying on the ground receiving IV fluid for loss of blood and shock, when he heard that his platoon was pinned down by an NVA machine gun. He tore the IV tubes from his arm, grabbed an M-16, and took out the enemy machine gun, saving the lives of many of his friends. He died doing it and was awarded a posthumous Navy Cross. Canada was different.

So was Jünger. He ran away from home in 1913 to join the French Foreign Legion and trained briefly in North Africa before returning to Germany. Over the course of the war, he was wounded fourteen times. He held an Iron Cross First Class and was the youngest person ever to be awarded Germany's highest medal for valor, the Pour le Merité, also known as the Blue Max. He could easily have found a safer billet or even managed on many occasions to get honorably invalided out of duty. Instead he chose to return, again and again. Toward the war's end, he was part of a new kind of infantry unit, Sturmtruppen, or storm troopers, who were specialists trained to attack in a method that successfully overcame the stalemate of trench warfare and whose tactics are now standard for all infantry units. When Germany entered World War II, Jünger volunteered to serve again, and he did, although he was too old for combat.

Storm of Steel, while widely acclaimed, has been criticized for glorifying war. I don't read it this way. Jünger's descriptions of carnage and filth are unadorned, neither lamented nor romanticized. What Jünger thought or felt at the time is largely absent in the narrative and hence unknown from this source. He offers no commentary on why Germany was fighting or why he was fighting for Germany. I think there are three reasons why he might have recorded his experiences in the way he did.

First, his memoir was taken from his diary, which was written *immediately after* the incidents occurred. In combat, humans are typically numb from the horror of it; this is what gets them through.

When I was in combat, I felt very little about carnage and death; I was terribly busy trying to get the job done and survive. Years later, I felt a great deal. *Storm of Steel* was published just two years after Jünger stopped fighting. There was no "years later" for him.

The second reason is that I think it was against Jünger's warrior code of honor to write about his experiences in other than a factual, nonjudgmental, noneditorialized way. I get the feeling that Jünger would have been dismayed, maybe even disgusted, at the way we emote about our experiences today. His warrior code of honor is evident throughout his memoir.

The third reason is that warriors, indeed most soldiers, are focused on staying alive and keeping their friends alive. They don't think or talk about whether war is moral. They don't ponder why they are fighting for their country or whether their country was right to put them in battle. They don't think about foreign policy—and they certainly don't make it. I once asked my father and one of my uncles, both veterans of World War II, if they thought about beating fascism and saving democracy when they were fighting in Europe. They both laughed out loud. My uncle said: "We just wanted to get it over with and come home in one piece. That's *all* we thought about."

Jünger was different in his attitude about wanting to get it over with and go home. After returning to the fighting in Flanders from a month's rest in Cambrai, he is subjected to intense artillery fire for days:

> In the evening, the shelling waxed to a demented fury. Ahead of us, coloured flares went up in a continual stream. Dust-covered runners reported that the enemy was attacking. After weeks of drumming [being shelled], the infantry battle was about to begin; we had come at the right time.

I would have said we had come at the *wrong* time.

But like Jünger, who observed the stream of colored flares, I can appreciate that, borrowing a phrase from Yeats, there is a terrible beauty about war, even though I'm not a born warrior. I remember watching enemy tracers seeming to float into the night sky over Laos, seeking to down one of our airplanes, in much the same way I'd watch fireworks. I remember even being enthralled, late in my tour when I'd been transferred to an air observer squadron, by green tracers flying by both windows of our OV-10 as we dived firing, head to head with an NVA antiaircraft gun. Jünger sees the beauty—it's everywhere in his memoir—and perhaps you will see it too. This doesn't need to change how you judge war; corral snakes and tsunamis are beautiful too.

In another scene, Jünger describes a fierce skirmish with Indian soldiers from the First Hariana Lancers:

> With only twenty men we had seen off a detachment several times larger, and attacking us from more than one side, and in spite of the fact that we had orders to withdraw if we were outnumbered. It was precisely an engagement like this that I'd been dreaming of during the *longueurs* of positional warfare.

I'd have been dreaming of my high school girlfriends.

"These short expeditions," Jünger writes, "where a man takes his life in his hands, were a good means of testing our mettle and interrupting the monotony of trench life. There's nothing worse for a soldier than boredom." I would say homesickness, hunger, hypothermia, getting gassed, gangrene, and trench foot, not to mention getting killed or maimed, would all be worse than boredom. But Jünger was different.

Jünger writes about many things other than combat, but all take us into the trenches as he saw them. He writes about fear and panic. He writes about nature—about having to live outside, just like a wild animal, in all of nature's cruelty and beauty. He writes about the code of honor and manliness that engenders mutual respect between soldiers on opposite sides of the battle, as when he encountered a young British officer just before Christmas during a poignant temporary truce that unfortunately went bad:

> We did, though, say much to one another that betokened an almost sportsmanlike admiration for the other, and I'm sure we should have liked to exchange mementoes.

At another point he writes:

> Throughout the war, it was always my endeavour to view my
> opponent without animus, and to form an opinion of him as
> a man on the basis of the courage he showed.

And he writes about the understated and often gallows humor
that goes hand in hand with the code of honor and manliness. I
remember in Vietnam a kid waiting to be medevaced, gasping for
air because he'd taken a bullet through one lung, saying, "You
know, sir, it ruined my whole day." Jünger often uses such humor:

> We suffered many casualties from the over-familiarity engen-
> dered by daily encounters with gunpowder.
> My dugout was somewhat changed as well . . . the British
> had fumigated it with a few hand-grenades.
> We were so abundantly graced with trench mortars . . .

And when describing the aforementioned Christmas truce
gone bad:

> It was all in all a less than merry Christmas.

In *Storm of Steel*, we read of a young soldier bearing with
courage, dignity, and humor the terrors of war in the trenches.
We watch him encounter a French girl and interact politely, even
genially, with families upon whom he is forcibly quartered. We
see a boy trying to become a man, as he defines one, and we see
him succeeding. Most of all, however, *Storm of Steel* is an articulate, often beautifully so, introduction to the worldview of a
different breed of man: the born warrior.

Karl Marlantes

Introduction

Storm of Steel (*In Stahlgewittern* is the original title) is one of the great books of World War I, if not the greatest. All sorts of trustworthy and unlikely people – and trustworthy often precisely *because* unlikely: cosmopolites, left-wingers, non-combatants – have stepped up to express their admiration, often in suitably embarrassed or bemused fashion: Böll and Borges, Enzensberger and Brecht, Gide and Moravia. In 1942, Gide wrote in his diary: 'Ernst Jünger's book on the 1914 War, *Storm of Steel*, is without question the finest book on war that I know: utterly honest, truthful, in good faith.' *no context or politics or stratgy*

Its contrast with most of the others is stark. It has no pacifist design. It makes no personal appeal. It is a notably *unconstructed* book. It does not set its author and his experience in any sort of context. It offers nothing in the way of hows and whys, it is pure where and when and of course, above all, what. There is nothing in it about the politics of the war – nothing even on its *join* *outcome* – and very little on the wider strategy of its conduct. It begins the moment Private Ernst Jünger first detrains in France, on 27 December 1914, at the age of nineteen, with (though we aren't told this) a rushed school-leaving certificate and a couple of months' training behind him, having volunteered on 1 August, the opening day of the war. (It is hard to imagine an English autobiographer or belletrist – a Graves or a Sassoon, amateur and holistic – wouldn't have included that, or indeed the fact that the year before, as a bored romantic youth full of wanderlust, he had run away to Algeria to join the French Foreign Legion!) It ends, in one of a bare handful of scenes that are away from the action, back in Germany four years later, when he is too badly hurt to carry on, a decorated lieutenant and the youngest-ever recipient of the *pour le Mérite*. War is all – fighting is all – everything else is cropped away. And, from first to last, in the affirmative. It is the work of a man whom the war made – and who, in World War II, was to be again – a professional soldier. It was published long before the likes of Blunden, Graves, Remarque and Sassoon, all of which appeared in the late 1920s, at a classic ten-year distance from the events they describe, giving their public and themselves time to recover; only Barbusse's novel *Le Feu* (*Under Fire*), from 1917, came out much before Ernst Jünger's account was first privately printed with a local firm (the family gardener, Robert Meier, was designated as the 'publisher') in 1920, at the instigation of Jünger's father. The impressively cumbersome original title was *In Storms of Steel: from the Diary of a Shock Troop Commander, Ernst Jünger, War Volunteer, and subsequently Lieutenant in the Rifle Regiment of Prince Albrecht of Prussia (73rd Hanoverian Regiment).*

The initial print-run was 2,000, the intended readership presumably members of the regiment and other veterans, and the work, in literary terms, was undistinguished and at times, apparently – hardly a surprise, considering its author's repeated rush to get out of school – 'even fell short of the required standard for a sixth-form essay'. The 'diary' element, though never entirely suppressed later, was initially mostly all there was, closely following the sixteen notebooks Jünger filled during the war. The book steadily sold through its small printings, but it wasn't the instant bestseller it is sometimes thought to have been. Jünger was recruited by Mittler & Son, a noted publisher of militaria in Berlin, and wrote more books on the war, including the viscerally – as well as headily – unpleasant treatise *On Battle as an Inner*

other books

Experience (1922) – of which I could not bring myself to read more than the excerpts I read years ago in a book on German history – and a couple of spin-offs covering material from *Storm of Steel* in a more lingering and opinionated way: *Copse 125* (1925) and *Fire and Blood* (1925). A shot at a novel, *Sturm* – after one of the characters, *nomen est omen* – was abandoned after a few instalments. In the mid 1920s, then, Jünger was already a prolific and established war writer before such a thing really existed. (His first non-war book, a memoir of his childhood, didn't appear until 1929.) Even so, acute observers were afraid they might lose Jünger the soldier to literature. On balance, I suppose, that's what happened, but it's a close call. Jünger has remained as much identified with World War I – or war in general – as with writing. I forget who it was who said they couldn't picture Jünger the author at all except in uniform. *Politicization of post-WWI Germany*

In the late 1920s, via Stahlhelm and the veterans' scene, he found himself as a publicist in nationalist politics. Because of the dearth of politics in Weimar, everything, paradoxically, was politicized; even the defeated generals, Ludendorff and Hindenburg, were rehabilitated as political figures. This is when Jünger made his notorious remark that he 'hated democracy like the plague', but to some extent that was what one might call 'Weimar talk'. Jünger was courted, not surprisingly, by the Nazis, and twice offered a seat in the Reichstag, but he wasn't interested. He didn't join the Deutsche Akademie der Dichtung (chaired for a year by the poet Gottfried Benn), nor was he ever a member of the Nazi Party. He and Hitler did exchange signed copies of their books, but even that seems like a mismatch: *My Struggle* for *Fire and Blood*. There was always something aloof and solipsistic about Jünger – the word 'aristocratic' is often misapplied to him – that meant that as a soldier and a writer and even an ideologue he was in it for himself, and never quite, at that. He was not a novelist or a politician or a *penseur*, though with elements of all three. He may have described himself as 'a field marshal of ideas',

Fought in WWII (Paris)

but, as Thomas Nevin drily remarks, 'he calls no philosophical system to attention'. It is hugely to Jünger's credit (though it is as much a matter of temperament as of choice) that he was never an opportunist – if anything, rather the opposite. The 1930s were a boom time for him – sales of *Storm of Steel* shot into six figures – but he retired from the public eye: left Berlin, wrote essays that – irritatingly for the Nazis – were aimed always beyond the present and the immediate future, wrote on entomology (the other passion of his life), travelled widely in Europe and further afield, lived quietly with his family in rural seclusion.

WWII

In 1939, he was back in uniform, and promoted to captain. He spent most of World War II with the German occupation in Paris, consorting with French intellectuals, eating and drinking and buying old books – and keeping a record of all these activities, and of a discreet political dissent, in his diaries, later published as *Strahlungen* (*Irradiations* might be the best English equivalent). These confirm (along with *Storm of Steel*, of course) that his gifts as a writer are primarily those of a diarist: descriptiveness and an ear for speech, attention to detail, mobility of perspective, intellectual stamina and disjunctiveness, at his best over medium distances, as a writer of passages rather than of books or sentences. After the war, Jünger's stock was predictably lower, and for a time he was not allowed to publish in Germany. But as early as 1955 he was (for the first time in his life) winning literary prizes, and in 1957 he began his association with the German publisher Klett that saw not one but two editions of his *Collected Works*, one completed in ten volumes in 1965, the second in eighteen in 1983. (Along with Wieland, Klopstock and Goethe, Jünger is one of only four German authors prolific and important and long-lived enough to see their own 'second edition'.) By the time of his death in 1998, at the age of a hundred and two, he had been heaped with virtually all the literary and civic honours Germany – and indeed Europe – had to bestow. He enjoyed a particularly devoted following in France, where one critic reckoned up an astonishing forty-eight of his works in print.

Age both softened and exacerbated Jünger's provocativeness. On the one hand, it provided him with distractions and luxuries, made him venerable and respectable (he was an incarnation of Yeats's senatorial 'smiling public man'); on the other, his mere continued existence was enough to goad to fury a wide band of literary and political enemies in Germany. Whether he wanted to or not – and he was often travelling the globe, researching unusual life-forms in remote settings – he remained a rallying-point and an object of fascination for the Fascist Right, and of horror and embarrassment for the Left. Honorific occasions involving Jünger, like the award of the Goethe Prize in 1982 – which at the time was compared to something that might have happened in Weimar – would invariably degenerate into *typisch deutsch* literary-political showdowns – very ugly and terribly principled. As an instance of the unbridled hatred felt for Jünger in certain quarters, in the 1990s, in Berlin – only in Berlin! – a gay musical version of *Storm of Steel* played to appreciative houses: a multiple and systematic persiflage of an experience and values that to him were sacred. One doesn't know whether to laugh or cry.

A very long life, like Jünger's (the name, by the way, does indeed mean 'younger'), brings with it a preoccupation with its form, with its meaning, with its straightness. This is something one sees as well in such survivor figures as the Norwegian Knut Hamsun (who lived to ninety-three), Ezra Pound (eighty-seven), or Boris Pasternak (a stripling seventy). Where Richard II says, 'Arm, my name,' Jünger seems to say, 'Arm, my age.' He refers, I don't know how humorously, to his early – pre-1930? – writing as his 'Old Testament'. He quotes Ranke on the desirability for historians of attaining a great age. It must be tempting – perhaps especially if one happens to be a diarist as well – to look down on younger people and say: what do they know? According to Octavio Paz, the claim to be the father of one's antagonist is a

8 versions

serious snub in Mexico. In 1984, a very old and spry Jünger turned out at Verdun with Helmut Kohl (whose favourite author he was) and François Mitterand (another admirer) to celebrate Franco-German reconciliation. Book titles underline his authority: *Siebzig verweht* (*Seventy Gone*, his journals of the 1970s), *Zwei Mal Halley* (*Halley Two Times*, a reference to the comet, which he saw in 1910, and again in 1986). Jünger made the claim that he had never regretted anything he had written, or taken anything back. In fact, his literary output and profile were subject to minute supervision and protection, by the author, his family, his publishers, his estate. (Cocteau observed pricelessly that Jünger 'didn't have dirty hands, he had no hands'.) Nothing resembling a biography appeared before the late 1980s. Some books of his were retired, others promoted. One of the English studies on him, by Elliot Neaman, has a section heading lapidarily called: '*Jünger revididus*'; it may not be good Latin, but it's a good joke.

The most revised of his books was the earliest of them, precisely *Storm of Steel*. Typically, there is as yet no full-length study of the changes that were made – though there is no shortage of adversarial and defensive and specialist writing on Jünger – but it seems there were as many as *eight* different published versions of the book: the earliest in 1920, for first publication, the latest in 1961, for the first edition of the *Collected Works*. No Jünger text, one critic groused, has ever been called definitive. (Even the copy I worked from seemed not to carry a date or ascription, although I'm sure it was the newest version.) In between, the most substantively different texts were those of 1924 and 1934. It is because of this that, even if I had wanted to, I couldn't have left out of my introduction all mention of Jünger's remaining eighty-odd years. *Storm of Steel* accompanied Jünger through most of his extremely long life, and he tinkered with it, one would have to say, obsessively. It was often tempting to put away the discussions of him once they got past the war, and pretend that

Jünger had died, or disappeared into obscurity or unconten-
tiousness, but because the later ideas and contexts have some
influence, to say the least, on a kind of text-*fleuve* that evolved
over the best part of sixty years, I had at least to allude to
them in passing. As well as being one of the earliest books on
World War I, *Storm of Steel* is also one of the newest, and it
seems likely that it gained in both respects. If one might put it
like this, in addition to outflanking the competition by getting in
ahead of them, *Storm of Steel* also outlasted them: the experience
it offers the reader is both more immediate and more considered,
more naively open-ended and more artistically complex, more
Sartre-ish and more – what shall I say? – Paterian.

The first revision was in 1924, when Jünger completely rewrote
his book for his new publisher. This first revised edition has been
called the first 'literary' version of *Storm of Steel*. It was also a
vigorously, even aggressively, Nationalist version, which may
have played well with the domestic audience of that time, but
perhaps less well abroad. It was, as luck would have it, this
version that was translated into English in 1929, and French in
1930. In the copy of Basil Creighton's English translation that I
have, there is a somewhat ingratiating 'Author's Preface to the
English Edition', with references to Gibraltar and Waterloo,
where Jünger's Hanoverian regiment – or, rather, their predecessors – had made common cause with the English against the
French, and careful compliments on the bravery and manliness
of the British: 'Of all the troops who were opposed to the
Germans on the great battlefields the English were not only
the most formidable but the manliest and the most chivalrous.'
But, once into the book, for instance in the chapter 'The Great
Offensive', there are passages like this:

It [the trench] seethed with English. I fired off my cartridges so fiercely
that I pressed [*sic*] the trigger ten times at least after the last shot. [. . .]
Only a few got away. A NCO was standing near me gaping at this

spectacle with mouth agog. I snatched the rifle from his hands in an uncontrollable need to shoot. My first victim was an Englishman whom I shot between two Germans at 150 metres. He snapped shut like the blade of a knife and lay still.

This explicit bloodlust is tempered by Jünger in later editions. Also gone is most of the generalizing and editorializing, much of it completely banal, as for example this sentence (earlier on in the same chapter): 'No one who has lived through moments like these can doubt that the course of nations in the last resort rises and falls with the destiny of war.' Gone too is the fanfare at the very end: 'Though force without and barbarity within conglomerate in sombre clouds, yet so long as the blade of a sword will strike a spark in the night may it be said: Germany lives and Germany shall never go under!' I suspect that it was the awareness that he was now read by an international public, as well as tact and personal maturity and a sense of the prevailing levels of violence and irresponsibility in public speech in Germany, that acted on Jünger. His 1934 revision was dubbed the 'quiet' version by one recent critic. The impartial dedication, 'For the fallen', was new. Just as it was ironic that it was the most bloody and rhetorical version of *Storm of Steel* that was spread abroad, so it was ironic that the Nazis presumably had to content themselves with this one when they boosted the book at home, in the years of the Third Reich.

To me, the metamorphoses of *Storm of Steel* on its journey from fighting to writing principally go to show one thing: that this is an indestructible book, clear, trustworthy, close to events and full of matter. Already it has survived its author, whose best-known work it will, I suspect, remain. It has also, I have to say, survived Basil Creighton's translation. In theory, it is always an advantage for a translator to be close to his original in time, and I imagine – though I don't know – that Creighton would also have fought – but his knowledge of German was patchy, his

Creighton translation

understanding of Jünger negligible, and his book seems much older and staler than his original. There are literally hundreds of coarsenesses, mistakes and nonsenses in his translation; open it at just about any page and you start to find them. These range from trivial mistakes over prepositions like, 'This typical forward movement made me sure that we were in for it *till* nightfall' (my italics), whereas what Jünger means, evidently, is 'that we were in for some action *before* nightfall' (p. 277); to errors of sense, like the 'unobtrusive' blowing up of church towers, to rob the enemy artillery of landmarks, where what is meant rather is their 'unceremonious' blowing up (p. 133), in such a way that it almost occasions casualties, or his 'airplanes tied with streamers', which should have been 'rosette-decorated aircraft' (i.e., Royal Air Force planes) (p. 170); the loss of tone, as in a description of a type of shell being 'different and far worse', when Jünger's typical bravado demands 'altogether more exciting[ly]' (p. 45), or Christmas being spent 'in this miserable fashion' (for 'recht ungemütlich'), instead of the cooler and less plaintive 'less than merry Christmas' (p. 59); to a failure to recognize German figurative speech, so that he has 'Unfortunately, the enemy was so plentifully supplied with munitions that at first it took our breath away,' and not 'Unfortunately, our opponents tended to have more munitions than ourselves, and so could play the game for longer' (the German phrase is 'einen langen Atem haben', literally, 'to have a long breath', and hence stamina) (p. 66), or 'We were soon beyond the zone of the light field guns and slackened our pace, as only a bird of ill-omen need expect to be hit by an isolated heavy,' which is incomprehensible, unless you know what it means: 'Before long, we were out of range of the light artillery, and could slow down, as the isolated heavy shells would only strike you if your number was up' (p. 253), which revolves around the German 'Pechvogel', or 'unlucky person or thing'. At the most entertaining extreme, it is the sort of 'howler' beloved of Classics masters, as in this sentence: 'The pleasure of my return was dashed by an unexpected alarm which had for me the peculiarly unpleasant consequence that I had to ride the company charger to Beaumont.' Was it really that bad? Creighton is only one letter out, but unfortunately, as it often does, it makes quite a difference: the German is 'Gefechtstross', not 'Gefechtsross'. What Jünger actually had to do was 'accompany the baggage train to Beaumont' (p. 131). An instance of a silent howler, a kind of literary whimper – mistranslation shows more commonly as fatuity than disgrace – is the following passage in Creighton: 'Streamers of black and white and red crossed the cloudless blue of the evening sky. The beams of the sunset dipped them in a tender rosy red so that they resembled a flight of flamingoes. We unfolded our trench-maps and spread them out to see how far we had penetrated the enemy lines.' This is not a children's party, or an – even for Jünger – unusually tender pastoral moment, rather it once again involves the air force:

The cloudless evening sky was crossed by a squadron of planes marked with our black, red and white. The last rays of the sun, which had already gone down, daubed them a shade of delicate pink, so they looked like flamingoes. We opened out our maps, and turned them face down, indicating to those above how far we had already pushed into the enemy line. (p. 249)

Creighton's translation has had a good long innings, but I fancy it's time it was retired.

If I might be allowed a couple of almost theoretical observations on what is a joyfully accessible and straight-ahead kind of book, I would like first to put the idea of a star shape in the reader's mind. The characteristic focus and form, it seems to me, of *Storm of Steel* is just such an in-and-out, the points and capes, the nooks and spines. It is not actually the most tightly drawn book one can imagine: that would have made it a small circle. Jünger is able, for instance, to accommodate the record of his brother Friedrich's ordeal at St-Pierre-Vaast; he generalizes beyond his own particular experience; he offers thoughts on the conduct of war, and of future wars; he does take us out of France and Flanders at moments; and, while the most characteristic depth of focus of the book is maybe ten yards or so – the interiors, the trenches and dugouts, the cars and lorries, the ruined houses, the beautiful, cultivated catalogues of war junk (like the one on p. 94) – still, there are also equally memorable distance shots, repeatedly of the sky, and of the colours and sounds of various ordnance, moments of eerie contemplation, like the background of a Renaissance portrait, and with just that in-and-out effect:

On the isolated heights on the way to Ransart was the ruin of a one-time *estaminet* – dubbed 'Bellevue' on account of the wide view of the front that was afforded from it – and that was a place I came to love, in spite of its exposed situation. From there, the view stretched over the dead land, whose defunct villages were linked by roads that had no traffic on them, and on which no living creature was to be seen. In the distance glimmered the outline of the abandoned city of Arras, and round to the right the shining chalk mine-craters of St Eloi. The weedy fields lay barren under the passing clouds and the shadows of clouds, and the tightly woven web of trenches spread its little white and yellow links, secured by lengthy communication trenches. From time to time, there was a puff of smoke from a shell, lobbed into the air as if by a ghostly hand; or the ball of a shrapnel hung over the wasteland like a great white flake slowly melting. The aspect of the landscape was dark and fantastic, the war had erased anything attractive or appealing from the scene, and etched its own brazen features, to appal the lonely onlooker. (pp. 38–9)

In terms of feeling, there is a similar story, describable in terms of 'hot' and 'cold': moments of resolute sang-froid and others of near-panic; being alone or with companions; being bored or in great danger or great exhilaration, that 'wild, unsuspected hilarity' he sees and feels in his first engagement (p. 24); anonymity and dandyishness, hebetude and exquisite sensitivity; nature and warfare; living in cosy near-domesticity and like animals in a hole in the ground. The same with the style, sometimes kept to the technicalities of a military situation report, and sometimes in the almost provocatively cultivated, French Symbolist notes on sound, colour, synaesthesia even, as in this notorious instance: 'Frequently, yellow rockets were shot off that blew up in the air, and sent a rain of fire cascading down, of a colour that somehow reminded me of the tone of a viola' (p. 114). Throughout, the book seems to me to have a hard, inorganic edge, which is why I have the impression of a star, rather than, say, an amoeba. The scenes, for example, with Jeanne, the girl living by herself in her cottage, seem ruthlessly trimmed back; or the references to friends and fellow officers of Jünger, or to home and family, which are never allowed to get blobby and out of hand. As I've shown already, the accounts of trench-fighting or assaults are similarly more disciplined and restrained than they once were. Even the composition of the book, veering between the minimalism of probably authentic diary entries in the chapter on 'Daily Life in the Trenches', and highly polished, written-up pieces of description that evolved much later, follows the jaggedness of the star shape. This, it seems to me, is one of Jünger's great freedoms and innovations.

The other is that, unlike any of the other World War I books I've read, *Storm of Steel* has found its way into natural epic form. The inspiration of most of the English books is lyrical or dramatic; they work with one-off contrasts and ironies; they fear repetition or excess of detail. They begin as they mean to go on, with misfortunes and reverses: Graves shelled by his own artillery; Blunden's grenade instructor blowing himself up with a bad grenade; Sassoon breaking a leg while riding before he ever gets to France. There is something bleakly – bracingly – comic about all three. At the most, they are *Entwicklungsromane*, narratives of the accrual of experience and the development of character. (There is nothing comic about Jünger whatsoever, and his few instances of rough humour do little to further German claims in that department.) *Storm of Steel* leaves all that behind: otherwise we should have had the escape to Algeria and much more. Similarly the twos and threes and fives of poetic and dramatic form are left behind: who can count the number of scenes and episodes in *Storm of Steel*? Jünger's first encounter with the war, after a few pages approaching it, is when the shell comes down in the gateway, and causes sudden carnage. There's nothing subversive about it, and nothing personal. It's not a book about survival, and I've never had that sense of that revelling (mistakenly) in one's own indestructibility that the political critics of Jünger say is a hallmark of Fascist writing. (It is there in other books of his.) There's a later, hyper-Nietzschean aphorism of Jünger's that goes: 'What doesn't kill me makes me stronger; and what kills me makes me incredibly strong.'

In the strangest way, *Storm of Steel* isn't really a personal book at all – it's about the war. In his World War II Diaries, there is this very suggestive idea: 'War isn't like a cake that the two sides divide up between them to the last crumb; there is always a piece left. That's the piece for the gods, and it remains outside the argument, and it elevates the fighting from sheer brutality and demonic violence. Homer knew and respected it.' *Storm of Steel* is about all of war, including that Olympians' share. Even the form of warfare in World War I – a mutual or reciprocal siege – seems somehow suitable for epic. As in *The Iliad*, it can be difficult to separate the momentous and the routine; that too is perhaps in the nature of war. Thomas Nevin notes: 'Marx had asked: "Is Achilles possible with gunpowder and lead?" Jünger had answered: "That was my problem."' Sometimes the progress seems slow and a little lumbering (Jünger's time as an observation officer I remember as a particularly quiet phase of the book), at other times the horror and excitement come pell-mell. There is repetition, there is detail of every sort, there is an effort to integrate war into nature, a military pastoral, the alternation of day and night, rain and shine, the wheel of the seasons: 'Each spring marked the beginning of a new year's fighting; intimations of a big offensive were as much part of the season as primroses and pussy-willows' (p. 141). All this is epic and celebratory. War and time and being are compounded into one great narcotic experience. (I could never understand, unless it was for doctrinal political reasons, why Sartre, asked about Jünger, said merely: 'I hate him.') At the same time, it's possible to read *Storm of Steel* without falling in thrall to war; one may even feel strengthened in one's pacifist convictions. It's a fair book, not a tract, and over the years and revisions I suspect it's become rather fairer. It has purpose – many purposes, even – but it's not designing or conniving.

Much of this is due to the way it ends. There is real weariness – the weariness, one might even conjecture, of a much older man – and a profoundly elegiac feeling in its last chapters. This is not a mendacious or literarily contrived withdrawal – Jünger is still attending to what's in front of him, and around him – but it is unexpected and, I think, deeply moving. It's the epic giving way to the tragic:

The nights brought heavy bombardments like swift, devastating summer thunderstorms. I would lie on my bunk on a mattress of fresh grass, and listen, with a strange and quite unjustified feeling of security, to the explosions all around that sent the sand trickling out of the walls. Or I would walk out to the fire-step to take in the mournful nocturnal scene, and the strange contrast between its heaviness and the fiery spectacle whose dance-floor it was.

At such moments, there crept over me a mood I hadn't known before. A profound reorientation, a reaction to so much time spent so intensely, on the edge. The seasons followed one another, it was winter and then it was summer again, but it was still war. I felt I had got tired, and used to the aspect of war, but it was from this familiarity that I observed what was in front of me in a new and subdued light. Things were less dazzlingly distinct. And I felt that the purpose with which I had gone out to fight had been used up, and no longer held. The war posed new, deeper puzzles. It was a strange time altogether. (p. 260)

It is still the Jünger repertoire, the contemplation, the casual fearlessness, the observation of huge and tiny things, the melancholy, the idea of the war-as-nature, the big metaphors, but with a new quality of introspection. (Though this too has a hard edge, it's momentary and continent and underplayed.) It's a moment of war-weariness, of *taedium belli*, surprising in such a one. For once, Jünger seems less like Achilles – sometimes he seems like Ajax – than like Hector. Influenza, enemy propaganda, bad food, silly accidents and foolish orders have all taken their toll, and twenty pages later, in the chapter called 'My Last Assault', there is what seems to me an utterly Homeric moment:

A figure in brown corduroy strode with equanimity across this fire-swept piece of terrain, and shook me by the hand. Kius and Boje, Captain Junker and Schaper, Schrader, Schläger, Heins, Findeisen, Höhlemann and Hoppenrath stood behind a hedge raked with lead and iron and talked through the attack. On many a day of wrath we had fought on one and the same battlefield, and today once more the sun, now low in the Western sky, was to gild the blood of all or nearly all.
[...]
It was our last storm. How many times over the last few years we had advanced into the setting sun in a similar frame of mind! Les Eparges, Guillemont, St-Pierre-Vaast, Langemarck, Passchendaele, Mœuvres, Vraucourt, Mory! Another gory carnival beckoned. (pp. 279–80)

Is this not majestic and surprising and beyond all contrivance in its sadness?
This is the reward of epic. A skimpier, less focused, less excessive,

less varied and venturesome book would never have mustered the layerings of repetition and endurance sufficient to produce this sudden deepening, this sudden *qualitative* change. The summaries (that 'hedge raked with lead and iron') might have been news, the heightening of the tone pretentious, the hint of alienation coquettish or already threadbare, and, in the two Homeric catalogues, the names might have been those of 'characters', and the sites of the battles pretty indistinguishable. Can you tell this, can you write about this? women queueing outside Stalin's prisons in the hope of seeing their sons and husbands asked the Russian poet Anna Akhmatova, there to see her own son, and, for whatever reason, she could. Ernst Jünger, for whatever reason, over decades, learned to tell his story of World War I.

Michael Hofmann
February 2003
Gainesville, Florida

Bibliography

General

Henri Barbusse, *Le Feu* (Paris, 1917)

Edmund Blunden, *Undertones of War* (London, 1928)

Geoff Dyer, *The Missing of the Somme* (London, 1994)

Paul Fussell, *The Great War and Modern Memory* (New York, 1975)

Robert Graves, *Goodbye to All That* (London, 1929)

Homer, *The Iliad*, trans. Robert Fagles (New York, 1990)

Ernst Jünger, *Auswahl aus dem Werk in Fünf Bänden*, Volume II
(*Das erste Pariser Tagebuch*; *Kaukasische Aufzeichnungen*; *Das zweite Pariser Tagebuch*) (Stuttgart, 1994)

——, *Copse 125*, trans. Basil Creighton (London, 1930)

——, *The Storm of Steel*, trans. Basil Creighton (London, 1929)

John Keegan, *The Face of Battle* (London, 1976)

Gert Ledig, *Die Stalinorgel* (Hamburg, 1955)

——, *Vergeltung* (Frankfurt, 1956)

——, *Faustrecht* (Munich, 1957)

Sven Lindqvist, *A History of Bombing*, trans. Linda Haverty Rugg
(London, 2001)

Robin Prior and Trevor Wilson, *The First World War* (London, 1999)

Erich Maria Remarque, *Im Westen nichts Neues* (Berlin, 1929)

Siegfried Sassoon, *The Complete Memoirs of George Sherston*
(London, 1937)

John Silkin (ed.), *The Penguin Book of First World War Poetry* (rev.
  edn., London, 1996)
Leon Wolff, *In Flanders Fields: Passchendaele 1917* (London, 1959)

Particular

Heinz Ludwig Arnold, *Krieger, Waldgänger, Anarch* (Göttingen,
  1990)
—— (ed.), *TEXT UND KRITIK # 105/106* (Göttingen, 1990)
Norbert Dietka, *Ernst Jünger – vom Weltkrieg zum Weltfrieden*
  (Bad Honnef, 1994)
Gerhard Loose, *Ernst Jünger* (Bloomington, 1974)
Steffen Martus, *Ernst Jünger* (Stuttgart, 2001)
Elliot Y. Neaman, *A Dubious Past: Ernst Jünger and the Politics of
  Literature after Nazism* (Berkeley and Los Angeles, 1999)
Thomas Nevin, *Ernst Jünger and Germany: Into the Abyss,
  1914–1945* (Durham, NC, 1996)
Paul Noack, *Ernst Jünger – Eine Biographie* (Berlin, 1998)
Heimo Schwilk (ed.), *Ernst Jünger – Leben und Werk in Bildern und
  Texten* (Stuttgart, 1988)
J. P. Stern, *Ernst Jünger* (New Haven, 1953)
Johannes Volmert, *Ernst Jünger: 'In Stahlgewittern'* (Munich, 1985)

Storm of Steel

For the fallen

In the Chalk Trenches of Champagne

The train stopped at Bazancourt, a small town in Champagne, and we got out. Full of awe and incredulity, we listened to the slow grinding pulse of the front, a rhythm we were to become mightily familiar with over the years. The white ball of a shrapnel shell melted far off, suffusing the grey December sky. The breath of battle blew across to us, and we shuddered. Did we sense that almost all of us – some sooner, some later – were to be consumed by it, on days when the dark grumbling yonder would crash over our heads like an incessant thunder?

We had come from lecture halls, school desks and factory workbenches, and over the brief weeks of training, we had bonded together into one large and enthusiastic group. Grown up in an age of security, we shared a yearning for danger, for the experience of the extraordinary. We were enraptured by war. We had set out in a rain of flowers, in a drunken atmosphere of blood and roses. Surely the war had to supply us with what we wanted; the great, the overwhelming, the hallowed experience. We thought of it as manly, as action, a merry duelling party on flowered, blood-bedewed meadows. 'No finer death in all the world than . . .' Anything to participate, not to have to stay at home!

'Form up by platoon!' Our heated fantasies cooled down on the march through the claggy soil of Champagne. Knapsacks, munition belts and rifles hung round our necks like lead weights. 'Ease up! Keep up at the back!'

5

Finally we reached Orainville, one of the typical hamlets of the region, and the designated base for the 73rd Rifles, a group of fifty brick and limestone houses, grouped round a château in parkland.

Used as we were to the order of cities, the higgledy-piggledy life on the village streets struck us as exotic. We saw only a few, ragged, shy civilians; everywhere else soldiers in worn and tattered tunics, with faces weatherbeaten and often with a heavy growth of beard, strolling along at a slow pace, or standing in little clusters in doorways, watching our arrival with ribald remarks. In a gateway there was a glowing field kitchen, smelling of pea soup, surrounded by men jingling their mess-tins as they waited to eat. It seemed that, if anything, life was a little slower and duller here, an impression strengthened by the evidence of dilapidation in the village.

We spent our first night in a vast barn, and in the morning were paraded before the regimental adjutant, First Lieutenant von Brixen, in the courtyard of the château. I was assigned to the 9th Company.

Our first day of war was not to pass without making a decisive impression upon us. We were sitting over breakfast in the school where we were quartered. Suddenly there was a series of dull concussions, and all the soldiers rushed out of the houses towards the entrance of the village. We followed suit, not really knowing why. Again, there was a curious fluttering and whooshing sound over our heads, followed by a sudden, violent explosion. I was amazed at the way the men around me seemed to cower while running at full pelt, as though under some frightful threat. The whole thing struck me as faintly ridiculous, in the way of seeing people doing things one doesn't properly understand.

Immediately afterwards, groups of dark figures emerged on to the empty village street, carrying black bundles on canvas stretchers or fireman's lifts of their folded hands. I stared, with a queasy feeling of unreality, at a blood-spattered form with a strangely contorted leg hanging loosely down, wailing 'Help! Help!' as if sudden death still had him by the throat. He was carried into a building with a Red Cross flag draped over the doorway.

What was that about? War had shown its claws, and stripped off its mask of cosiness. It was all so strange, so impersonal. We had barely begun to think about the enemy, that mysterious, treacherous being somewhere. This event, so far beyond anything we had experienced, made such a powerful impression on us that it was difficult to understand what had happened. It was like a ghostly manifestation in broad daylight.

A shell had burst high up over the château entrance, and had hurled a cloud of stone and debris into the gateway, just as the occupants, alerted by the first shots, were rushing out. There were thirteen fatalities, including Gebhard the music master, whom I remembered well from the promenade concerts in Hanover. A tethered horse had had a keener sense of the approaching danger than the men, and had broken free a few seconds before, and galloped into the courtyard, where it remained unhurt.

Even though the shelling could recommence at any moment, I felt irresistibly drawn to the site of the calamity. Next to the spot where the shell had hit dangled a little sign where some wag had written 'Ordnance this way'. The castle was clearly felt to be a dangerous place. The road was reddened with pools of gore; riddled helmets and sword belts lay around. The heavy iron château gate was shredded and pierced by the impact of the explosive, the kerbstone was spattered with blood. My eyes were drawn to the place as if by a magnet; and a profound change went through me.

Talking to my comrades, I saw that the incident had rather blunted their enthusiasm for war. That it had also had an effect on me was instanced by numerous auditory hallucinations, so that I would mistake the trundling of a passing cart, say, for the ominous whirring of the deadly shell.

next pt better

"Hearing" "Shelling"

This was something that was to accompany us all through the war, that habit of jumping at any sudden and unexpected noise. Whether it was a train clattering past, a book falling to the floor, or a shout in the night – on each occasion, the heart would stop with a sense of mortal dread. It bore out the fact that for four years we lived in the shadow of death. The experience hit so hard in that dark country beyond consciousness, that every time there was a break with the usual, the porter Death would leap to the gates with hand upraised, like the figure above the dial on certain clock towers, who appears at the striking of the hour, with scythe and hourglass.

The evening of that same day brought the long-awaited moment of our moving, with full pack, up to battle stations. The road took us through the ruins of the village of Betricourt, looming spectrally out of the half-dark, to the so-called 'Pheasantry', an isolated forester's house, buried in some pine woods, where the regimental reserve was housed, of which, to this point, the 9th Company had formed a part. Their commander was Lieutenant Brahms.

We were welcomed, divided up into platoons, and before long found ourselves in the society of bearded, mud-daubed fellows, who greeted us with a kind of ironic benevolence. They asked us how things were back in Hanover, and whether the war might not be over soon. Then the conversation turned, with us all listening avidly, to short statements about earthworks, field kitchens, stretches of trench, shell bombardment, and other aspects of stationary warfare.

After a little while, a shout rang out in front of our cottage-like billet to 'Turn out!' We formed up into our platoons, and on the order 'Load and safety!' we felt a little twinge of arousal as we rammed clips of live ammunition into our magazines.

Then silent progress, in Indian file, through the landscape dobbed with dark patches of forest to the front. Isolated shots rang out from time to time, or a rocket flared up with a hiss to leave us in deeper darkness following its short spectral flash. Monotonous clink of rifles and field shovels, punctuated by the warning cry: 'Watch it, barbed wire!'

Then a sudden jingling crash and a man swearing: 'Dammit, why couldn't you tell me there's a crater!' A corporal shuts him up: 'Pipe down, for Christ's sake, do you think the French are wearing earplugs?' More rapid progress. The uncertain night, the flickering of flares and the slow crackling of rifle fire produce a kind of subdued excitement that keeps us strangely on our toes. From time to time, a stray bullet whines past chilly into the distance. How often since that first time I've gone up the line through dead scenery in that strange mood of melancholy exaltation!

At last we dropped into one of the communication trenches that wound their way through the night like white snakes to the front. There I found myself standing between a couple of traverses, lonely and shivering, staring hard into a line of pines in front of the trench, where my imagination conjured up all sorts of shadowy figures, while the occasional stray bullet slapped into the boughs and somersaulted down with a whistle. The only diversion in this seemingly endless time was being collected by an older comrade, and trotting off together down a long, narrow passage to an advance sentry post, where, once again, it was our job to gaze out into the terrain in front. I was given a couple of hours to try to find an exhausted sleep in a bare chalk dugout. When the sky lightened, I was pale and clay-daubed, and so was everyone else; I felt I had lived this sort of mole's life for many months already.

The regiment had taken up a position winding through the chalky Champagne soil, facing the village of Le Godat. On the right, it abutted a tattered area of woodland, the so-called 'Shell Wood', and from there it zigzagged across vast sugar-beet fields, where we could see the luminous red trousers of dead French attackers dotted about, to the course of a stream, across which

communications with the 74th Regiment were kept open by
patrols at night. The stream poured over the weir of a destroyed
mill ringed by brooding trees. For months, its water had been
laving the black parchment faces of the dead of a French colonial
regiment. An eerie place, especially at night, when the moon cast
moving shadows through breaks in the clouds, and the sounds
of the rushes and the murmuring water were joined by others less
easily accounted for.

The regimen was taxing, beginning at dusk, for which the
entire complement was made to stand to in the trench. Between
ten at night and six in the morning, only two men out of each
platoon were allowed to sleep at a time, which meant that we got
two hours a night each, though they were eaten into by being
woken early, having to fetch straw, and other occupations, so
that there were only a few minutes left as a rule.

Guard duty was either in the trench or else in one of the
numerous forward posts that were connected to the line by long,
buried saps; a type of insurance that was later given up, because
of their exposed position.

The endless, exhausting spells of sentry duty were bearable so
long as the weather happened to be fine, or even frosty; but it
became torture once the rain set in in January. Once the wet
had saturated the canvas sheeting overhead, and your coat and
uniform, and trickled down your body for hours on end, you got
into a mood that nothing could lighten, not even the sound of
the splashing feet of the man coming towards you to relieve you.
Dawn lit exhausted, clay-smeared figures who, pale and teeth
chattering, flung themselves down on the mouldy straw of their
dripping dugouts.

Those dugouts! They were holes hacked into the chalk, facing
the trench, roofed over with boards and a few shovelfuls of earth.
If it had been raining, they would drip for days afterwards; a
desperate waggishness kitted them out with names like 'Stalactite
Cavern', 'Men's Public Baths', and other such. If several men

Sleeping in trench dugouts

wanted to rest at the same time, they had no option but to stick their legs out into the trench, where anyone passing was bound to trip over them. In the circumstances, there was not much chance of sleep in the daytime either. Besides, we had two hours ✓ of sentry duty in the day too, as well as having to make running repairs to the trench, go for food, coffee, water, and whatever else. *1 battle = old stager*

Clearly, this unaccustomed type of existence hit us hard, especially since most of us had had only a nodding acquaintance with real work. Furthermore, we were not received out here with open arms, as we'd expected. The old-stagers took every opportunity to pull our legs, and every tedious or unexpected assignment was put the way of us 'war-wantons'. That instinct, which had survived the switch from barracks yard to war, and which did nothing to improve our mood, ceased after the first battle we fought in side by side, after which we saw ourselves as 'old-stagers'. *Reserve in earthen huts*

The period in which the company lay in reserve was not much cosier. We dwelt in fir-branch camouflaged earth huts round the 'Pheasantry' or in the Hiller Copse, whose dungy floors at least gave off a pleasant, fermenting warmth. Sometimes, though, you would wake up lying in several inches of water. Although 'roomy-dizzy' was just a name to me, after only a few nights of this involuntary immersion I felt pain in every one of my joints. I dreamed of iron balls trundling up and down my limbs. Nights here were not for sleeping either, but were used to deepen the *Digging* many communication trenches. In total darkness, if the French flares happened not to be lighting us up, we had to stick to the heels of the man in front with somnambulistic confidence if we weren't to lose ourselves altogether, and spent hours traipsing around the labyrinthine network of trenches. At least the digging was easy; only a thin layer of clay or loam covered the mighty thicknesses of chalk, which was easily cut by the pickaxe. Sometimes green sparks would fly up if the steel had encountered one of the fist-sized iron pyrite crystals that were sprinkled through-out the soft stone. These consisted of many little cubes clustered together, and, cut open, had a streakily goldy gleam.

A little ray of sunshine in all this monotony was the nightly arrival of the field kitchen in the corner of the Hiller Copse. When the cauldron was opened, it would release a delicious aroma of peas with ham, or some other wonder. Even here, though, there was a dark side: the dried vegetables, dubbed 'wire entangle-ments' or 'damaged crops' by disappointed gourmets.

In my diary entry for 6 January, I even find the irate note: 'In the evening, the field kitchen comes teetering up, with some god-awful pigswill, probably frozen beets boiled up.' On the 14th, by contrast: 'Delicious pea soup, four heavenly portions, till we groaned with satisfaction. We staged eating contests, and argued about the most favourable position. I contended that it was standing up.'

There were liberal helpings of a pale-red brandy, which had a strong taste of methylated spirits, but wasn't to be sneezed at in the cold wet weather. We drank it out of our mess-tin lids. The tobacco was similarly strong, and also plentiful. The image of the soldier that remains with me from those days is that of the sentry with his spiked, grey helmet, fists buried in the pockets of his greatcoat, standing behind the shooting-slit, blowing pipe smoke over his rifle butt.

Most pleasant were days off in Orainville, which were spent catching up on sleep, cleaning our clothes and gear, and drilling. The company was put in a vast barn that had only a couple of hen-roost ladders to facilitate entrances and exits. Although it was still full of straw, there were braziers lit in it. One night I rolled up against one, and was woken only by the efforts of several comrades pouring water over me. I was horrified to see that the back of my uniform was badly charred, and for some time to come I had to go around in what bore a passing resemblance to a pair of tails.

Disillusionment & Boredom

DEFENSIVE – Thinking

After only a short time with the regiment, we had become thoroughly disillusioned. Instead of the danger we'd hoped for, we had been given dirt, work and sleepless nights, getting through which required heroism of a sort, but hardly what we had in mind. Worse still was the boredom, which is still more enervating for the soldier than the proximity of death. *gets to front when trenches began*

We pinned our hopes on an attack; but we had picked a most unfavourable moment to join the front, because all movement had stopped. Even small-scale tactical initiatives were laid to rest as the trenches became more elaborate and the defensive fire more destructive. Only a few weeks before our arrival, a single company had risked one of these localized attacks over a few hundred yards, following a perfunctory artillery barrage. The French had simply picked them off, as on a shooting-range, and only a handful had got as far as the enemy wire; the few survivors spent the rest of the day lying low, till darkness fell and they were able to crawl back to their starting-point.

A contributory factor in the chronic overtiring of the troops was the way that trench warfare, which demanded a different way of keeping one's strength up, was still a novel and unexpected phenomenon as far as the officer corps was concerned. The great number of sentries and the incessant trench-digging were largely unnecessary, and even deleterious. It's not a question of the scale of the earthworks, but of the courage and condition of the men behind them. The ever-deeper trenches might protect against the odd head wound, but it also made for a defensive and security-conscious type of thinking, which we were loath to abandon later. Moreover, the demands made by the maintenance of the trenches were becoming ever-more exorbitant. The most disagreeable contingency was the onset of thaw, which caused the frost-cracked chalk facings of the trenches to disintegrate into a sludgy mess.

Of course we heard bullets whistling past our trench, and sometimes we got a few shells from the forts at Rheims, but these little trifling reminders of war came a long way below our expectations. Even so, we were occasionally reminded of the deadly earnest that lurked behind this seemingly aimless business. On 8 July, for instance, a shell struck the 'Pheasantry', and killed our battalion adjutant, Lieutenant Schmidt. The officer in command of the French artillery was, apparently, also the owner of that hunting lodge.

The artillery was still in an advanced position, just behind the front; there was even a field gun incorporated in the front line, rather inadequately concealed under tarpaulins. During a conversation I was having with the 'powderheads', I was surprised to notice that the whistling of rifle bullets bothered them much more than the crumps. That's just the way it is; the hazards of one's own line of service always seem more rational and less terrifying.

On the stroke of midnight, on 27 January,* we gave the Kaiser three cheers, and all along the front sang 'Heil dir im Siegerkranz' ['Hail thee mid the conquerors' round']. The French responded with rifle fire.

Some time round about then, I had a disagreeable experience which might have brought my military career to a premature and somewhat inglorious end. The company was on the left of the line, and towards dawn, following a night on duty, a comrade and I were detailed to go on double sentry duty by the stream bed. On account of the cold, I had, in breach of regulations, wrapped a blanket round my head, and was leaning against a tree, having set my rifle down in a bush next to me. On hearing a sudden noise behind me, I reached for my weapon – only to find it had disappeared! The duty officer had snuck up on me and taken it without my noticing. By way of punishment, he sent me, armed only with a pickaxe, towards the French posts about a hundred yards away – a cowboys-and-Indians notion that almost did for me. For, during my bizarre punishment watch, a troop of

* The birthday of Kaiser Wilhelm II (1859–1941).

14

three volunteers ventured forward through the wide reed bed, creating so much rustling that they were spotted right away by the French, and came under fire. One of them, a man called Lang, was hit and never seen again. Since I was standing hard by, I got my share of the then-fashionable platoon salvoes, so that the twigs of the willow tree I was standing next to were whipping round my ears. I gritted my teeth and, out of sheer cussedness, remained standing. As dusk fell, I was brought back to my unit.

We were all mightily pleased when we learned that we would finally leave this position, and we celebrated our departure from Orainville with a beery evening in the big barn. On 4 February, we marched back to Bazancourt, and a regiment of Saxons took our place.

From Bazancourt to Hattonchâtel

in cities)

In Bazancourt, a dull little town in Champagne, the company was quartered in the school, which, as a result of our exceptional tidiness, soon came to resemble a peacetime barracks. There was an orderly sergeant, who woke everyone punctually, barracks duty, and roll-call every evening, held by the corporal. In the morning, the companies moved out for a couple of hours' brisk drill and exercise on the barren fields outside town. I was taken out of this environment after a few days; my regiment was sending me on a training course to Recouvrence.

Recouvrence was a remote little village, nestling in pretty chalk hills, to where all the regiments in the division dispatched a few of their young men to receive a thorough schooling in military matters from a staff of hand-picked officers and NCOs. We of the 73rd had cause to be grateful to Lieutenant Hoppe for this – and for much else besides.

Life in this secluded hamlet was a strange mixture of barracks drill and academic leisure, attributable to the fact that the bulk of the participants had, until a few months before, been attending various lecture halls and faculties all over Germany. By day, the young people were honed into soldiers by all the rules of the art, while in the evenings, they and their teachers assembled around vast barrels brought over from the stores at Montcornet to display much the same degree of discipline and commitment – to drinking. When the various units trickled back from their respective

most = students

ALCOHOL

watering-holes in the early hours, the little chalk village houses were treated to the unfamiliar sight of student high jinks. The course director, a captain, had the pedagogical habit of expecting redoubled efforts in class the following morning.

On one occasion, we were even kept going for forty-eight hours straight. It was for the following reason. We had the respectful custom, at the end of a night's drinking, of giving our captain an escort home. One evening, an ungodly drunken fellow, who reminded me of Magister Laukhard,* was entrusted with this important task. He was back in next to no time, grinning widely and reporting that he had dropped the 'old man' off, not in his billet but in the cowshed.

Our comeuppance was not slow to follow. Just as we had got back to our own quarters for a good lie-down, the alarm was raised by the local watch. Swearing, we buckled on our gear and ran to our stations. We found the captain already there, in a towering temper, as might be imagined, and displaying an extraordinary zeal. He greeted us with the call: 'Fire-practice, the watch-house is on fire!' Physical punishment

Before the eyes of the astonished villagers, the fire-engine was trundled out of the fire station, the hose attached to it, and the guardroom was inundated with well-aimed sprays of water. The 'old man' stood on the stone steps with increasing ire, directing the exercise, and calling on us for unstinting efforts. Every so often, he bawled out some soldier or civilian who happened to provoke him especially, and gave orders for whoever it was to be led off. The unhappy fellow in question was quickly hauled off behind the building, safely out of sight. As dawn broke, we were still standing there, knees shaking, manning the pump. At last we were allowed to dismiss, though only to get ready for morning drill.

---

* A debased version of a Renaissance man (1758–1822): theologian, drunkard, soldier and spy. He fought in the Prussian army against Napoleon, was captured in 1792, and in 1795 managed to escape and return to Germany.

When we reached the drill ground, the old man was already there, clean-shaven, fresh and alert, all ready to devote himself with particular zeal to our training.

Relations between the men were very cordial. It was here that I made close friendships, which were to stand the test of many battlefields, with several outstanding fellows, among them Clement, who fell at Monchy, with the painter Tebbe (at Cambrai), and with the Steinforth brothers (at the Somme). Three or four of us roomed together, and shared a household. I particularly remember our regular scrambled egg and fried potato suppers. On Sundays, we ran to rabbit – a local speciality – or chicken. As I was the one in charge of making the purchases, our landlady once showed me a number of vouchers or promissory notes she had received from soldiers requisitioning food; a wonderful selection of earthy humour, generally to the effect that rifleman A. N. Other, having paid his homage to the charms of the daughter of the house, had needed a dozen eggs to help him recoup his strength.

ability to speak French

The villagers were quite astonished that we simple soldiers could all speak more or less fluent French. The circumstance gave rise to the occasional droll incident. Once, for instance, I was at the village barber's with Clement, when one of the waiting Frenchmen called out in his thick Champagne accent to the barber, who was just shaving Clement: 'Eh, coupe la gorge avec!' complete with sawing motions at his throat.

To his horror, Clement calmly replied: 'Quant à moi, j'aimerais mieux la garder,'* showing the kind of sang-froid that a warrior ought to have.

In mid-February, we of the 73rd felt consternation to hear of heavy losses taken by the regiment at Perthes, and felt desperate to be so far from our comrades at the time. The fierce defence of

---

* 'Why don't you just cut his throat with it!' . . . 'If it's all one to you, I'd just as soon hang on to it.'

our sector of the front in that 'witches' cauldron' got us the sobriquet 'The Lions of Perthes' that was to accompany us wherever we went on the Western Front. Besides that, we were also known as 'Les Gibraltars', on account of the blue Gibraltar colours we wore in memory of the regiment from which we traced our descent, the Hanoverian Guards, who defended the island fortress against the French and Spanish from 1779 to 1783.

The heavy news reached us in the middle of the night, as we were carousing as usual under the eye of Lieutenant Hoppe. One of the revellers, 'Beanpole' Behrens, the selfsame man who had dropped the captain off to bed in the cowshed, wanted to walk out the instant he heard, 'because the beer had lost its taste'. Hoppe held him back, observing that to do so would be unsoldierly. And Hoppe was right too; he himself fell a few weeks later at Les Eparges, in front of his company's extended line.

On 21 March, following a little exam, we were returned to our regiment, which was once more at Bazancourt. Then, following a big parade and a valedictory address from General von Emmich, we left the 10th Army Corps. On 24 March, we were put on trains and taken towards Brussels, where we were amalgamated with the 76th and 164th Regiments, to form the 111th Infantry Division, which is what we remained till the end of the war.

Our battalion was billeted in the little town of Hérinnes, set in a cosy Flemish landscape. On 29 March, I celebrated my twentieth birthday.

Although the Belgians had room enough in their houses, our company was installed in a large and draughty barn, which the cutting sea wind whistled through on the cold March nights. That apart, our stay in Hérinnes was quite restorative, with plenty of drill, but good victualling, and the food also very cheap to buy.

The half-Flemish, half-Walloon population was very friendly. I had frequent conversations with the owner of one particular *estaminet*, a keen Socialist and freethinker of a distinctively Belgian type. On Easter Sunday, he invited me to lunch, and would take no money, even for what we drank. Before long, all of us had struck up our various friendships and relationships, and on our afternoons off we could be seen striding through the countryside, making for this or that farmstead, to take a seat in a sparkling clean kitchen round one of the low stoves, on whose round tops a big pot of coffee was kept going. We chatted away in a blend of Flemish and Lower Saxon.

Towards the end of our stay, the weather improved, and we happily went for walks in the attractive, rather watery countryside. The landscape, in which yellow marsh marigolds seemed to have sprouted overnight, was set off by the sight of numbers of half-naked soldiers along the poplar-lined river banks, all with their shirts over their knees, busily hunting for lice. Fairly unscathed myself thus far by that scourge, I helped my comrade Priepke, an exporter from Hamburg, wrap his woollen waistcoat – as populous as once the garment of the adventurous Simplicissimus* – round a heavy boulder, and for mass-extermination, dunk it in the river. Where, since we left Hérinnes very suddenly, it will have mouldered away quietly ever since.

On 12 April 1915, we were put on trains at Hal, and, to mislead any possible spies, took a wide detour across the northern part of the front to the battlefield of Mars-la-Tour. In the village of Tronville, the company moved into its customary barn quarters, in a boring and squalid dump typical of the Lorraine, put together from flat-roofed, windowless stone crates. Because of the danger from aeroplanes, we were forced to stay in the crowded township most of the time; once or twice, though, we managed to get to the renowned nearby sites of Mars-la-Tour and Gravelotte. Only a few hundred yards away from the village, the road from

---

* Eponymous hero of the novel by Grimmelshausen (1622–1676), a picaresque set during the Thirty Years War.

Gravelotte crossed the frontier, where a smashed French border marker lay on the ground. In the evenings, we sometimes took melancholy satisfaction from going on walks to Germany.

Our barn was so ramshackle that you had to pick your way carefully over the joists if you weren't to crash through the mouldy planking on to the threshing-floor beneath. One evening, as our unit, under our decent Corporal Kerkhoff, was busy doling out portions on a manger, a huge lump of oak detached itself from the rafters and came crashing down. It was pure chance that it stuck fast a little way over our heads in the crook of two walls. We were more frightened than hurt; only our precious meat portions lay covered in rubble and debris. Then, no sooner had we crawled into the straw after this ill omen, than there was a pounding on the gate, and the alarming voice of the sergeant-major got us out of our resting-places in no time. First off, as always with these surprises, there was a moment of silence, then total confusion and din: 'My helmet!' 'Where's my haversack?' 'I can't get into my boots!' 'You stole my ammunition!' 'Shut up, August!'

In the end, we were all ready, and we marched off towards the station at Chamblay, from where a train took us, minutes later, to Pagny-sur-Moselle. The next morning, we were climbing the hills of the Moselle, and stopped in Prény, a charming hill village, with the ruins of a château looming over it. Our barn this time turned out to be a stone construction filled with fragrant mountain hay. Through its window-slits we had a view out over the wine-grown slopes of the Moselle, on to the little valley town of Pagny, which was regularly targeted by shells and aerial bombardment. Several times, shells landing in the river brought up vast columns of water.

The balmy spring weather was enlivening, and spurred us on to long walks in the wonderful hill country. So exuberant were we that we carried on larking about long into the evening, before finally settling to sleep. One much-loved prank was

Marching

pouring water or coffee from a canteen into a snoring sleeper's mouth.

On the evening of 22 April, we marched out of Prény and covered over twenty miles to the village of Hattonchâtel, without registering any footsoreness, in spite of our heavy packs. We pitched camp in the woods on the right of the famous Grande Tranchée. All the indications were that we would be fighting in the morning. Bandage packs were issued, extra tins of beef, and signalling flags for the gunners.

I sat up for a long time that night, in the foreboding eve of battle mood of which soldiers at all times have left report, on a tree stump clustered round with blue anemones, before I crept over the ranks of my comrades to my tent. I had tangled dreams, in which a principal role was played by a skull.

In the morning, when I told Priepke about it, he said he hoped it was a French skull.

Les Eparges

The tender green of young leaves shimmered in the flat light. We followed hidden, twisting paths towards a narrow gorge behind the front line. We had been told that the 76th was to attack after a bombardment of only twenty minutes, and that we were to be held in reserve. On the dot of noon, our artillery launched into a furious bombardment that echoed and re-echoed through the wooded hollows. For the first time, we heard what was meant by the expression 'drumfire'. We sat perched on our haversacks, idle and excited. A runner plunged through to the company commander. Brisk exchange. 'The three nearest trenches have fallen to us, and six field guns have been captured!' Loud cheers rang out. A feeling of up-and-at-'em.

At last, the longed-for order. In a long line, we moved forward, towards the pattering of heavy rifle fire. It was getting serious. To the side of the forest path, dull thumps came down in a clump of firs, bringing down a rain of branches and soil. One nervous soldier threw himself to the ground, while his comrades laughed uneasily. Then Death's call slipped through the ranks: 'Ambulancemen to the Front!'

A little later, we passed the spot that had been hit. The casualties had already been removed. Bloody scraps of cloth and flesh had been left on bushes around the crater – a strange and dreadful sight that put me in mind of the butcher-bird that spikes its prey on thorn bushes.

Medics

Troops were advancing at the double along the Grande Tranchée. Casualties huddled by the roadside, whimpering for water, prisoners carrying stretchers came panting back, limbers clattered through fire at a gallop. On either side, shells spattered the soft ground, heavy boughs came crashing down. A dead horse lay across the middle of the path, with giant wounds, its steaming entrails beside it. In among the great, bloody scenes there was a wild, unsuspected hilarity. A bearded reservist leaned against a tree: 'On you go now, boys, Frenchie's on the run!'

death

We entered the battle-tramped realm of the infantryman. The area round the jumping-off position had been deforested by shells. In the ripped-up no man's land lay the victims of the attack, still facing the enemy; their grey tunics barely stood out from the ground. A giant form with red, blood-spattered beard stared fixedly at the sky, his fingers clutching the spongy ground. A young man tossed in a shell-crater, his features already yellow with his impending death. He seemed not to want to be looked at; he gave us a cross shrug and pulled his coat over his head, and lay still.

Our marching column broke up. Shells came continually hissing towards us in long, flat arcs, lightnings whirled up the forest floor. The shrill toot of field artillery shells I had heard quite often even before Orainville; it didn't strike me as being particularly dangerous. The loose order in which our company now advanced over the broken field had something oddly calming about it; I thought privately that this baptism of fire business was actually far less dangerous than I'd expected. In a curious failure of comprehension, I looked alertly about me for possible targets for all this artillery fire, not, apparently, realizing that it was actually ourselves that the enemy gunners were trying for all they were worth to hit.

confusion in war

'Ambulancemen!' We had our first fatality. A shrapnel ball had ripped through rifleman Stolter's carotid artery. Three packets of lint were sodden with blood in no time. In a matter of seconds he had bled to death. Next to us, a couple of ordnance pieces loosed off shells, drawing more fire down on us from the enemy. An artillery lieutenant, who was in the vanguard, looking for wounded, was thrown to the ground by a column of steam that spurted in front of him. He got to his feet and made his way back with notable calm. We took him in with gleaming eyes.

It was getting dark when we received orders to advance further. The way now led through dense undergrowth shot through by shells, into an endless communication trench along which the French had dropped their packs as they ran. Approaching the village of Les Eparges, without having any troops in front of us, we were forced to hew defensive positions in solid rock. Finally, I slumped into a bush and fell asleep. At moments, half asleep, I was aware of artillery shells, ours or theirs, describing their ellipses in a trail of sparks.

'Come on, man, get up! We're moving out!' I woke up in dew-sodden grass. Through a stuttering swathe of machine-gun fire, we plunged back into our communication trench, and moved to a position on the edge of the wood previously held by the French. A sweetish smell and a bundle hanging in the wire caught my attention. In the rising mist, I leaped out of the trench and found a shrunken French corpse. Flesh like mouldering fish gleamed greenishly through splits in the shredded uniform. Turning round, I took a step back in horror: next to me a figure was crouched against a tree. It still had gleaming French leather harness, and on its back was a fully packed haversack, topped by a round mess-tin. Empty eye-sockets and a few strands of hair on the bluish-black skull indicated that the man was not among the living. There was another sitting down, slumped forward towards his feet, as though he had just collapsed. All around were dozens more, rotted, dried, stiffened to mummies, frozen in an eerie dance of death. The French must have spent months in the proximity of their fallen comrades, without burying them.

During the morning, the sun gradually pierced the fog, and

spread a pleasant warmth. After I'd slept on the bottom of the trench for a while, curiosity impelled me to inspect the unoccupied trench we'd captured the day before. It was littered with great piles of provisions, ammunition, equipment, weapons, letters and newspapers. The dugouts were like looted junk-shops. In amongst it all were the bodies of the brave defenders, their guns still poking out through the shooting-slits. A headless torso was jammed in some shot-up beams. Head and neck were gone, white cartilage gleamed out of reddish-black flesh. I found it difficult to fathom. Next to it a very young man lay on his back with glassy eyes and fists still aiming. A peculiar feeling, looking into dead, questioning eyes – a shudder that I never quite lost in the course of the war. His pockets had been turned inside out, and his emptied wallet lay beside him.

Unmolested by any fire, I strolled along the ravaged trench. It was the short mid-morning lull that was often to be my only moment of respite on the battlefield. I used it to take a good look at everything. The unfamiliar weapons, the darkness of the dugouts, the colourful contents of the haversacks, it was all new and strange to me. I pocketed some French ammunition, undid a silky-soft tarpaulin and picked up a canteen wrapped in blue cloth, only to chuck it all away again a few steps further along. The sight of a beautiful striped shirt, lying next to a ripped-open officer's valise, seduced me to strip off my uniform and get into some fresh linen. I relished the pleasant tickle of clean cloth against my skin.

Thus kitted out, I looked for a sunny spot in the trench, sat down on a beam-end, and with my bayonet opened a round can of meat for my breakfast. Then I lit my pipe, and browsed through some of the many French magazines that lay scattered about, some of them, as I saw from the dates, only sent to the trenches on the eve of Verdun.

Not without a certain shudder, I remember that during my breakfast I tried to unscrew a curious little contraption that I

26

unawareness of closeness to death
feelings of invincibility
LES EPARGES

found lying at my feet in the trench, which for some reason I took to be a 'storm lantern'. It wasn't until a lot later that it dawned on me that the thing I'd been fiddling around with was a live hand-grenade.

As conditions grew brighter, a German battery opened up from a stretch of woods just behind the trench. It didn't take long for the enemy to reply. Suddenly I was struck by a mighty crash behind me, and saw a steep pillar of smoke rising. Still unfamiliar with the sounds of war, I was not able to distinguish the hisses and whistles and bangs of our own gunnery from the ripping crash of enemy shells, and hence, to get a sense of the lines of engagement. Above all, I could not account for the way I seemed to be under fire from all sides, so that the trajectories of the various shells were criss-crossing apparently aimlessly over the little warren of trenches where a few of us were holed up. This effect, for which I could see no cause, disquieted me and made me think. I still viewed the machinery of conflict with the eyes of an inexperienced recruit – the expressions of bellicosity seemed as distant and peculiar to me as events on another planet. This meant I was unafraid; feeling myself to be invisible, I couldn't believe I was a target to anyone, much less that I might be hit. So, returned to my unit, I surveyed the terrain in front of me with great indifference. In my pocket-diary I wrote down – a habit of mine later on as well – the times and the intensity of the bombardment.

Towards noon, the artillery fire had increased to a kind of savage pounding dance. The flames lit around us incessantly. Black, white and yellow clouds mingled. The shells with black smoke, which the old-timers called 'Americans' or 'coal boxes', ripped with incredible violence. And all the time the curious, canary-like twittering of dozens of fuses. With their cut-out shapes, in which the trapped air produced a flute-like trill, they drifted over the long surf of explosions like ticking copper toy clocks or mechanical insects. The odd thing was that the little birds in the forest seemed quite untroubled by the myriad noise; they sat peaceably over the smoke in their battered boughs. In the short intervals of firing, we could hear them singing happily or ardently to one another, if anything even inspired or encouraged by the dreadful noise on all sides.

In the moments when the shelling was particularly heavy, the men called to each other to remain vigilant. In the stretch of trench that I could see, and out of whose walls great clumps of mud had already been knocked here and there, we were in complete readiness. Our rifles were unlocked in the shooting-slits, and the riflemen were alertly eyeing the foreground. From time to time they checked to left and right to see whether we were still in contact, and they smiled when their eyes encountered those of comrades.

I sat with a comrade on a bench cut into the clay wall of the trench. Once, the board of the shooting-slit through which we were looking splintered, and a rifle bullet flew between our heads and buried itself in the clay.

By and by, there were casualties. I had no way of knowing how things stood in other sectors of the labyrinthine trench, but the increasing frequency of the calls for 'Ambulancemen!' showed that the shelling was starting to take effect. From time to time, a figure hurried by with its head or neck or hand wrapped in fresh, clean and very visible bandages, on its way to the rear. It was a matter of urgency to get the victim out of the way, because of the military superstition by which a trifling wound or hit, if not immediately dealt with, is certain to be followed by something rather worse.

My comrade, volunteer Kohl, kept up that North German sang-froid that might have been made for such a situation. He was chewing and squeezing on a cigar that refused to draw, and apart from that looked rather sleepy. Nor did he allow himself to be upset when, suddenly, to the rear of us, there was a clattering as of a thousand rifles. It turned out that the intensity of the shelling had caused the wood to catch fire. Great tongues of flame climbed noisily up the tree trunks.

While all this was going on, I suffered from a rather curious anxiety. I was envious of the old 'Lions of Perthes' for their experience in the 'witches' cauldron', which I had missed out on through being away in Recouvrence. Therefore, each time the coal-boxes came down especially thick and fast in our neck of things, I would turn to Kohl, who had been there, and ask:

'Hey, would you say this was like Perthes now?'

To my chagrin, he would reply each time with a casually dismissive gesture:

'Not by a long chalk!'

When the shelling had intensified to the extent that now our clay bench had started to sway with the impact of the black monsters, I yelled into his ear:

'Hey, is it like Perthes *now*?'

Kohl was a conscientious soldier. He began by standing up, looked about himself carefully, and then roared back, to my satisfaction:

'I think it's getting there!'

The reply filled me with foolish delight, as it confirmed to me that this was my first proper battle.

At that instant, a man popped up in the corner of our sector: 'Follow me left!' We passed on the command, and started along the smoke-filled position. The ration party had just arrived with the chow, and hundreds of unwanted mess-tins sat and steamed on the breastwork. Who could think to eat now? A crowd of wounded men pushed past us with blood-soaked bandages, the excitement of the battle still etched on their pale faces. Up on the edge of the trench, stretcher after stretcher was swiftly lugged to the rear. The sense of being up against it began to take hold of us. 'Careful of my arm, mate!' 'Come along, man, keep up!'

I spotted Lieutenant Sandvoss, rushing past the trench with distracted staring eyes. A long white bandage trailing round his

neck gave him a strangely ungainly appearance, which probably
explains why just at that moment he reminded me of a duck.
There was something dreamlike about the vision – terror in the
guise of the absurd. Straight afterwards, we hurried past Colonel
von Oppen, who had his hand in his tunic pocket and was issuing
orders to his adjutant. 'Aha, so there is some organization and
purpose behind all this,' it flashed through my brain.

The trench debouched into a stretch of wood. We stood irresolutely under huge beech trees. A lieutenant emerged from dense
undergrowth and called to our longest-serving NCO: 'Have them
fall out towards the sunset, and then take up position. Report to
me in the dugout by the clearing.' Swearing, the NCO took over.

We fell out in extended order, and lay down expectantly in a
series of flattish depressions that some predecessors of ours had
scooped out of the ground. Our ribald conversations were suddenly cut off by a marrow-freezing cry. Twenty yards behind us,
clumps of earth whirled up out of a white cloud and smacked
into the boughs. The crash echoed through the woods. Stricken
eyes looked at each other, bodies pressed themselves into the
ground with a humbling sensation of powerlessness to do anything else. Explosion followed explosion. Choking gases drifted
through the undergrowth, smoke obscured the treetops, trees
and branches came crashing to the ground, screams. We leaped
up and ran blindly, chased by lightnings and crushing air pressure,
from tree to tree, looking for cover, skirting around giant tree
trunks like frightened game. A dugout where many men had
taken shelter, and which I too was running towards, took a direct
hit that ripped up the planking and sent heavy timbers spinning
through the air.

Like a couple of squirrels having stones thrown at them, the
NCO and I dodged panting round a huge beech. Quite mechan-
ically, and spurred on by further explosions, I ran after my
superior, who sometimes turned round and stared at me, wild-
eyed, yelling: 'What in God's name are those things? What are

they?' Suddenly there was a flash among the rootwork, and a blow on the left thigh flung me to the ground. I thought I had been struck by a clump of earth, but the warm trickle of blood indicated that I'd been wounded. Later, I saw that a needle-sharp piece of shrapnel had given me a flesh wound, though my wallet had taken the brunt of it. The fine cut, which before slicing into the muscle had split no fewer than nine thicknesses of stout leather, looked as though it might have been administered by a scalpel. Shrapnel

I threw down my haversack and ran towards the trench we had come from. From all sides, wounded men were making tracks towards it from the shelled woods. The trench was appalling, choked with seriously wounded and dying men. A figure stripped to the waist, with ripped-open back, leaned against the parapet. Another, with a triangular flap hanging off the back of his skull, emitted short, high-pitched screams. This was the home of the great god Pain, and for the first time I looked through a devilish chink into the depths of his realm. And fresh shells came down all the time.

I lost my head completely. Ruthlessly, I barged past everyone on my path, before finally, having fallen back a few times in my haste, climbing out of the hellish crush of the trench, to move more freely above. Like a bolting horse, I rushed through dense undergrowth, across paths and clearings, till I collapsed in a copse by the Grande Tranchée.

It was already growing dark by the time a couple of stretcher-bearers who were looking for casualties came upon me. They picked me up on their stretcher and carried me back to their dressing-station in a dugout covered over with tree branches, where I spent the night, pressed together with many other wounded men. An exhausted medic stood in the throng of groaning men, bandaging, injecting and giving calm instructions. I pulled a dead man's coat over me, and fell into a sleep that incipient fever lit with lurid dreams. Once, in the middle of the night, I awoke, and saw the doctor still working by the light of a lamp. A Frenchman was screaming incessantly, and next to me a man growled: 'Bloody Frenchies, never happy if they've not got something to moan about!' And then I was asleep again.

As I was being carried away the following morning, a splinter bored a hole through the stretcher canvas between my knees.

Along with other wounded men, I was loaded on to one of the ambulance wagons that shuttled between the battlefield and the main dressing-station. We galloped across the Grande Tranchée, which was still under heavy fire. Behind the grey canvas walls we careered through the danger that accompanied us with giant stamping strides.

On one of the stretchers on which – like loaves of bread into an oven – we had been pushed into the back of the cart lay a comrade with a shot in the belly that occasioned him intense pain. He appealed to every one of us to finish him off with the ambulanceman's pistol that hung in the wagon. No one answered. I was yet to experience the feeling where every jolt seems like a hammer blow on a bad injury.

The chief dressing-station was in a forest clearing. Long rows of straw had been laid out and covered with foliage. The stream of wounded was proof, if proof were needed, that a significant engagement was in progress. At the sight of the surgeon, who stood checking the roster in the bloody chaos, I once again had the impression, hard to describe, of seeing a man surrounded by elemental terror and anguish, studying the functioning of his organization with ant-like cold-bloodedness.

Supplied with food and drink, and smoking a cigarette, I lay in the middle of a long line of wounded men on my spill of straw, in that mood which sets in when a test has been got through, if not exactly with flying colours, then still one way or another. A short snatch of conversation next to me gave me pause.

'What happened to you, comrade?'

'I've been shot in the bladder.'

'Is it very bad?'

'Oh, that's not the problem. I can't stand it that I can't fight . . .'

Later that same morning, we were taken to the main collection point in the village church at St Maurice. A hospital train was there, already getting up steam. We would be back in Germany in two days. From my bed on the train, I could see the fields just coming into spring. We were well looked after by a quiet fellow, a philosophy scholar in private life. The first thing he did for me was to take out his penknife and cut the boot off my foot. There are people who have a gift for tending others, and so it was with this man; even seeing him reading a book by a night-light made me feel better.

The train took us to Heidelberg.

NAT'LISM

At the sight of the Neckar slopes wreathed with flowering cherry trees, I had a strong sense of having come home. What a beautiful country it was, and eminently worth our blood and our lives. Never before had I felt its charm so clearly. I had good and serious thoughts, and for the first time I sensed that this war was more than just a great adventure.

The battle at Les Eparges was my first. It was quite unlike what I had expected. I had taken part in a major engagement, without having clapped eyes on a single live opponent. It wasn't until much later that I experienced the direct coming together, the climax of battle in the form of waves of attackers on an open field, which, for decisive, murderous moments, would break into the chaos and vacuity of the battlefield.

Douchy and Monchy

Two weeks later, my wound was healed. I was released to the reserve battalion in Hanover, and was given a short home leave there to get used to walking again.

'Why not report as a gentleman-cadet?' my father suggested to me on one of my first mornings at home, as we were walking round the orchard to see how the trees would bear; and I did as he suggested, even though it had seemed much more attractive to me at the beginning of the war to be a simple rifleman, responsible only for myself.

So the regiment sent me off to Döberitz, on another course, which I left six weeks later with the rank of ensign. From the hundreds of young men who had come from all over Germany, I could tell that the country was not short of good fighting stock. While the training I had received in Recouvrence had been directed at the individual, here we were instructed in various ways of moving across terrain in small groups.

In September 1915, I travelled back to my regiment. I left the train in the village of St Léger, the divisional headquarters, and marched at the head of a small detachment of reservists to Douchy, where the regiment was based. Ahead of us, the French autumn offensive was in full swing. The front manifested itself as a long, billowing cloud over open country. Overhead the machine-guns of the air squadrons pattered away. Sometimes, when one of the French planes came down very low – their

34

colourful rosettes seeming to scan the ground like big butterflies' eyes – my little troop and I took cover under the poplars that lined the road. The anti-aircraft guns threaded long fleecy lines through the air, and whistling splinters pinged into the tilth.

This little march was to give me an opportunity of putting my newly acquired skills into practice right away. We knew we had been spotted, probably by one of the many captive balloons whose yellow forms glimmered in the Western sky, because, just as we were turning into the village of Douchy, the black cone of a shell exploded in our faces. It struck the entrance to the little village cemetery, just beside the road. For the first time, I found myself in the position of having to react to an unexpected development with an immediate decision.

'To the left – in extended order – quick march!'

The column spilled out over the fields at the double; we formed up again to the left, and entered the village by a large detour.

Douchy, where the 73rd Rifles were billeted, was a middle-sized village that had not, as yet, suffered much from the war. This place, nestled on the wavy ground of Artois, became, over the year and a half of stationary warfare in that region, a kind of second garrison to the regiment, a place of rest and recreation after gruelling days of fighting and working on the front line. How many a time we drew a deep breath to see the lonely light at the entrance to the village winking towards us through the black and rainy night! It meant having a roof over our heads again, and a bed in the dry. We could sleep without having to go out into the night four hours later, and without being pursued even into our dreams by the fear of a surprise attack. It made us feel reborn, on the first day of a rest spell, when we'd had a bath, and cleaned our uniforms of the grime of the trenches. We exercised and drilled out on the meadows, to return suppleness to our rusty bones, and to reawaken the *esprit de corps* of individuals isolated over the long watches of the night. That gave us the ability to resist during the long and taxing days ahead. At first, the companies took it in turn to march to the front for work on the fortifications. The strenuous double roster was dropped later on, on the orders of our understanding Colonel von Oppen. The security of a position depends less on the elaborate construction of its approach routes and the depths of the firing trench than on the freshness and undiminished courage of the men defending it.

For off hours, Douchy had much to commend it to its grey inhabitants. Numerous bars were still plentifully provided with eatables and drinkables; there was a reading room, a coffee bar and, later on, a cinema was improvised from a large barn. The officers enjoyed an excellently equipped mess-room and a bowling alley in the rectory garden. There were regular company parties, in which officers and men, in the timeless German fashion, vied with one another in drinking. Not to forget the killing days, for which the company pigs, kept fat on the refuse from the field kitchens, gave their lives.

Since the civilian population was still living in the village, it was important to exploit all available space. Gardens were partly taken up with huts and various temporary dwellings; a large orchard in the middle of the village was turned into a public square, another became a park, the so-called Emmichplatz. A barber and dentist were installed in a couple of dugouts covered with branches. A large meadow next to the church became a burial ground, to which the company marched almost daily, to take their leave of one or more comrades to the strains of mass singing.

In the space of a single year, a crumbling rural village had sprouted an army town, like a great parasitical growth. The former peacetime aspect of the place was barely discernible. The village pond was where dragoons watered their horses, infantry exercised in the orchards, soldiers lay in the meadows sunning themselves. All the peacetime institutions collapsed, only what was needed for war was maintained. Hedges and fences were

impact on locals

broken through or simply torn down for easier access, and everywhere there were large signs giving directions to military traffic.
While roofs caved in, and furniture was gradually used up as
firewood, telephone lines and electricity cables were installed.
Cellars were extended outwards and downwards to make bomb
shelters for the residents; the removed earth was dumped in
the gardens. The village no longer knew any demarcations or
distinctions between thine and mine.

The French population was quartered at the edge of the village,
towards Monchy. Children played on the steps of dilapidated
houses, and old people made hunched figures, slinking timidly
through the new bustle that had remorselessly evicted them from
the places where they had spent entire lifetimes. The young people
had to stand-to every morning, and were detailed to work the
land by the village commandant, First Lieutenant Oberländer.
The only time we came into contact with the locals was when we
brought them our clothes to be washed, or went to buy butter
and eggs.

One of the more remarkable features of this army town was
the way a couple of young orphaned French boys followed the
troops around. The two boys, of whom one was eight or so, the
other twelve, went around clad entirely in field grey, and both
spoke fluent German. They referred to their compatriots as the
soldiers did, as 'Schangels'.* Their keenest desire was to go with
'their' company up the line. They drilled faultlessly, saluted
their superior officers, formed up on the left flank for roll-call,
and put in for leave when it was time to accompany the kitchen-
helpers on shopping expeditions to Cambrai. When the 2nd
Battalion went to Quéant for a couple of weeks of instruction,
one of the two, Louis, was ordered by Colonel von Oppen to
remain behind in Douchy; no one spotted him anywhere on the
way, but when the battalion arrived, there he was leaping happily

* I would hazard, derived from the German pronunciation of the French 'Jean'.

out of the baggage cart where he had been hiding. The elder of the two, I was told, was later sent to petty-officer school in Germany.

Barely an hour's march from Douchy lay Monchy-au-Bois, where the regiment's two reserve companies were billeted. In the autumn of 1914, it had been bitterly fought over, and had ended up in German possession, as the battle slowly fought to a standstill in a half-circle round the ruins of this once-affluent town.

Now the houses were burned down and shot up, the neglected gardens raked by shells, and the fruit trees snapped. The rubble of stones had been heaped into a defensive installation with the aid of trenches, barbed wire, barricades and concrete strongpoints. All the approach roads could be covered by machine-gun fire from a pillbox called 'Torgau Redoubt'. Another strongpoint went by the name of 'Altenburg Redoubt', an entrenched post to the right of the village that was home to a detachment of company reserves. Also pivotal to the defence was a quarry that in peacetime had provided the limestone for the village houses, and which we had stumbled upon rather by chance. A company cook who had lost his water-pail in a well had had himself lowered after it, and had noticed a spreading cavern-like hole. The place was investigated and, after a second entrance had been knocked through, it offered bomb-proof accommodation for a large number of fighters.

On the isolated heights on the way to Ransart was the ruin of a one-time *estaminet* – dubbed 'Bellevue' on account of the wide view of the front that was afforded from it – and this was a place I came to love, in spite of its exposed situation. From there, the view stretched over the dead land, whose defunct villages were linked by roads that had no traffic on them, and on which no living creature was to be seen. In the distance glimmered the outline of the abandoned city of Arras, and round to the right the shining chalk mine-craters of St Eloi. The weedy fields lay barren under the passing clouds and the shadows of clouds, and the tightly woven web of trenches spread its little white and yellow links, secured by lengthy communication trenches. From time to time, there was a puff of smoke from a shell, lobbed into the air as if by a ghostly hand; or the ball of a shrapnel hung over the wasteland like a great white flake slowly melting. The aspect of the landscape was dark and fantastic, the war had erased anything attractive or appealing from the scene, and etched its own brazen features, to appal the lonely onlooker. *Destruction*

The desolation and the profound silence, sporadically broken by the crump of shells, were heightened by the sorry impression of devastation. Ripped haversacks, broken rifles, scraps of cloth, counterpointed grotesquely with children's toys, shell fuses, deep craters from explosions, bottles, harvest implements, shredded books, battered household gear, holes whose gaping darkness betrayed the presence of basements, where the bodies of the *dead bodies* unlucky inhabitants of the houses were gnawed by the particularly assiduous swarms of rats; a little espaliered peach tree despoiled of its sustaining wall, and spreading its arms pitifully; in the cattle byres and stables and barns the bones of livestock still dangling from their chains; trenches dug through the ravaged gardens, in among sprouting bulbs of onions, wormwood, rhubarb, narcissus, buried under weeds; on the neighbouring fields grain barns, through whose roofs the grain was already sprouting; all that, with a half-buried communication trench running through it, and all suffused with the smell of burning and decay. Sad thoughts are apt to sneak up on the warrior in such a locale, when he thinks of those who only recently led their lives in tranquillity.

As already mentioned, the front line described a semi-circle around the village, connected to it by an array of communication trenches. It was divided in two, Monchy South and Monchy West. These in turn were formed up into six company sections, from A to F. The bulge in the front afforded the British a good ✓ opportunity for flanking fire, the skilful use of which occasioned

Trenches

us heavy losses. They deployed a gun hidden immediately behind their own lines that sent out little shrapnels, which seemed to be fired and to reach us practically simultaneously. Out of the blue a hail of lead balls would flash down over the length of a trench, as often as not taking a sentry with it.

Next, let us take a quick turn through the trenches as they were at that time, to familiarize the reader with some of the recurring terminology.

To reach the front line, the firing trench, we take one of the many 'saps', or communication trenches, whose job it is to afford the troops some protection on their way to battle stations. These, often very long, trenches are broadly perpendicular to the front, but, to make it less easy to rake them with fire, they most often follow a zigzag or curving course. After a quarter of an hour's march, we enter the second trench, the support trench, which is parallel to the firing trench, and serves as a further line of defence should that be taken.

The firing trench is wholly unlike those frail constructions that were dug in the early days of the war. Nor is it just a simple ditch either, but it is dug to a depth of ten or twenty feet. The defenders move around as on the bottom of a mine gallery; to observe the ground in front of the position, or to fire out, they climb a set of steps or a wide wooden ladder to the sentry platform, which is set at such a height in the earth that a man standing on it is a head taller than the top of the rampart. The marksman stands at his sentry post, a more or less armoured niche, with his head protected by a wall of sandbags or a steel plate. The actual lookout is through tiny slits through which a rifle barrel is pushed. The quantities of earth that were dug out of the trench are piled up in a wall behind the trench, a parados affording protection from the rear; machine-gun emplacements are built into these earthworks. On the front side of the trench, the earth is kept level, so as to leave the field of vision as clear and uncluttered as possible.

In front of the trench, often in multiple lines, is a wire entanglement, a complicated web of barbed wire designed to keep the
attacker busy, so that he presents an easy target for the defensive
sentries.

Rank weeds climb up and through the barbed wire, sympto-
matic of a new and different type of flora taking root on the
fallow fields. Wild flowers, of a sort that generally make only an
occasional appearance in grain fields, dominate the scene; here
and there even bushes and shrubs have taken hold. The paths too
are overgrown, but easily identified by the presence on them of
round-leaved plantains.* Bird life thrives in such wilderness,
partridges for instance, whose curious cries we often hear at night,
or larks, whose choir starts up at first light over the trenches.

To keep the firing trench from being raked by flanking fire, it's
laid out in a meandering line, forever doubling and tripling back
on itself. Each of these turns forms a traverse, to catch any shells
fired from the side. The fighter is thus protected from behind,
from the side and, of course, from the front.

To rest in, there are dugouts, which have evolved by now
from rudimentary holes in the ground to proper enclosed living
quarters, with beamed ceilings and plank-cladded walls. The
dugouts are about six feet high, and at a depth where their floors
are roughly level with the bottom of the trench outside. In effect,
there is a layer of earth on top of them thick enough to enable
them to survive oblique hits. In heavy fire, though, they are
death-traps, and it's better to be in the depths of the shelters.

The shelters are braced with solid wood joists. The first is fixed
in the front wall of the trench, level with the bottom, and from
this entrance each successive joist is set a couple of hand's
breadths lower, so that the amount of protection is rapidly

* German *Wegerich*: the weed plantain (etymologically derived from the French
plante, 'sole of the foot') which flourishes along footpaths, rather than the
tropical vegetable of the same name (from the Spanish *platano*, 'banana'). Anna
Akhmatova's 1921 book of poems was called *Plaintain* in the same sense.

increased. By the thirtieth step, there are nine yards of earth overhead, twelve counting the depth of the trench. Then there are slightly wider frames set straight ahead or perpendicular to the steps; these constitute the actual living quarters. Communication is possible by lateral tunnels, while branchings-off towards the enemy lines are used for mining or listening posts.

The whole thing should be pictured as a huge, ostensibly inert installation, a secret hive of industry and watchfulness, where, within a few seconds of an alarm being sounded, every man is at his post. But one shouldn't have too romantic an idea of the atmosphere; there is a certain prevailing torpor that proximity to the earth seems to engender.

I was sent to the 6th Company, and, a few days after my arrival, moved into line at the head of a platoon, where I was straightaway welcomed by a few English 'toffee-apples'. These are brittle iron shells, filled with high explosive, somewhat resembling fruit on a stalk; or imagine a fifty-kilogram dumbbell, with one of the weights missing. They went off with a muffled thud, and, moreover, were often masked by machine-gun fire. It therefore made an eerie impression on me when sudden flames lit up the trench just next to us, and a malignant wave of air pressure shook us. The men quickly pulled me back into the platoon dugout, which we were just passing. We felt the next five or six mortar thumps from within. The mine doesn't actually impact, it seems more to nestle down; the calmness of its devastation was somehow the more unsettling. The following day, when I first inspected the trench by daylight, I saw those big emptied steel casings hanging up by their stalks outside dugouts, serving as alarm gongs.

C Sector, which our company held, was the regiment's most forward sector. In Lieutenant Brecht, who had hurried back from the United States at the outbreak of war, we had the very man to defend such a position. He loved danger, and he died in battle.

Life in the trenches was a matter of unbending routines; I will now describe the course of a single day of the kind that we had, one after another, for a year and a half, except when normal levels of fire were intensified to what we called 'turbulence'.

Day in the trenches begins at dusk. At seven o'clock someone from my platoon comes in to wake me from my afternoon nap, which, with a view to night duty, I like to have. I buckle on my belt, stick a Verey-light pistol in it and some bombs, and leave my more or less cosy dugout. As I walk through the by now highly familiar sector, I automatically check that the sentries are all in position. The password is given in low tones. By now, it is night-time, and the first silvery flares climb aloft, while peeled eyes scrutinize no man's land. A rat skitters about among the tin cans thrown over the ramparts. Another joins it with a squeak, and, before long, the whole place is swarming with the lithe shapes emerging from their holes in ruined village basements or among the shot-up bomb shelters. Hunting rats is a much-loved change from the tedium of sentry duty. A piece of bread is put out as bait, and a rifle is levelled at it, or gunpowder from dud shells is sprinkled in their holes and torched. Then they come squeaking out with singed fur. They are repellent creatures, and I'm always thinking of the secret desecrations they perform on the bodies in the village basements. Once, as I was striding through the ruins of Monchy on a warm night, they came oozing out of their hiding-places in such indescribable numbers that the ground was like a long carpet of them, patterned with the occasional white of an albino. Some cats have moved in with us from the ruined villages around; they love the proximity of humans. One large white tom with a shot-off front paw is frequently seen ghosting about in no man's land, and seems to have been adopted by both sides.

Of course, I was telling you about trench duty. But one loves these digressions; it's an easy matter to start nattering, to fill up a dark night and the slow hours. I would many times stop and listen to the tales of some character from the front, or a fellow

43

NCO, and take in his chatter with rapt attention. As an ensign, I am often engaged in conversation by a kindly duty officer, who suffers equally from the boredom. Yes, the man even gets to be quite pally, talks in a soft, low voice, reveals secrets and desires. And I attend, because I too feel oppressed by the heavy black walls of the trenches; I too am yearning for warmth, for something human in this eerie desolation. At night, the landscape emanates a curious cold; a sort of emotional cold. It makes you start to shiver when you cross an unoccupied part of the trench that is reserved for sentries; and if you cross the wire entanglements, and set foot in no man's land, the shivering intensifies to a faint, teeth-rattling unease. The novelists haven't done justice to this teeth-chattering; there's nothing dramatic about it, it's more like having a feeble electric current applied to you. Most of the time you're just as unaware of it as you are of talking in your sleep at night. And, for another thing, it stops the moment anything actually happens.

The conversation winds down. We are tired. Sleepily we stand in a fire-bay, propped against the trench, and stare at our cigarettes glimmering in the dark.

When there's frost, you stomp up and down so hard that the earth echoes. The sound of incessant coughing carries for miles through the cold air. Often enough, if you're creeping forward in no man's land, that coughing is your first warning that you're nearing enemy lines. Or a sentry will be whistling or humming to himself, in contrast to yourself, creeping up on him with murderous intent. Or again it's raining, in which case you stand sadly with your collar turned up under the eaves of the dugout entrance, listening to the regular drip drip drip. But if you hear the footfall of a superior on the duckboards, you step out smartly, walk on, suddenly swing about, click your heels together, and report: 'NCO on duty. Sector all quiet, sir!' because standing in doorways is not permitted.

Your thoughts drift. You look at the moon, and think of lovely, cosy days at home, or of the big city miles to the rear, where people are just now streaming out of the cafés, and big arc lamps light up the lively commotion of the city centre. It feels like something in a dream – incredibly remote.

Something rustles in front of the trench, a couple of wires clink together. Straightaway all your dreams are out the window, your senses are stretched to the point of pain. You climb on to the fire-step, fire off a tracer round: nothing stirs. It must have been a rabbit or a pheasant, nothing more.

Often you can hear the enemy working on his wire entanglements. Then you empty your magazine in his direction. Not only because those are the standing instructions, but also because you feel some pleasure as you do it. 'Let them feel the pressure for a change. Who knows, perhaps you even managed to hit one of them.' We too go unspooling wire most nights, and take a lot of casualties. Then we curse those mean British bastards. *dehumanize*

On some sectors of the line, say at the sap heads, the sentries are barely thirty yards apart. Here you sometimes get personally acquainted with your opposite numbers; you get to know Tommy or Fritz or Wilhelm by his cough or his whistle or his singing voice. Shouts are exchanged, often with an edge of rough humour.

'Hey, Tommy, you still there?' *talking to other side*
'Yup!'

'Then get your head down, I'm about to start shooting at you!'

Sometimes you hear a whistling, fluttering sound, following a dull discharge. 'Watch out, trench mortar!' You rush to the *MORTARS* nearest dugout steps and hold your breath. The mortars explode differently, altogether more excitingly than common-or-garden shells. There's something violent and devious about them, something of personal vitriol. They are treacherous things. Rifle-grenades are a scaled-down version of them. One rises like an arrow out of the opposite lines, with its reddish-brown metal head scored into squares like chocolate, to make it splinter better. If the horizon lights up at night in certain places, all the sentries leap up from their posts, and take cover. They know from long experience where the mortars trained on C Sector are.

At last the luminous dial shows that two hours are up. Now wake up the relief, and head for the dugout. Maybe the ration party will have brought post, or a parcel, or a newspaper. It's a strange feeling to read news from home, and their peacetime anxieties, while the shadows cast by a flickering candle flame brush over the rough low beams. After scraping off the worst of the mud from my boots with a piece of stick, and giving them a finishing touch against a leg of the crudely fashioned table, I lie down on my pallet, and pull the blanket over my head for a quick four-hour 'gargle', as the slang has it. Outside, the shots monotonously ring against the parapet, a mouse scrabbles over my face and hands, nothing disturbs my sleep. Even the 'wee-er beasties' don't bother me, it's only a few days since we thoroughly fumigated the dugout.

Twice more, I am torn from my sleep to do my duty. During the last watch, a bright streak behind the sky to the east announces the coming day. The contours of the trench are sharpened; in the flat light, it makes an impression of unspeakable dreariness. A lark ascends; its trilling gets on my wick. Leaning against the parapet, I stare out at the dead, wire-scarred vista with a feeling of tremendous disillusion. These last twenty minutes seem to go on for ever. At last there's the clatter of the coffee-bringers coming down the communication trench: it's seven o'clock in the morning. The night-watch is over.

I head for the dugout and drink coffee, and wash in an old herring can. That freshens me up; I no longer want to lie down. At nine o'clock, after all, I need to go to my platoon and give them the day's tasks. We're real Renaissance men who can turn our hands to anything, and the trenches make their thousandfold demands of us every day. We sink deep shafts, construct dugouts and concrete pillboxes, rig up wire entanglements, devise drainage systems, revet, support, level, raise and smooth, fill in latrines;

levelling of soc classes

in a word, we do all possible tasks ourselves. And why wouldn't we, given that we have representatives of every rank and calling in our midst? If one man doesn't know, then another will. Only lately a miner took the pick out of my hand as I was working on our platoon dugout, and remarked: 'Keep cutting at the bottom, the dirt at the top will come down by itself!' Strange not to have thought of something so elementary oneself. But here, stood in the middle of the bleak landscape, suddenly compelled to take cover, to wrap up against wind and weather, to knock together beds and tables, to improvise stoves and steps, we soon learn to use our hands. The value of skills and crafts is there for all to see. ✓

At one o'clock, lunch is brought up from the kitchens, which are in a basement in Monchy, in large containers that were once milk churns and jam boilers. The food is of martial monotonousness, but plentiful enough, provided the ration parties don't 'evaporate' it on the way, and leave half of it on the ground. After lunch, we nap or read. Gradually the two hours approach that are set aside for the trench duty by day. They pass more quickly than their nocturnal counterparts. We observe the front line opposite through binoculars or periscopes, and often manage to get in a head shot or two through a sniper's rifle. But careful, because the British also have sharp eyes and useful binoculars.

2 hr day duty

random deaths

A sentry collapses, streaming blood. Shot in the head. His comrades rip the bandage roll out of his tunic and get him bandaged up. 'There's no point, Bill.' 'Come on, he's still breathing, isn't he?' Then the stretcher-bearers come along, to carry him to the dressing-station. The stretcher poles collide with the corners of the fire-bays. No sooner has the man disappeared than everything is back to the way it was before. Someone spreads a ✓ few shovelfuls of earth over the red puddle, and everyone goes back to whatever he was doing before. Only a new recruit maybe leans against the revetment, looking a little green about the gills. He is endeavouring to put it all together. Such an incredibly brutal assault, so sudden, with no warning given. It can't be

some really love fighting

possible, can't be real. Poor fellow, if only you knew what was in store for you.

Or again, it's perfectly pleasant. A few apply themselves with sportsmanlike enthusiasm. With connoisseurial expressions, they follow the bursts of our artillery in the enemy trench. 'Bull's-eye!' 'Wow, did you see the dirt go up after that one! Poor old Tommy! There's mud in your eye!' They like lobbing rifle-grenades and light mortar-bombs across, to the disapproval of more timorous souls. 'Come on, stop that nonsense, we're getting enough of a pounding as it is!' But that doesn't keep them from pondering incessantly about how best to propel grenades with handmade catapults or some other hellish contraptions to imperil the ground in front of the trench. Now, they might clear a small passage in the wire in front of their sentry post, so that the easy access might lure some unsuspecting scout in front of their sights; another time, they creep across and tie a bell to the wire on the other side, and pull on it with a long string to drive the British sentries crazy. They get kicks out of fighting.

At teatime, things can get quite cosy. The ensign is often required to provide company for one or other of the senior officers. Things are done with formality and some style; a couple of china cups on a hessian tablecloth. Afterwards, the officer's batman will leave a bottle and glasses out on the wobbly table. Conversation becomes more personal. It's a curious thing that even here other people remain the most popular subject of conversation. Trench gossip flourishes in these afternoon sessions, almost as in a small town garrison. Superiors, comrades and inferiors may all be subjected to vigorous criticism, and a fresh rumour makes its way through all six commanders' dugouts along the line in no time at all, it seems. The observation officers, spying on the regimental position with field glasses and sketch pad, are not without some of the responsibility. In any case, the position is not hermetically sealed; there's a perpetual coming and going. During the quiet morning hours, staff officers come

('DRILLS')

round and make work, much to the fury of the poor grunt, who
has just lain down following his last watch, only to hear the call:
'The divisional commander is present in the trench!' and plunges
out of his dugout looking fairly impeccable once more. Then,
after that, there's the pioneer and the trench-construction and
the drainage officer – all of them carrying on as if the trench
existed only for their particular specialism. The artillery observer
gets a frosty reception a little later, as he seeks to hold a trial
barrage, because no sooner has he gone, taking his periscope
with him – having stuck it up out of the trench at various points,
like an insect its antennae – than the British artillery will start up,
and the infantry are always the ones who catch it. And then the
commanders of the advance party and the entrenching detachments put in an appearance as well. They sit in the platoon
commander's dugout until it's completely dark, drinking grog
and smoking and playing Polish lotto, until they've cleaned up
as thoroughly as a band of rats. Then, at some ungodly hour, a
little chappie comes ghosting down the trench, creeps up behind
the sentry, shouts 'Gas attack!' in his ear, and counts how many
seconds it takes the fellow to get into his mask. He, obviously, is
the gas-attack protection officer. In the middle of the night,
there's one more knock on the plank door of the dugout:
'What's going on here? You asleep already? Here, will you sign
receipt of twenty knife-rests and half a dozen dugout frames?'
The carrying-party is there. So, on quiet days anyway, there's
a continual coming and going, enough finally to induce the
poor inhabitant of the dugout to sigh: 'Oh, if only there'd be a
bit of bombardment so we could get some peace!' It's true too: a
couple of heavy bombs only contribute to the overall feeling of
cosiness: we're left to ourselves, and the tedious pen-pushing
stops.

'Lieutenant, permission to take my leave, sir, I'm going on duty
in half an hour!' Outside, the clay walls of the parados are
gleaming in the dying rays of the sun, and the trench itself is

completely in shadow by now. Soon the first flares will go up, and the night sentries will begin their back and forth.

The new day for the trench warrior begins.

Daily Life in the Trenches

And so our days passed in strenuous monotony, interspersed with short rest periods in Douchy. But even in the front line, there were some good times to be had. Often I would sit with a feeling of cosy seclusion at the table in my little dugout, whose unplaned gun-hung plank walls had for me something of the Wild West about them, drinking a cup of tea, smoking and reading, while my orderly busied himself at the tiny stove, and the aroma of toasting bread gradually filled the air. What trench warrior has not experienced the sensation? Outside, along the fire-bays, came the heavy rhythmic tramp of feet, and a rough shout when sentry met sentry in the trench. My desensitized hearing no longer took in the incessant rifle fire, the smart impacts of bullets thudding into cover, or the flares expiring with a slow hiss beside the opening of my air-shaft outside. Then I would take my notebook out of my map pocket, and jot down the salient events of the day.

And so there came about, as part of my diary, a conscientious account of life in C Sector, the small zigzag part of the long front where we were at home, where we knew every overgrown bit of trench and every ramshackle dugout. Round about us in the mounds of earth rested the bodies of dead comrades, every foot of ground had witnessed some sort of drama, behind every traverse lurked catastrophe, ready day and night to pluck its next chance victim. And yet we all felt a strong bond to our sector, as though we had grown together with it. We had seen it when it was a black ribbon winding through the snowy landscape, when the florid thickets round about flooded it with narcotic scents at noontide, and when pallid moonbeams wove webs round its dark corners, while squeaking clusters of rats went about their ghastly business. We sat on long summer evenings cheerfully on its clay ramparts, while the balmy air wafted the sounds of our busy hammering and banging and our native songs in the direction of the enemy; we plunged over beams and chopped wire while Death with his steel club assaulted our trenches and slothful smoke slunk out of our shattered clay ramparts. Many times, the colonel wanted to transfer us out to a quieter section of the regimental line, but each time the company begged him as one man to let us remain in C Sector. There now follows a selection from my diary entries taken down at the time, from those nights at Monchy.

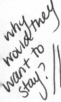 why would they want to stay?

7 October 1915. Standing at dawn on the fire-step opposite our dugout next to the sentry when a rifle bullet ripped through his forage cap without harming a hair of his head. At the same time, two pioneers were wounded on the wires. One had a ricochet through both legs, the other a ball through his ear.

In the morning, the sentry on our left flank was shot through both cheekbones. The blood spurted out of him in thick gouts. And, to cap it all, when Lieutenant von Ewald, visiting our sector to take pictures of sap N barely fifty yards away, turned to climb down from the outlook, a bullet shattered the back of his skull and he died on the spot. Large fragments of skull were left littering the sentry platform. Also, a man was hit in the shoulder, but not badly.

19 October. The middle platoon's section of trench was attacked with six-inch shells. One man was hurled against a post by the blast so hard that he sustained serious internal injuries, and a splinter of wood punctured the artery in his arm.

In the early morning fog, as we were repairing our wires on

the right, we came upon a French corpse that must have been there for many months.

That night, two men were wounded while unspooling wire. Gutschmidt was shot in both hands and one thigh, Schafer took a bullet in the knee.

30 October. Following a torrential downpour in the night, all the traverses came down and formed a grey sludgy porridge with the rain, turning the trench into a deep swamp. Our only consolation was that the British were just as badly off as we were, because we could see them baling out for all they were worth. Since our position has a little more elevation than theirs, we even managed to pump our excess their way. Also, we used rifles with telescopic sights on them.

The crumbled trench walls exposed a line of bodies left there from the previous autumn's fighting.

9 November. Was standing next to Territorial Wiegmann in front of Altenburg Redoubt when a long shot passed through his bayonet, which he was carrying over his shoulder, and gave him a bad wound in the groin. Those British bullets with their brittle points are dumdum* by any other name.

Staying in these little earthworks tucked into the landscape, where I am based with half a platoon, offers more freedom of movement than the front line. A gentle slope comes between us and the front; behind us there's an ascent to the wooded hill of Adinfer. Fifty paces behind the fortifications, in a rather poorly selected location, is our latrine – a long beam supported on two trestles over a ditch. The men like to spend time there, either reading the paper, or for companionship, in the manner of canaries, say. This is the font of all the various sinister rumours that course around the front, and that go by the name of 'bog

---

* 'A soft-nosed bullet (1897); f. *Dum Dum*, name of a military station and arsenal near Calcutta, India' (*Oxford Dictionary of Etymology*). They have been, at different times, disapproved of and declared illegal.

talk'. In one instance, admittedly, the cosiness is shattered by the fact that the place, while not overlooked by the enemy, is still vulnerable to fire over the low rise. If they aim just over the ridge, the bullets pass through the dip at chest height, and a man has to lie flat on the floor to be safe. So it sometimes happens that in the same 'session', two or three times, more or less clothed, you have to measure your length, to allow a machine-gun burst, like a musical scale, to pass over your head. It's the occasion for all sorts of ribaldry, of course.

hunting

Among the more positive aspects of our situation is the availability of game, in particular pheasants, untold numbers of which inhabit the fallow fields. For want of shotguns, we have to try and sneak up on the rather dim 'cookpot volunteers' and blow their heads off, otherwise there's not too much left to eat. You have to remember not to get too carried away in the heat of the chase, otherwise the huntsman risks becoming the quarry, if the trenches below get a sight of you.

Rats we go after with steel traps. Admittedly, the beasts are so strong that they try and take the traps with them; their noisy efforts bring us charging out of our dugouts to finish them off with clubs. We've even devised a type of hunt for the mice who nibble our bread; we all but empty a cartridge, and, using a paper pellet for a bullet, we try to shoot them with that.

shooting games

Last but not least, with a fellow NCO, I've thought up another type of shooting sport, quite exciting though again not without its perils. In conditions of fog, we go out collecting up unexploded shells, little ones and big ones, some weighing a hundredweight or more, all usually in plentiful supply. We set these up at some distance away, and then, hidden behind shooting-slits, we bang away at them. We don't need anyone to examine the targets to tell us how we've done, because a hit – a shot on the fuse – announces itself right away with a hideous blast, which is greatly increased if it's a case of 'all nine'; in other words, if the explosion carries through a whole row of these unexploded duds.

14 November. Last night I dreamed I was shot in the hand. As a result I'm more than usually careful all day.

21 November. I was leading an entrenchment party from Altenburg Redoubt to C Sector. Then Territorial Diener climbed up on a mound behind the trench to shovel some soil over the defences. No sooner had he got up there than a bullet fired from the sap went right through his head, and dropped him dead in the trench. He was a married man with four children. His comrades stayed a long time at their shooting-slits afterwards, hoping to exact revenge. They were weeping with frustration. They seemed to feel personal enmity for the Britisher who had fired the mortal shot.

24 November. A machine-gunner was gravely wounded in the head in our sector. Half an hour later, another man in our company had his cheek laid open by infantry fire.

On 29 November our battalion moved back for a fortnight to the little town of Quéant, in the back area of the division, which later was to achieve such bloody renown, to drill and indulge in some of the blessings afforded by the hinterland. During our stay there, my commission as lieutenant came through, and I was posted to the 2nd Company.

In Quéant and its environs, we were often invited to drinking sessions by the local commandants, and I was given an insight into the near-absolute authority these local bosses exercised over their subordinates and the local populations. One Captain of Horse dubbed himself the King of Quéant, and made his appearance every night at our round table, where he was greeted by upraised right hands and a thunderous 'Long Live the King!' He held sway over us till daybreak, a moody monarch, punishing every breach of etiquette and every violation of his infinitely subtle conduct regulations with the imposition of a round of drinks. We grunts, as new arrivals, had a predictably hard time of it. The following day, we would see him after lunch, a little the worse for wear, touring his estates in a dogcart, and paying *drunkenness*

his respects to neighbouring monarchs (with many libations to Bacchus), in readiness for the evening ahead. These visits he referred to as 'ambuscades'. On one occasion, he got into a tiff with the King of Inchy, and had a mounted MP call out an official feud between them. After several engagements, in the course of which rival detachments of squires bombarded each other with clods of earth from their respective fortified trenches, the King of Inchy was incautious enough to regale himself with Bavarian beer at the mess in Quéant, and was apprehended while visiting a lonely place. He was forced to purchase a vast tun of beer by way of ransom. And so ended the epic war between the two monarchs.

On 11 December, I went over the top to the front line, to report to Lieutenant Wetje, the commander of my new company, which occupied C Sector in turn about with my former company, the 6th. As I was about to leap into the trench, I was shocked at the change to the position in just a fortnight. It had collapsed into a huge, mud-filled pit in which the occupants sloshed around miserably. Already up to my hip in it, I thought ruefully back to the round table of the King of Quéant. We poor grunts! Almost all the dugouts had collapsed, and the shelters were inundated. We had to spend the next weeks working incessantly, merely to get something resembling *terra firma* underfoot. For the time being, I stayed with Lieutenants Wetje and Boje in a shelter, whose ceiling – in spite of tarpaulins suspended beneath it – leaked like a sieve, so that the servants had to carry the water out in buckets every half-hour.

leaking

When I left the shelter completely sodden the following morning, I couldn't believe the sight that met my eyes. The battlefield that previously had borne the stamp of deathly emptiness upon it was now as animated as a fairground. The occupants of both trenches had emerged from the morass of their trenches on to the top, and already a lively exchange of schnapps, cigarettes, uniform buttons and other items had commenced between the two barbed-wire lines. The throng of khaki-clad figures emerging from the hitherto so apparently deserted English lines seemed as eerie as the appearance of a ghost in daylight.

Suddenly a shot rang out that laid one of our men dead in the mire, whereupon both sides quickly scuttled back into their trenches. I went to that part of our line which fronted on to the British sap, and called out that I wanted to speak to an officer. And lo, I saw several British soldiers going back, and returning with a young man from their firing trench who had on, as I was able to see through my field glasses, a somewhat more ornate cap than they did. We negotiated first in English, and then a little more fluently in French, with all the men listening. I reproached him for the fact that one of our men had been killed by a treacherous shot, to which he replied that that hadn't been his company, but the one adjacent. 'Il y a des cochons aussi chez vous!'* he remarked when a few shots from the sector next to ours plugged into the ground not far from his head, causing me to get ready to take cover. We did, though, say much to one another that betokened an almost sportsmanlike admiration for the other, and I'm sure we should have liked to exchange mementoes.

For clarity's sake, we gave a solemn mutual declaration of war, to commence three minutes after the end of our talks, and following a 'Good-night!' on his part, and an 'Au revoir!' on mine, to the regret of my men I fired off a shot that pinged against his steel loophole, and got one myself that almost knocked the rifle out of my hands.

It was the first time I had been given an opportunity of surveying the battlefield in front of the sap, seeing as otherwise one couldn't even show the peak of one's cap in such a perilous place. I saw that immediately in front of our entanglements there was a skeleton whose bleached bones glimmered out of scraps of blue

* 'There are some unscrupulous bastards on your side too!'

uniform. From the British cap-badges seen that day, we were able to tell that the regiment facing ours were the 'Hindustani' Leicestershires.

Shortly after our negotiations were concluded, our artillery fired off a few rounds at the enemy positions, whereupon, before our eyes, four stretchers were carried across the open field without a single shot being loosed off at them from our side. I must say I felt proud.

Throughout the war, it was always my endeavour to view my opponent without animus, and to form an opinion of him as a man on the basis of the courage he showed. I would always try and seek him out in combat and kill him, and I expected nothing else from him. But never did I entertain mean thoughts of him. When prisoners fell into my hands, later on, I felt responsible for their safety, and would always do everything in my power for them.

As Christmas approached, the weather seemed to worsen; we had recourse to pumps in our efforts to do something about the water. During this muddy phase, our losses also worsened. So, for instance, I find in my diary for 12 December: 'Today we buried seven men in Douchy, and two more were shot.' And for 23 December: 'Mud and filth are getting the better of us. This morning at three o'clock an enormous deposit came down at the entrance to my dugout. I had to employ three men, who were barely able to bale the water that poured like a freshet into my dugout. Our trench is drowning, the morass is now up to our navels, it's desperate. On the right edge of our frontage, another corpse has begun to appear, so far just the legs.'

We spent Christmas Eve in the line, and, standing in the mud, sang hymns, to which the British responded with machine-gun fire. On Christmas Day, we lost one man to a ricochet in the head. Immediately afterwards, the British attempted a friendly gesture by hauling a Christmas tree up on their traverse, but our angry troops quickly shot it down again, to which Tommy replied with rifle-grenades. It was all in all a less than merry Christmas.

On 28 December, I was back in command of the Altenburg Redoubt. On that day, rifleman Hohn, one of my best men, lost his arm to a shell fragment. Heidotting received a bad thigh wound from one of the many bullets that were whizzing round our earthworks in the hollow. And my faithful August Kettler, the first of many servants to die in my service, fell victim to a shrapnel that passed through his windpipe as he was on his way to Monchy to get my lunch. As he was setting off with the mess-tins, I had called out to him: 'August, mind how you go, won't you.' 'I'll be fine, Lieutenant!' And then I was summoned and found him lying on the ground close to the dugout, gurgling, as the air passed through the wound into his chest with every breath he took. I had him carried back; he died a few days later in hospital. It was a feature of his case, as it was of quite a few others, that his inability to speak made him even more pathetic, as he stared at the nurses in bewilderment like a tormented animal.

The road from Monchy to Altenburg Redoubt cost us a lot of blood. It led along the rear slope of a modest elevation, perhaps five hundred paces behind our front line. Our opponents, perhaps alerted by aerial photographs to the fact that this road was indeed much frequented, set themselves to rake it at intervals with machine-gun fire, or to unload shrapnels over the area. Even though there was a ditch running along beside the road, and there were strict orders to walk in the ditch, sure enough everyone tended to stroll along this dangerous road, without any cover, with the habitual insouciance of old soldiers. Generally, we got away with it, but on many days fate snatched a victim or two, and over time they added up. Here, too, stray bullets from all directions seemed to have arranged a rendezvous for themselves at the latrine, so that we were often compelled to flee, holding a newspaper and trousers at half-mast. And for all that, it seemed not to have occurred to anyone to move this indispensable facility to a place of greater safety.

MUD

January also was a month of back-breaking work. Each platoon began by removing the mud from the immediate vicinity of its dugout, by means of shovels, buckets and pumps, and then, having firm ground underfoot once more, set about establishing communications with its neighbours. In the Adinfer forest, where our artillery was positioned, teams of woodcutters were set to strip the branches off young trees and split them into long struts. The trench walls were sloped off and entirely reveted with this material. Also, numerous culverts, drainage ditches and sumps were dug, so that things were once more made bearable. What really made a difference were those deep sumps that were dug through the surface clay and enabled water to drain into the absorptive chalk beneath.

On 28 January 1916, a man in my unit was wounded in the body by a splinter from a bullet that shattered against his plate. On the 30th, another got a bullet in the thigh. When we were relieved on 1 February, the communication trenches were subjected to intense fire. A shrapnel shell landed at the feet of rifleman Junge, my former cleaner in the 6th Company, failed to go off, but flared up instead with a tall flame, so that he had to be carried away with grave burns.

desensitized

It was round about then too that an NCO with the 6th, whom I knew well, and whose brother had fallen only days before, was fatally injured by a 'toffee-apple' that he had found. He had unscrewed the fuse, and, noticing that the greenish powder he tipped out was highly inflammable, he put a lit cigarette in at the opening. The mortar of course blew up, and he received fifty separate wounds. We suffered many casualties from the over-familiarity engendered by daily encounters with gunpowder. A rather alarming neighbour in this respect was Lieutenant Pook, who was housed by himself in a dugout in the maze of trenches behind our left flank. He had collected a number of enormous

dud shells, and amused himself by unscrewing their fuses, and
tinkering with them as if they were bits of clockwork. Every time
I had to go past his lair I made a wide detour. Even when the men
were only chipping the copper rings off the shells to work them
into paper-knives or bracelets, there were incidents. *SHELLING*

On the night of 3 February we were back in Douchy, following
a taxing time at the front. The next morning, I was enjoying my
first morning of ease, drinking a cup of coffee in my billet on the
Emmichplatz, when a monster of a shell, the herald of a heavy
bombardment, went off outside my door and sent the window
glass jangling into my room. With three bounds I was in the
cellar, where the other inhabitants also presented themselves in
quick time. Since the cellar was half above ground, and was only
separated from the garden by a thin wall, we all pressed together
into a short tunnel that had been embarked on only a few days
previously. With animal instincts, my sheepdog forced his whimpering way between the tight-pressed bodies into the deepest,
furthest corner of the shelter. Far in the distance, we could hear
the dull thud of a series of discharges, then, when we'd counted
to thirty or so, the whining approach of the heavy iron lumps,
ending in crashing explosions all round our little abode. Each
time, there was an unpleasant surge of pressure through the cellar
window, and clods of earth and shards came clattering on the
tiled roof, while the anxious horses whinnied and stamped in
their stables near by. The dog whined throughout, and a fat
bandsman screamed as if he were having a tooth pulled each time
a whistling bomb approached.

At last the storm was over, and we could risk going out in the
open again. The wrecked village street was swarming like a
disturbed anthill. My quarters looked in a bad way. The earth
had been blown open in several places against the cellar wall, fruit
trees were snapped, and smack in the middle of the path lay a
long and malign-looking shell that hadn't gone off. The roof was
riddled with holes. A big fragment of shell had removed half the

chimney. In the regimental office next door, a few sizeable splinters had drilled through the walls and the large wardrobe, shredding the uniforms that were kept there for wear on home leave.

On 8 February, the sector received a vigorous pummelling. It began early in the morning when our own artillery dropped a dud on the dugout of my right flank, to the consternation of those within, pushing through the door and toppling the stove. This event, which could have passed off so much worse, was immortalized in a sketch of eight men trying to get out past the smoking stove through the shattered door, while the bomb lay in the corner, rolling its eyes wickedly. In the afternoon, three more dugouts were hit, but luckily only one man was slightly hurt in the knee, because all the others, except for the sentries, had withdrawn into the shelters. The following day, Fusilier Hartmann from my platoon was fatally hit in the side by the flanking battery.

On 25 February, we were particularly affected by a fatality that robbed us of an outstanding comrade. Just before we were to be relieved, I was brought the news in my dugout that volunteer Karg had just fallen in the shelter next door. I went there, to see, as so often before, a serious-looking group of men around a motionless figure, lying with rigid fingers on the bloodied snow, staring at the darkening winter sky with glassy eyes. Another victim for the flanking battery! Karg had been in the trench when it had started up, and had straightaway leaped into the shelter. A shell had struck the opposite wall of the trench high up, and at just such an angle as to cast a large splinter into the entrance to the shelter. Karg, who must have thought he had already reached safety, was struck on the back of the head; his death was instant and unexpected.

That flanking battery was quite a feature of those days. On average once an hour, it would fire a round at us, out of the blue, whose fragments precisely swept out the trench. In the six days from 3 to 8 February, it cost us three dead and seven wounded, three of them seriously. Even though it was located on a hillside no more than a mile away from our left flank, our artillery seemed to be unable to do anything about it. We therefore tried, by adding to the number of traverses and building them higher, to restrict its effectiveness to small parts of the trench at any given time. Those stretches that were visible from it, we masked with screens of hay or material. Also, we beefed up the sentry posts with wooden beams and slabs of reinforced concrete. But even then, because of the way the trench was used as a thoroughfare, the odds favoured the English gunners in their effort to 'pick us off' without excess use of munitions.

By early March, we had seen the worst of the mud. The weather turned dry, and the trench was now securely supported. Every night, I sat in my dugout at a little desk, reading, or chatting if I had company. There were four of us officers, including the company commander, and we lived together very harmoniously, drinking coffee in one or other of our dugouts, or having supper together, often over a bottle or two, smoking, playing cards, and enjoying rather baronial conversations. On some days, there was herring with boiled potatoes and dripping, which was considered quite a feast. In the memory, such congenial hours made up for other days of blood, filth and work. Also, they were only possible in this long stationary phase of the war, where we had all bonded together, and an almost peacetime routine had evolved. Our principal source of pride was our building work, which HQ broadly left us to get on with by ourselves. Through constant work, one thirty-step shelter after another was dug out of the chalk and clay soil, and linked by cross-passages, so that we could go from right to left of our frontage in safety and comfort, entirely underground. My own favourite project was a sixty-yard underground passage linking my dugout with the company commander's, with other dormitories and munitions depots off to either side, just like a regulation corridor. All this was to come in handy in the fighting to come.

When we met in the trenches after morning coffee – we even had newspapers delivered to the front, at least some of the time – all clean and with our footrules in our hands, we compared progress, and our talk was of shelter-frames, dugout designs, rate of progress, and other such matters. A popular subject was the construction of my 'boudoir', a little cubby-hole off the underground passage, dug into dry chalk; a sort of warren where we could have happily dozed through the end of the world. For a mattress I had set aside some fine-meshed wire, and the wall-coverings were of some special sandbag material.

On 1 March, as I was standing by Territorial Ikmann, who was to fall not long afterwards, a shell landed the other side of a tarpaulin next to us. The splinters fizzed past us without hurting either of us. When we examined them later, we found hideously long and sharp steel needles that had sliced through the cloth. We called these things 'whizz-bangs' or 'grapeshot', because we could never hear them coming; it was like suddenly being in the middle of a whirring cloud of splinters.

On 14 March, the sector on our right took a direct hit from a six-inch shell, and three men were killed, three others badly wounded. One simply vanished off the face of the earth, another was burned black. On the 18th, the sentry in front of my dugout was struck by a shell fragment that cut open his cheek and took off the tip of his ear. On the 19th, on our left flank, Fusilier Schmidt II was shot in the head. On the 23rd, to the right of my dugout, Fusilier Lohmann fell, shot in the head. That same evening, a sentry reported that an enemy patrol were stuck in our wire. I led a party to look see, but we found no one.

On 7 April, on the right flank, Fusilier Kramer received head wounds from some bullet fragments. This type of wounding was very common, because the English munitions were so soft as to fragment on contact. In the afternoon, the area immediately around my dugout came in for some heavy and sustained bombardment. The skylight was smashed, and, on every new impact,

a hail of dried clay came sprinkling through the opening, though
we made a point of finishing our coffee together.

Afterwards, we fought a duel with a daredevil Englishman,
whose head peeped out over the rim of a trench that couldn't
have been more than a hundred yards away, and who sent a
stream of extremely well-aimed shots pinging round our shooting-slits. I returned fire with a few of the men, but immediately a
shrewdly aimed ball on the edge of our plate kicked sand in our
faces, and gave me a scratch on the neck. We weren't to be
put off, though, popping up suddenly, taking swift aim, and
disappearing again. Then a bullet smashed the rifle of Fusilier
Storch, the splinters bloodying his face in at least a dozen places.
The next shot nicked a piece out of our armour plating; and
another shattered the mirror we were using for observation, but
we had the satisfaction of having our opponent disappearing for
good after a series of shots had struck the clay ramparts directly
in front of his face. For good measure, with three rounds of hard
munitions, I made a mess of the armour behind which this fellow
had done his mischievous worst.

On 9 April, two British planes flew repeatedly low over our
position. All the men raced out of their dugouts and started
banging away into the sky like crazy. I was just remarking to
Lieutenant Sievers: 'I hope to God the flanking battery don't get
any ideas!' and already the steel shreds were flying about our
ears, and we had to leap into the nearest shelter. Sievers was
standing by the entrance; I urged him to go further in, and smack!
an inch-thick splinter dug itself into the damp clay in front of his
feet, still smoking. For afters, we were sent shrapnel mortars,
whose black balls exploded over our heads with great violence.
One man was hit in the armpit by a piece of one, no bigger than
the head of a pin, but extremely painful. In return, I planted
a few 'pineapples' in the British trenches, as we called those
five-pound mortars that resembled tropical fruit. There was a
tacit agreement between the infantry on both sides to restrict

themselves to rifle fire; all recourse to explosives was punished by a double load back. Unfortunately, our opponents tended to have more munitions than ourselves, and so could play the game for longer.

To get over the shock, we downed several bottles of red wine in Sievers's dugout, which got my dander up to such a degree that I took the high road back to my cubby-hole, in spite of the bright moon. Before long, I lost my way, wound up in a vast shell-hole, and heard the British working in their trench hard by. After causing a breach of the peace with a couple of hand-grenades, I hurriedly withdrew into our trench, in the process catching my hand on the prong of one of our lovely mantraps. These consist of four sharp iron spears assembled in such a way that one of them is always vertical. We left them out on scouting paths.

There was a lot of activity in the field altogether in those days, some of it not without its funny – or bloody funny – side. For instance, a soldier on one of our patrols was shot at because he had a stammer and couldn't get the password out in time. Another time, a man who had been celebrating in the kitchens in Monchy till past midnight, clambered over the wire, and started blazing away at his own lines. After he'd shot off all his ammunition, he was taken in and given a sound beating.

The Beginning of the Battle of the Somme

In mid-April 1916, I was detailed to attend an officer-training course under the overall direction of the divisional commander, Major-General Sontag, at Croisilles, a little town behind the divisional lines. There, we received instruction in a variety of practical and theoretical military subjects. Particularly fascinating were the tactical excursions on horseback, under Major von Jarotzky, a fat little staffer, who would get terribly excited about things. We called him the 'Pressure-cooker'. A series of excursions and inspection visits to the very often improvised units in the hinterland gave us, who were in the habit of viewing slightly askance everything that happened there, an insight into the incredible work that goes on behind a line of fighting men. And so we visited the abattoir, the commissariat and gunnery repair workshop in Boyelles, the sawmill and pioneer park in the woods of Bourlon, the dairy, pig farm and rendering plant in Inchy, the aviation park and bakery in Quéant. On Sundays we went to the nearby towns of Cambrai, Douai and Valenciennes, to remind ourselves of what 'ladies in hats' looked like.

It would be rather mean of me, in this book that has so much blood in it, if I were to withhold from you an account of a scrape in which my part was a somewhat comical one. Back in winter, when our battalion was a guest of the King of Quéant, I had, as a young officer, been called upon to inspect the guard for the first time. On the edge of town, I had promptly lost my way, and, meaning to ask for directions to the little station guard post, I had walked into a tiny cottage that stood there all by itself. Living there, I found, all alone, as her father had lately died, was a seventeen-year-old girl by the name of Jeanne. When she gave me directions, she laughed, and when I asked what was so funny, she said: 'Vous êtes bien jeune, je voudrais avoir votre devenir.'* – Because of the spiritedness of her remark, I had dubbed her Jeanne d'Arc, and in the subsequent trench-fighting, I had occasionally thought of that isolated little house.

One evening in Croisilles, I suddenly felt an urge to go over there. I had a horse saddled up, and before long had left the town behind me. It was a May evening, perfect time for a ride. The clover lay like heavy burgundy cushions on the fields stitched with hawthorn, and outside the village gates the huge candles of flowering chestnuts flickered in the gloaming. I rode through Bullecourt and Ecoust, never guessing that in two years' time I would find myself making ready to attack the hideous ruins of these villages, now nestling so peaceably among ponds and hills at eventide. At the little station I had inspected in the winter, civilians were still busy unloading cylinders of propane. I greeted them, and watched them for a while. Before long, the house appeared in front of me, with its reddish-brown, bemossed roof. I rapped on the shutters, which were already bolted shut.

'Qui est là?'

'Bonsoir, Jeanne d'Arc!'

'Ah, bonsoir, mon petit officier Gibraltar!'

I was made as pleasantly welcome as I'd hoped I would be. After tying up my horse, I went inside and was asked to share her supper of eggs, white bread and butter, all nicely laid out on a large cabbage leaf. Seeing such things, one really doesn't need a second invitation.

Everything would have been fine and dandy, but as I stepped

* 'You're so young, I wish I could have your future.'

out to leave, I found a torch shining in my eyes, and a military policeman asking me for my documentation. My talking to the civilians, the attentiveness with which I'd observed the gas cylinders, my unexplained appearance in this sparsely garrisoned district, all had aroused the suspicion of espionage. Of course I hadn't brought my service-book with me, and so had to be led before the King of Quéant, who was, as usual at this time of night, presiding over his round table.

Luckily, I found a sympathetic ear there. I was identified and made welcome. On this occasion, I came away with a rather different impression of the king; the hour was late, and he was talking about tropical jungles where he had spent a lot of time in charge of the building of a railway line.

On 16 June, the general sent us back to our units with a little speech, from which we were given to understand that our opponents were preparing a large-scale offensive on the Western Front, with its left flank facing our own position. This was our first inkling of what was to be the Battle of the Somme. It marked the end of the first and mildest part of the war; thereafter, it was like embarking on a different one altogether. What we had, admittedly almost unbeknown to ourselves, been through had been the attempt to win a war by old-fashioned pitched battles, and the stalemating of the attempt in static warfare. What confronted us now was a war of *matériel* of the most gigantic proportions. This war in turn was replaced towards the end of 1917 by mechanized warfare, though that was not given time fully to develop.

The sense that something was imminent hardened once we returned to our regiments, because our comrades told us of the increasing activity of the enemy. The British had twice, albeit unsuccessfully, essayed a raid in force against C Sector. We had retaliated with a well-prepared assault by three officers' patrols against the so-called trench triangle, in the course of which we had taken several prisoners. While I'd been away, Wetje had been wounded by a shrapnel ball on the arm, but resumed command of the company shortly after my return. My dugout was somewhat changed as well, a direct hit had just about halved its dimensions. During the aforementioned raid, the British had fumigated it with a few hand-grenades. My replacement had managed to squeeze his way out through the skylight, while his batman had perished. His blood was still visible in great brown stains across the lining boards.

On 20 June I was ordered to eavesdrop on the enemy trenches, to find out whether they were trying to undermine us, and with Ensign Wohlgemut, Lance-Corporal Schmidt and Fusilier Parthenfelder, I set out a little before midnight across our own, pretty high wire entanglements. The first stretch we did hunched forward, and then we crept side by side over the densely grown field. Fourth-form memories of Karl May* came to me as I slithered along on my front through dewy grass and thistles, anxious to avoid the slightest rustle, with the British lines visible barely fifty yards in front of us as a black stroke against the grey. From a great distance, a spray of machine-gun bullets came down almost perpendicularly on top of us; an occasional flare went up and threw its chill light on our already rather inhospitable patch of land.

Then there was a loud rustling behind us. Two shadows were dashing between the trenches. Even as we made ready to throw ourselves upon them, they had disappeared. Moments later, the thunder of two hand-grenades in the British trenches indicated that we had brushed past some of our own. We continued to creep forward.

Suddenly the ensign gripped my arm: 'Watch out, right, very close, ssh, ssh!' And then, no more than ten paces away, I heard sundry rustlings in the grass. We had lost our orientation, and

---

* German author and polygrapher (1842–1912), whose tendentious, patriotic, neo-colonialist tales were routinely read by generations of young Germans.

Prowling btw trenches

had been creeping along parallel to the English lines; presumably the enemy had heard us, and had now emerged from his trenches to see what was going on.

These moments of nocturnal prowling leave an indelible impression. Eyes and ears are tensed to the maximum, the rustling approach of strange feet in the tall grass is an unutterably menacing thing. Your breath comes in shallow bursts; you have to force yourself to stifle any panting or wheezing. There is a little mechanical click as the safety-catch of your pistol is taken off; the sound cuts straight through your nerves. Your teeth are grinding on the fuse-pin of the hand-grenade. The encounter will be short and murderous. You tremble with two contradictory impulses: the heightened awareness of the huntsman, and the terror of the quarry. You are a world to yourself, saturated with the appalling aura of the savage landscape.

A line of dim forms surfaced, their whispers carried across to us. We turned to look at them; I heard the Bavarian Parthenfelder biting the blade of his knife.

They took a few more steps towards us, and then started working on their wires, seemingly not having noticed us. We crept very slowly backwards, keeping our eyes fixed on them. Death, which had already loomed up expectantly between us, slunk away dejectedly. After a little, we stood up and went on, till we reached our sector safely.

Our expedition's fortunate conclusion gave us the idea of taking a prisoner, and we decided to go again the next night. I had just lain down, therefore, for an afternoon nap when I was startled up by a thunderous din outside my dugout. The British were lobbing 'toffee-apples' across, which, even though they made very little noise as they were fired, were so heavy that their splinters ripped away the massive posts of the revetment. Swearing, I clambered up from my bed and went into the trench, only, the next time I saw one of the black weights arcing towards us, to shout: 'Mortar coming left!' and nip into the nearest shelter.

In the course of the next few weeks, we were so abundantly graced with trench mortars of all shapes and sizes that we got in the habit, each time we found ourselves walking along the trench, of keeping one eye aloft, and the other on the entrance to the nearest deep dugout.

That night, my three companions and I once more crept out between the trenches. We crawled along on our toes and elbows till right up to the British entanglements, where we hid behind clumps of grass. After a while, some British came out, dragging a roll of wire after them. They stopped close in front of us, put the roll down, snipped at it with wire-cutters, and talked in whispers. We sidled together, and had a hasty discussion: 'Toss a hand-grenade in there, and pick up the pieces!' 'Come on, there's four of them!' 'Don't talk rubbish!' 'Quiet! Quiet down!' My warning came too late; as I looked up, the British were darting lizard-like under their wires, and disappeared into their trench. The feeling now got a little clammy. The thought: 'Now they're going to bring up a machine-gun' gave me a bad taste in my mouth. The others entertained similar fears. We slid back as quickly as we could, with quite a jangle. The British lines woke up. Drumming of feet, whispers, running hither and thither. Pssht ... a flare. All around it was as bright as day, while we tried to press our heads into the grass. Another flare. Tricky moments. You wish the earth would swallow you up, you'd rather be anywhere than where you are, ten yards in front of enemy lines. Another one. Paow! Paow! The unmistakably crisp and deafening report of rifle shots fired at almost point-blank range. 'Christ! They've seen us!'

No longer worried about making a noise, we called to each other to run for our lives, and leapt up and raced towards our lines through the now pattering gunfire. After a few bounds, I stumbled and landed in a small and very shallow crater, while the other three raced past me, thinking I was done for. I pressed myself to the ground, pulled in my head and my legs, and allowed

shell crater

the bullets to brush over me. Every bit as menacing were the burning lumps of magnesium from the flares, which burned down very close to me in some cases, and which I tried to pat away with my cap. Eventually the shooting relented, and, after a further quarter of an hour, I left my hiding-hole, slowly and cautiously to begin with, and then as fast as my hands and feet could carry me. Since the moon had set by now, I soon became utterly disorientated and had no idea where the British or the German lines were. Not even the distinctive shape of the ruined mill at Monchy was visible against the horizon. The odd bullet from one side or the other streaked over the ground. In the end I lay down in the grass and determined to wait for morning. Suddenly I heard some whispers very close by. I prepared to do battle, and then cautiously made a series of indeterminate natural sounds that I thought might pass equally well for English as German. I resolved to reply to the first English call I received with a hand-grenade. Then, to my delight, it turned out that the whispering was that of my little troop, who were just in the process of taking off their belts, to carry my body back. We sat a while longer in a bomb-crater, and were overjoyed at seeing each other again. Then we made our way back to our trenches. All told, our adventure had taken three hours.

I was back on trench duty again at five. In No. 1 Platoon's part of the line, I ran into Sergeant Hock standing outside his dugout. When I expressed surprise at seeing him out so early, he informed me that he was lying in wait for a large rat whose gnawing and rustling had kept him up all night. And from time to time he would look ruefully at his absurdly small dugout, which he had christened 'Villa Fat-of-the-Land Chicken'.

While we were standing together, we heard a distant sound of firing, which boded nothing in particular to us. But Hock, who the day before had almost been brained by a large mortar-bomb, and was therefore very apprehensive, dived into the nearest shelter, sliding down the first fifteen steps in his haste, and finding space in the next fifteen for three virtuoso somersaults. I stood up by the entrance, laughing so hard I forgot all about mortars and shelters, when I heard the poor chap bewailing this painfully curtailed rat-hunt, all the while rubbing various sore joints and attempting to put back a dislocated thumb. The unhappy man went on to tell me he'd just been sitting down to eat the night before when the mortar-bomb had come along. As a result he'd got grit all over his dinner, and had made a first painful acquaintance with the flight of steps. He had just arrived here from home, and wasn't yet used to our roughneck ways.

After this incident, I betook myself to my dugout, but today too there was no chance of any restorative kip. From early morning on, our trench was subjected to mortar attack, at shorter and shorter intervals. By noon, I'd had enough. With a few other fellows, I got our Lanz mortar set up, and aimed at our opponent's trenches – a pretty feeble reply, admittedly, to the heavy bombs we'd been ploughed with. Sweating, we squatted on a little dip in the trench – the clay baked hard by the June sun – and sent bomb after bomb towards their lines.

Since the British seemed quite unperturbed, I went with Wetje to the telephone, where, after some thought, we agreed on the following form of words: 'Helen's spitting in our trenches. We need potatoes, big ones and little ones!' We used this type of language when there was a chance that the enemy might be listening in; and before long we were pleased to hear back from Lieutenant Deichmann that the fat policeman with the stiff moustaches and a couple of his little friends would be brought up, and before long the first of our two-hundredweight bombs flew into the enemy trench, followed by a few units of field artillery, with the result that we were left in peace for the rest of the day.

Midday the following day the dance began again, but significantly intensified. At the first shot, I took my subterranean passage to the second line, and from there to the communications trench where we had set up our own mortar emplacement. We opened fire in such a way that every time we received a 'toffee-apple' we replied with a Lanz. After exchanging about forty mortars, the enemy gunner seemed to be finding his range. His missiles were coming down to the right and left of us, without being able to interrupt our activity until one was seen heading straight for us. At the very last moment we pulled our trigger one last time, and then ran as fast as we could. I had just made it to a mucky, wired stretch of trench when the monster blew up just behind me. The enormous air pressure threw me over a bundle of barbed wire into a shell-hole full of greenish water, and sent a sprinkling of hard clay shards on top of me. I picked myself up, feeling very groggy and dishevelled. My boots and trousers were ripped by the barbed wire, my hands and my uniform were stuck with thick clay, and my knee was bleeding from a long wound. Rather the worse for wear, I slunk back through the trench to my dugout to get over the experience.

Other than that, the mortars hadn't done much in the way of damage. The trench had taken a battering in a few places, a Priester mortar was smashed, and the 'Villa Fat-of-the-Land Chicken' was no more. It had received a direct hit, while its unlucky owner was down in the deep dugout, otherwise in all probability he would have practised his third freestyle descent of the steps.

The firing went on all afternoon without a break, and by evening it had been increased to drumfire by numbers of cylindrical bombs. We referred to these missiles as 'wash-basket mortars' because it sometimes looked as though they had been shaken down from the sky by the basketload. The best way of picturing their design is imagining a rolling-pin with two short handles on it. Apparently they were fired from special revolver-like drums and were sent spinning end over end through the air, making a somewhat laboured wheezing sound. From a distance they resembled flying sausages. These came down so thick and fast that their landing was like the torching of a batch of rockets. The 'toffee-apples' had something crushing or stamping about them, these had more of a rending effect on the nerves.

We sat tensed and ready in the shelter entrances, prepared at any moment to repel invaders with rifles and hand-grenades, but the bombardment died back after half an hour. In the night we had two more bouts of firing to withstand, during which our sentries stood at their posts and indomitably kept watch. As soon as the gunning relented, numerous flares lit up the defenders charging out from their shelters, and a brisk fire persuaded the enemy that there was still life in our lines.

In spite of the heavy bombardment, we lost only one man, Fusilier Diersmann, whose skull was smashed by a mortar-bomb landing on the parapet in front of him. Another man was wounded in the back.

On the day after this unquiet night, numerous bursts of firing prepared us for an imminent attack. In that time, our trenches really were shot to pieces, and the smashed timber from their revetment made them almost impassable; a number of dugouts were also flattened.

Brigade headquarters sent an intelligence report to the front: 'Intercepted British telephone message: the British have precise descriptions of the gaps in our lines, and have requested "Steel Helmets". It is not known whether "Steel Helmet" is code for heavy mortars. Be prepared!'

We resolved to be on the alert for anything the coming night, and agreed that anyone who didn't give his name in response to a 'Hallo!' would be immediately fired at. Every officer had his pistol loaded with a red flare, to alert the artillery.

The night was still wilder than the last. In particular, one concentration of fire at quarter past two outdid anything there had been up to that point. A hail of heavy shells struck all round my dugout. We stood fully armed on the shelter steps, while the light of our little candle stumps reflected glitteringly off the wet, mildewed walls. Blue smoke streamed in through the entrances, and earth crumbled off the ceiling. 'Boom!' 'Good God!' 'A light! A light!' 'Get everything ready!' Everyone's hearts were in their mouths. Hands darted to release the pins on bombs. 'That was the last of them!' 'Let's go!' As we charged out of the entrance, a mine with a delay fuse went off, and hurled us back inside. All the same, as the last of the iron birds came whooshing down, all the sentry positions were manned by us. Bright as day, a firework display of flares lit the cloud-swathed field. These instants, in which the entire complement of men stood behind the traverses, tensed and ready, had something magical about them; they were like the last breathless second before a hugely important performance, as the music is turned off and the big lights go up.

For several hours that night, I stood leaning against the entrance to my dugout, which, irregularly, faced the enemy, from time to time looking at my watch, to take down notes about the levels of fire. I eyed the sentry, an older man with children, standing completely impassive with his rifle, lit from time to time by the flash of an explosion.

Oddly, it was after the shooting had subsided that we took another casualty. Fusilier Nienhauser suddenly fell from his sentry post, and came crashing down the shelter steps to join his comrades who were all assembled at the bottom. When they inspected the eerie arrival, all they could find on him was a small wound on the forehead, and a puncture over the right nipple from which blood was flowing. It remained unclear whether the wound or the sudden fall had killed him.

At the end of this night of terror, we were relieved by the 6th. In the grumpy mood produced by the appearance of the sun following a sleepless night, we marched down the communications trench to Monchy, and from there to the reserve line set back at the edge of the Adinfer forest, that afforded us box seats for the overture to the Somme battles. The sectors to our left were still swathed in black and white smoke, one massive explosion after another sent the dirt spewing up past rooftop height; and over them, hundreds of speedy lightnings produced by bursting shrapnels. Only the coloured signals, the mute appeals to the artillery for help, indicated that there was still life in the trenches. This was the first time I had seen artillery fire to match a natural spectacle.

In the evening, just as we hoped for a good night's sleep at last, we were given orders to load trench-mortar ammunition at Monchy, and had to spend all night waiting up in vain for a lorry that had got stuck, while the British made various, fortunately unsuccessful, attempts on our lives, either by means of high-angled machine-gun fire or sweeping the road with shrapnels. We were especially irritated by one machine-gunner who sprayed his bullets at such an angle that they came down vertically, with acceleration produced by sheer gravity. There was absolutely no point in trying to duck behind walls.

That night, the enemy gave us an example of his painstaking observation skills. In the second line, perhaps a mile and a quarter from the enemy, we had left a heap of chalk in front of what was to be a subterranean munitions dump. The British drew the unfortunately correct conclusion that this dump was to be masked over in the course of the night, and fired a group of shrapnels at it, succeeding in gravely wounding three of our men.

In the morning, I was shaken out of my sleep yet again by the order to lead my platoon on a digging detail to C Sector. My sections were broken up and divided among the 6th Company. I accompanied some of them back to the Adinfer woods, to get them chopping timber. On the way back to the trench, I stopped in my dugout for a quick catnap. But it was no good, I was unable to get any rest in those days. No sooner had I pulled off my boots, than I heard our artillery firing with unwonted animation from their position on the edge of the woods. At the same time my batman Paulicke materialized in the entrance to the shelter, and shouted down: 'Gas attack!'

THE BEGINNING OF THE BATTLE OF THE SOMME

I broke out the gas mask, got into my boots, buckled up, ran out and saw a huge cloud of gas hanging over Monchy in thick white swathes, and drifting under a slight breeze in the direction of Point 124 on the low ground.

Since my platoon was for the most part in the front line, and an attack was probable, there wasn't much time to stop and think. I leaped over the ramparts of the reserve line, raced forward, and soon found myself enveloped in the gas cloud. A penetrating smell of chlorine confirmed for me that this was indeed fighting gas, and not, as I had briefly thought, artificial fog. I therefore donned my mask, only to tear it off again right away because I'd been running so fast that the mask didn't give me enough air to breathe; also the goggles misted over in no time, and completely whited out. All this of course was hardly the stuff of 'What To Do in a Gas Attack', which I'd taught so often myself. Since I felt pain in my chest, I tried at least to put the cloud behind me as fast as I could. At the entrance to the village, I needed to get through a barrage of gunfire, whose impacts, topped by numerous clouds of shrapnel, drew a long and even chain across the barren and otherwise unfrequented fields.

Artillery fire in open country never has the same effect, either physically or on one's morale, as it does among dwellings or fortifications. I had therefore broken through the line of fire, and found myself in Monchy, which lay under an extraordinary hail of shrapnel. A shower of balls, splinters and fuses came hissing and whizzing through the branches of the fruit trees in the neglected gardens, or smacked against the masonry.

In a dugout in the garden, I saw my company comrades Sievers and Vogel sitting; they had lit a merry wood fire, and were leaning over the cleansing flame to escape the effects of the chlorine. I joined them there, until the fire had slackened off a little, and then went forward down communication trench 6.

As I went on, I looked at all the little animals lying in the pit of the trench, killed by the chlorine, and thought: 'The barrage *heavy bombardment*

is bound to start up again any moment, and if you continue taking your time, you'll be caught in the open, like a mouse in a trap.' And yet, I continued phlegmatically at my own pace.

Exactly what I had anticipated happened: not more than fifty yards away from the company shelter, I found myself in a whole new and much worse bombardment, in which it seemed completely impossible to get through even this short stretch of trench without being hit. Luckily for me, I saw right by me one of the occasional niches that were carved into the trench walls for dispatch runners. Three dugout frames, not a whole lot, but better than none at all. So I pressed myself in there and allowed the storm to pass.

Unwittingly, I seemed to have chosen the liveliest corner going. Light and heavy 'toffee-apples', Stokes bombs, shrapnels, rattles, shells of all kinds – I could no longer identify everything that was buzzing and whizzing and crashing around me. I was reminded of my corporal at Les Eparges, and his exclamation: 'What in God's name are those things?'

Occasionally my ears were utterly deafened by a single fiendish crashing burst of flame. Then incessant hissing gave me the sense of hundreds of pound weights rushing down at incredible speed, one after the other. Or a dud shell landed with a short, heavy ground-shaking thump. Shrapnels burst by the dozen, like dainty crackers, shook loose their little balls in a dense cloud, and the empty casings rasped after they were gone. Each time a shell landed anywhere close, the earth flew up and down, and metal shards drove themselves into it.

It's an easier matter to describe these sounds than to endure them, because one cannot but associate every single sound of flying steel with the idea of death, and so I huddled in my hole in the ground with my hand in front of my face, imagining all the possible variants of being hit. I think I have found a comparison that captures the situation in which I and all the other soldiers who took part in this war so often found ourselves: you must imagine you are securely tied to a post, being menaced by a man swinging a heavy hammer. Now the hammer has been taken back over his head, ready to be swung, now it's cleaving the air towards you, on the point of touching your skull, then it's struck the post, and the splinters are flying – that's what it's like to experience heavy shelling in an exposed position. Luckily, I still had a bit of that subliminal feeling of optimism, 'it'll be all right', that you feel during a game, say, and which, while it may be quite unfounded, still has a soothing effect on you. And indeed even this shelling came to an end, and I could go on my way once more, and, this time, with some urgency.

At the front, the men were all busy greasing their rifles in accordance with the nostrums of 'What To Do in a Gas Attack', because their barrels had been completely blackened by chlorine. An ensign dolefully showed me his new sword-knot, which had quite lost its silver sheen, and had turned a greenish black.

Since our opponents seemed not to be making a move, I took my troops back to the rear. Outside the company office in Monchy, we saw a lot of men affected by gas, pressing their hands against their sides and groaning and retching while their eyes watered. It was a bad business, because a few of them went on to die over the next several days, in terrible agony. We had had to withstand an attack with chlorine, which has a burning, corrosive effect on the lungs. Henceforth, I resolved never to go anywhere without my gas mask, having previously, incredibly foolishly, often left it behind in my dugout, and used its case – like a botanist – as a container for sandwiches. Seeing this taught me a lesson.

On the way back, meaning to buy something, I had gone into the 2nd Battalion canteen, where I found a dejected canteen boy standing surrounded by broken crockery. A shell had come through the ceiling and gone off in the store, converting its treasures into a *mélange* of jam, liquid soap and punctured containers of this and that. He had just, with Prussian pernicketiness, done his accounts, showing a loss of 82 marks and 58 pfennigs.

In the evening, because of the uncertain position, my platoon, which had so far been withdrawn to the second line, was moved forward to the village, and was housed in the quarry. We settled ourselves into its numerous nooks and crannies, and lit an enormous fire, whose smoke went up through the well-shaft, greatly to the annoyance of some of the company cooks, who were almost asphyxiated as they pulled up their buckets of water. Since we had been issued with strong grog, we sat on limestone blocks round the fire, and sang and talked and smoked.

Round about midnight, all hell was let loose in the curved front enclosing Monchy. Dozens of alarm clocks rang, hundreds of rifles went off, and white and green flares went up unceasingly. Next, a barrage of fire went off, heavy trench mortars crashed, drawing plumes of fiery sparks after them. Wherever in the maze of ruins there was a human soul, the long-drawn-out cry went up: 'Gas attack! Gas attack! Gas! Gas! Gaaas!'

By the light of the flares, a dazzling flow of gas billowed over the black jags of masonry. Since there was a heavy smell of chlorine in the quarry as well, we lit large straw fires at the entrances, whose acrid smoke almost drove us out of our refuge, and forced us to try and cleanse the air by waving coats and tarpaulins.

The next day, we were able to marvel at the traces the gas had left. A large proportion of the plants had withered, snails and moles lay dead, and the horses that were stabled in Monchy for use by the messengers, had watering eyes and muzzles. The shells and ammunition splinters that lay all over the place had a fetching green patina. The cloud had been noticed as far away as Douchy, where rattled civilians had assembled outside Colonel von Oppen's quarters and demanded gas masks. Instead, they were loaded on to lorries, and driven to towns and villages set back from the front.

The following night we were in the quarry again; in the evening,

Battle

I was given news that coffee would be provided at quarter past four in the morning, as an English deserter had said an attack was planned for five. And, indeed, no sooner had the coffee-bringers roused us the next morning than the almost familiar shout of 'Gas attack!' rang out. There was a sweetish smell in the air; and, as we were later to find out, this was phosgene to which we were being treated. In the ring around Monchy, powerful drumfire was raging, but that ebbed away before long.

This anxious hour turned into a bracing morning. From communication trench 6, Lieutenant Brecht emerged on to the village street, with a bloody bandage wrapped round his hand, accompanied by a soldier with fixed bayonet and an English captive. Brecht was given a triumphant reception in Headquarters West, and told us the following:

The British had let off clouds of gas and smoke at five in the morning, and had gone on to rattle our trench with mortar fire. Our soldiers, as was their custom, had leapt out of their shelters while the bombing was still in progress, and we had taken more than thirty casualties. Then, still hidden in the smoke, two large British raiding parties had appeared, one of which had got into the trench, and taken a wounded NCO of ours. The other never made it past the wire entanglement. The single exception Brecht – who, before the war, had been a plantation owner in America – now seized by the throat, and greeted with the words, 'Come here, you son of a bitch!' The captive was presently being treated to a glass of wine, and looking with half-frightened, half-puzzled eyes at the previously deserted village street, now filling with ration parties, ambulancemen, dispatch-carriers and various nondescript onlookers. He was a tall fellow, very young, fresh-faced, and with fair hair. 'What a shame to have to shoot at such people!' went through my head as I saw him.

Soon a long line of stretchers arrived at the dressing-station. A lot of wounded men came from Monchy South as well, because the enemy had also succeeded in breaking into the line – briefly

83

– in E Sector. One of the assailants must have been an amazing character. He had leaped into the trench, apparently unremarked, and run along it, past the backs of the sentries, who all had their eyes on the field in front of them. One after the other, he leaped on them from behind – the gas masks restricted further their field of vision – and, having felled a number of them with blows of a club or rifle butt, returned, equally unremarked, to the British lines. When the trench was tidied up later, eight sentries were found with broken skulls.

Around fifty stretchers, with men lying groaning on them in blood-soaked bandages, were laid out in front of some sheets of corrugated metal, under which the doctor did his business, with sleeves rolled up.

One young fellow, whose blue lips shone rather ominously from his ghostly white face, was mumbling to himself: 'I'm too badly . . . they won't be able . . . I'm sure – I'll die.' A fat NCO from the medical corps looked at him pityingly, and several times breathed a comforting: 'Come on, mate, come on!'

Even though the British had thoroughly prepared this little attack – designed to tie up our forces here, to favour their offensive on the Somme – with plenty of trench-mortar attacks and clouds of poison gas, they only managed to take alive a single, wounded, prisoner, whereas they left plenty of dead on our wires. Of course our losses were also substantial; the regiment later that morning mourned over forty dead, among them three officers, and a good number of wounded as well.

The following afternoon we finally moved back for a few days to our beloved Douchy. That same evening, we celebrated the success of the engagement with several well-earned bottles.

On 1 July, it was our sorry task to bury a proportion of our dead in our churchyard. Thirty-nine wooden coffins, with the names written in pencil on the unplanned planks, were laid side by side in the pit. The minister spoke on the text: 'They have fought a good fight,' beginning with the words, 'Gibraltar, that is your motto, and why not, for have you not stood firm like the rock in the sea surge!'

It was in the course of these days that I learned to appreciate these men, with whom I was to be together for two more years of the war. What was at stake here was a British initiative on such a small scale as barely to find mention in the histories of both armies, intended to commit us to a sector where the main attack was not to be. Nor did the men have very much to do, only cover the very small amount of ground, from the entrance of the shelter to the sentry posts. But these few steps needed to be taken in the instant of a great crescendo of fire before an attack, the precise timing of which is a matter of gut instinct and feeling. The dark wave that so many times in those nights welled up to the traverses through raging fire, and without even an order being possible, remained with me in my heart as a personal yardstick for human trustworthiness.

Especially strongly marked is the memory of the position, broken and still steaming, as I walked through it shortly after the attack. The day's sentries were already in position while the trenches had yet to be cleared. Here and there, the sentry posts were covered with dead, and, in among them, as it were, arisen from their bodies, stood the new relief with his rifle. There was an odd rigidity about these composites – it was as though the distinction between alive and dead had momentarily been taken away.

On the evening of 3 July, we moved back up to the front. It was relatively quiet, but there were little indications that there was something afoot. There was soft and insistent hammering from the mill at all times, as though metal were being fashioned. We intercepted numerous telephone calls to an English pioneer officer at the very front, concerning gas cylinders and explosions. From dawn to the last gleam of light at the end of the day, English aeroplanes kept up a dense pattern of overflying, to keep us and the hinterland apart. The trench bombardments were substantially harder than usual; also, there was a suspicious change of target, as though new batteries were set to finding their range. In spite of it all, we were relieved on 12 July, without too much disagreeableness, and went into the reserve in Monchy.

On the evening of the 13th, our dugouts in the garden came under fire from a ten-inch naval gun, whose massive shells rumbled at us in a low arc. They burst with a terrific bang. At night, we were woken up by intense fire and a gas attack. We sat round the stove in the dugout in our gas masks, all except Vogel, who had lost his, and was running around like a madman, looking in all the corners, while a few sadistic fellows whom he'd given a hard time reported that the smell of gas was getting stronger and stronger. In the end, I gave him my refill, and he sat for an hour behind the smoking stove, holding his nose, and sucking on the mouthpiece.

On that same day I lost two men from my platoon, wounded as they went around the village: Hasselmann had a bullet through the arm, while Maschmeier caught a shrapnel ball through the throat.

There was no attack that night; even so, the regiment lost another twenty-five dead and a great many wounded. On the 15th and 17th, we had further gas attacks to endure. On the 17th, we were relieved and twice suffered heavy bombardment in Douchy. One of them came just as we were having an officers' meeting with Major von Jarotzky in an orchard. It was dangerous, but it was still ridiculous to watch the company suddenly burst apart, fall on their faces, force their way through hedges in an absolute trice, and disappear under various cover before you could count to ten. A shell falling in the garden of my lodgings killed a little girl who had been digging around for rubbish in a pit.

On 20 July we moved back up. On the 28th, I arranged with Ensign Wohlgemut and Privates Bartels and Birkner to go on another one of our patrols. We had nothing more in mind than to wander around between the lines and see what was new in no man's land, because we were beginning to get a bit bored with the trench. In the afternoon, Lieutenant Brauns, the officer in the 6th Company who was relieving me, paid me a call in my dugout, bringing a fine Burgundy with him. Towards midnight we broke up; I went out into the trench, where my three companions were already assembled in the lee of a traverse. After I'd picked out a few bombs that looked dry and in working order, I climbed over the wire in a high good humour, and Brauns called out a jovial: 'Break a leg!' after me.

In quick time, we had crept up to the enemy barrier. Just before it, we came across a pretty stout and well-insulated wire in some long grass. I was of the opinion that information was important here, and instructed Wohlgemut to cut off a piece and take it with him. While he was sawing away at it with – for want of more appropriate tools – a cigar clipper, we heard something jingling the wire; a few British soldiers appeared and started working without noticing us, pressed as we were in the long grass.

Mindful of our hard time on the previous expedition, I breathed: 'Wohlgemut, toss a hand-grenade in that lot!'

'Lieutenant, shouldn't we let them work a bit more first?'

'Ensign, that was an order!'

Even here, in this wasteland, the magic words took effect. With the sinking feeling of a man embarking on an uncertain adventure, I listened to the dry crackle of the pulled fuse, and watched Wohlgemut, to offer less of a target, trundle, almost roll the grenade at the British group. It stopped in a thicket, almost in the middle of them; they seemed not to have seen anything. A few moments of great tension ticked by. 'C-crashh!' A flash of lightning lit up their sprawling figures. With a shout of '*You are prisoners!*' we launched ourselves like tigers into the dense white smoke. A desperate scene developed in fractions of seconds. I held my pistol in the middle of a face that seemed to loom out of the dark at me like a pale mask. A shadow slammed back against the barbed wire with a grunt. There was a ghastly cry, a sort of

'Wah!' – of the kind that people only produce when they've seen a ghost. On my left, Wohlgemut was banging away with his pistol, while Bartels in his excitement was throwing a hand-grenade in our midst.

After one shot, the magazine had clicked out of my pistol grip. I stood yelling in front of a Briton who in his horror was pressing his back into the barbed wire, and kept pulling the trigger. Nothing happened – it was like a dream of impotence. Sounds came from the trench in front of us. Shouts rang out, a machine-gun clattered into life. We jumped away. Once more I stopped in a crater and aimed my pistol at a shadowy form that was pursuing me. This time, it was just as well it didn't fire, because it was Birkner, whom I had supposed to be safely back long ago.

Then we raced towards our lines. Just before our wire, the bullets were coming so thick and fast that I had to leap into a water-filled, wire-laced mine-crater. Dangling over the water on the swaying wire, I heard the bullets rushing past me like a huge swarm of bees, while scraps of wire and metal shards sliced into the rim of the crater. After half an hour or so, once the firing had abated, I made my way over our entanglements and leaped into our trench, to an enthusiastic reception. Wohlgemut and Bartels were already back; and another half an hour later, so was Birkner. We were all pleased at the happy outcome, and only regretted that once again our intended captive had managed to get away. It was only afterwards that I noticed that the experience had taken its toll on my nerves, when I was lying on my pallet in my dugout with teeth chattering, and quite unable to sleep. Rather, I had the sensation of a sort of supreme awakeness – as if I had a little electric bell going off somewhere in my body. The following morning, I could hardly walk, because over one knee (over other, historic injuries) I had a long scrape from the barbed wire, while the other had caught some shards from Bartels's hand-grenade.

These short expeditions, where a man takes his life in his hands, were a good means of testing our mettle and interrupting the monotony of trench life. There's nothing worse for a soldier than boredom.

On 11 August there was a black riding stallion loose outside Berles-au-bois, which a territorial was finally able to kill with three bullets. The British officer it had escaped from wouldn't have been too pleased to see it in that condition. In the night, Fusilier Schulz caught a spent part of an English bullet in his eye. In Monchy, too, there were more casualties, as the walls brought down by shelling now afforded less and less protection from random sprays of machine-gun bullets. We started to dig trenches right across the village, and erected new walls near the most dangerous places. In the neglected gardens, the berries were ripe, and tasted all the sweeter because of the bullets flying around us as we ate them.

The 12th of August was the long-awaited day when, for the second time in the war, I had a home furlough. No sooner had I got home and settled in, though, than a telegram came winging after me: 'Return immediately, further details from local command Cambrai.' And three hours later, I was on the train. On the way to the station, three girls in light dresses swayed past me, clutching tennis racquets – a shining last image of that sort of life, which was to stay with me for a long time.

On the 21st I was back in familiar country, the roads swarming with soldiers on account of the departure of the 111th and the arrival of a new division. The 1st Battalion was based in the village of Ecoust-St-Mein, whose wreckage we were to reoccupy on our advance two years from now.

I was welcomed by Paulicke, whose days were also numbered. He told me that the young fellows from my platoon must have inquired about a dozen times whether I wasn't back yet. It stirred and revived me to hear that; I realized that in the hot days that were ahead of us, I had a following based not only on rank, but also on character.

That night I was put up with eight other officers in the loft of an empty house. We stayed up a long time, and, for want of anything stronger, sat drinking coffee that a couple of French-women made for us in the house next door. We knew there was a battle impending, the like of which the world had not seen. We felt no less aggressive than the troops who had marched over the border two years before, but we were more experienced and therefore more dangerous. We were up for it, in the best and most cheerful condition, and expressions like 'avoid contact with the enemy' were not in our vocabulary. Anyone seeing the men round this jolly table would have to tell themselves that positions entrusted to them would only be lost when the last defender had fallen.

And that indeed proved to be the case.

Guillemont

On 23 August 1916, we were put on lorries and driven as far as Le Mesnil. Even though we had already heard we were to be posted to the legendary heart of the Battle of the Somme, namely the village of Guillemont, the mood was extraordinarily high. Jokes and witticisms flew from one vehicle to another, to the general merriment of all.

During one stop on the way, a driver split his thumb in the course of crank-starting his lorry. The sight of the wound almost made me ill, I have always been sensitive to such things. I mention this because it seems virtually unaccountable as I witnessed such terrible mutilation in the course of the following days. It's an example of the way in which one's response to an experience is actually largely determined by its context.

From Le Mesnil we marched, after dark, to Sailly-Saillisel, where the battalion took off their knapsacks in a large meadow and prepared a storm pack.

Ahead of us rumbled and thundered artillery fire of a volume we had never dreamed of; a thousand quivering lightnings bathed the western horizon in a sea of flame. A continual stream of wounded, with pale, sunken faces, made their way back, often barged aside by clattering guns or munitions columns heading the other way.

A runner from a Württemberg regiment reported to me to guide my platoon to the famous town of Combles, where we were to be held in reserve for the time being. He was the first German soldier I saw in a steel helmet, and he straightaway struck me as the denizen of a new and far harsher world. Sitting next to him in the roadside ditch, I questioned him avidly about the state of the position, and got from him a grey tale of days hunkered in craters, with no outside contact or communications lines, of incessant attacks, fields of corpses and crazy thirst, of the wounded left to die, and more of the same. The impassive features under the rim of the steel helmet and the monotonous voice accompanied by the noise of the battle made a ghostly impression on us. A few days had put their stamp on the runner, who was to escort us into the realm of flame, setting him inexpressibly apart from us.

'If a man falls, he's left to lie. No one can help. No one knows if he'll return alive. Every day we're attacked, but they won't get through. Everyone knows this is about life and death.'

Nothing was left in this voice but equanimity, apathy; fire had burned everything else out of it. It's men like that that you need for fighting.

We were marching along a wide road, which ran in the moonlight like a white ribbon across the dark countryside, towards the thunder of guns, whose voracious roar grew ever more immeasurable. Abandon all hope! What gave the scene a particularly sinister aspect was the way all the roads were clearly visible, like a network of white veins in the moonlight, and there was no living being on them. We marched as on the gleaming paths of a midnight cemetery.

Before long the first shells landed left and right of us. Conversations grew quieter and stopped altogether. We listened to the whining approach of each shell with the strange tenseness that seems somehow to sharpen one's hearing. The first real challenge that confronted us was crossing Frégicourt-Ferme, a small cluster of houses just past the graveyard at Combles. That was where the noose that had been drawn around Combles was tightest.

Everyone wanting to enter or leave the town had to pass through
here, and so incessant very heavy fire, like the focused beams of
a magnifying glass, was concentrated on this one little lifeline.
Our guide had warned us about this notorious bottleneck;
we passed through it at the double, while the ruins clattered
around us.

Over the ruins, as over all the most dangerous parts of the
terrain, lay a heavy smell of death, because the fire was so intense
that no one could bother with the corpses. You really did have
to run for your life in these places, and when I caught the smell
of it as I ran, I was hardly surprised – it belonged to there.
Moreover, this heavy sweetish atmosphere was not merely
disgusting; it also, in association with the piercing fogs of
gunpowder, brought about an almost visionary excitement,
that otherwise only the extreme nearness of death is able to
produce.

Here, and really only here, I was to observe that there is a
quality of dread that feels as unfamiliar as a foreign country. In
moments when I felt it, I experienced no fear as such but a kind
of exalted, almost demoniacal lightness; often attended by fits of
laughter I was unable to repress. *ruined towns*

So far as we were able to see in the dark, Combles was a mere
skeleton of its former self. Great amounts of wood and jettisoned
household objects told us that its destruction was very recent.
After crossing numerous piles of junk, sped on our way by a
stream of shrapnels, we reached our quarters, a large house
riddled with holes, which I chose for my base with three of my
sections, while the other two settled into the basement of a ruin
across the way.

At four o'clock already we were roused from our beds put
together from bits of furniture, to be given our steel helmets.
Coincidentally, we also stumbled upon a sack of coffee beans
hidden in the cellar – a discovery swiftly followed by an eager
brew-up.

After breakfast, I took a little look around the place. In the course of a very few days, heavy artillery had transformed a peaceable town in the hinterland to the image of dread. Whole houses had been flattened or ripped apart by shells, so that the rooms and their furnishings were left hanging over the chaos like theatre flats. The smell of corpses oozed from some buildings, because the first abrupt assault had taken the inhabitants by surprise, and buried many of them in the ruins before they could leave their dwellings. On one doorstep lay a little girl, stretched out in a lake of crimson.

All that was left of the streets were narrow footpaths that went snaking through huge mounds of beams and masonry. Fruit and vegetables were mouldering away in the ravaged gardens.

After lunch, which we put together in the kitchen from an over-supply of iron rations, and which was concluded, of course, by a potent cup of coffee, I went and stretched out in an armchair upstairs. From letters that were lying around I saw that the house had belonged to a brewer by the name of Lesage. There were open cupboards and wardrobes in the room, an upset washstand, a sewing-machine and a pram. On the walls hung smashed paintings and mirrors. On the floor were drifts, sometimes several feet deep, of drawers pulled out of chests, linen, corsets, books, newspapers, nightstands, broken glass, bottles, musical scores, chair legs, skirts, coats, lamps, curtains, shutters, doors off their hinges, lace, photographs, oil paintings, albums, smashed chests, ladies' hats, flowerpots and wallpaper, all tangled together.

looting

Through the splintered shutters, the view was of a square furrowed by bombs, under the boughs of a ragged linden. This confusion of impressions was further darkened by the incessant artillery fire that was raging round the town. From time to time, the gigantic impact of a fifteen-inch shell drowned out all other noise. Clouds of shards washed through Combles, splattering against the branches of the trees, or striking the few intact roofs, sending the slates slithering down.

In the course of the afternoon, the bombing swelled to such a pitch that all that was left was the feeling of a kind of oceanic roar, in which individual sounds were completely subordinated. From seven o'clock, the square and the houses on it were subjected to fifteen-inch-shell bombardment at thirty-second intervals. There were many that did not go off, whose short, dull thumps shook the house to its foundations. Throughout, we sat in our basement, on silk-upholstered armchairs round a table, with our heads in our hands, counting the seconds between explosions. The witticisms dried up, and finally the boldest of us had nothing to say. At eight o'clock the house next door came down after taking two direct hits; its collapse occasioned a huge cloud of dust.

From nine till ten, the shelling acquired a demented fury. The earth shook, the sky seemed like a boiling cauldron. Hundreds of heavy batteries were crashing away at and around Combles, innumerable shells criss-crossed hissing and howling over our heads. All was swathed in thick smoke, which was in the ominous underlighting of coloured flares. Because of racking pains in our heads and ears, communication was possible only by odd, shouted words. The ability to think logically and the feeling of gravity, both seemed to have been removed. We had the sensation of the ineluctable and the unconditionally necessary, as if we were facing an elemental force. An NCO in No. 3 Platoon went into a frenzy.

At ten o'clock, this infernal carnival gradually seemed to calm itself, and settled into a sedate drumfire, in which, admittedly, one still was not able to make out an individual shot.

At eleven o'clock, a runner arrived with orders to take the men out on to the church square. We joined up with the other two platoons in marching order. A fourth platoon, under Lieutenant Sievers, had dropped out because they were to take provisions up to the front. They now ringed us as we assembled in this perilous location, and loaded us with bread, tobacco and canned meat. Sievers insisted I take a pan of butter, shook hands, and wished us luck.

Lost way

Then we marched off in Indian file. Everyone was under strict orders absolutely to stay in touch with the man in front. No sooner were we out of the village, than our guide realized he'd gone wrong. We were forced, under heavy shrapnel fire, to retrace our steps. Then, mostly at a jog, we crossed open country, following a white ribbon laid out to guide us, though it was shot in pieces. We were forced to stop periodically, often in the very worst places, when our guide lost his way. To keep the unit together, we were not allowed to lie down or take cover.

bombing

Even so, the first and third platoon had suddenly vanished. On, on! In one violently bombarded defile, the sections backed up. Take cover! A horribly penetrating smell told us that this passage had already taken a good many lives. After running for our lives, we managed to reach a second defile which concealed the dugout of the front line commanding officer, then we lost our way again, and in a painful crush of excited men, had to turn back once more. At the most five yards from Vogel and me, a middle-sized shell struck the bank behind us with a dull thump, and hurled mighty clods of earth over us, as we thought our last moment had come. Finally, our guide found the path again – a strangely constellated group of corpses serving as landmark. One of the dead lay there as if crucified on the chalk slope. It was impossible to imagine a more appropriate landmark.

(loss of landmarks)

On, on! Men collapsed while running, we had to threaten them to use the last energy from their exhausted bodies. Wounded men went down left and right in craters – we disregarded their cries for help. We went on, eyes implacably on the man in front, through a knee-high trench formed from a chain of enormous craters, one dead man after another. At moments, we felt our feet settling on soft, yielding corpses, whose form we couldn't make out on account of the darkness. The wounded man collapsing on the path suffered the same fate; he too was trampled underfoot by the boots of those hurrying ever onwards.

And always the sweetish smell! Even little Schmidt, my orderly, who had accompanied me on the odd perilous reconnaissance, was beginning to reel. I snatched his rifle out of his hands, which even in his extremity, the good lad tried to resist.

At last we reached the front line, which was occupied by men huddled together in little holes. Their dull voices trembled with joy when they learned that we were come to relieve them. A Bavarian sergeant handed over the sector and his flare pistol to me with a few words.

My platoon's sector was on the right flank of the regiment's position, and consisted of a defile hammered by constant shelling into little more than a dip, running through open country from a couple of hundred paces to the left of Guillemont, to a little less than that to the right of the Bois de Trônes. Some five hundred paces separated us from the troops to our right, the 76th Infantry. The shelling here was so heavy that nothing could survive.

Suddenly the Bavarian sergeant had disappeared, and I stood all alone, with my flare pistol in my hand, in the midst of that eerie cratered landscape, masked now by patches of creeping fog. Behind me I heard a stifled, unpleasant sound; with a degree of calm that astonished me, I registered that it came from a bloated disintegrating corpse.

Since I had no idea as to the enemy's possible whereabouts, I went back to my men and told them to be ready for the worst. All of us stayed awake; I spent the night with Paulicke and my two orderlies in a foxhole no bigger than a cubic yard.

When morning paled, the strange surroundings gradually revealed themselves to our disbelieving eyes.

The defile proved to be little more than a series of enormous craters full of pieces of uniform, weapons and dead bodies; the country around, so far as the eye could see, had been completely ploughed by heavy shells. Not a single blade of grass showed itself. The churned-up field was gruesome. In among the living defenders lay the dead. When we dug foxholes, we realized that they were stacked in layers. One company after another, pressed together in the drumfire, had been mown down, then the bodies had been buried under showers of earth sent up by shells, and then the relief company had taken their predecessors' place. And now it was our turn.

The defile and the land behind was strewn with German dead, the field ahead with British. Arms and legs and heads stuck out of the slopes; in front of our holes were severed limbs and bodies, some of which had had coats or tarpaulins thrown over them, to save us the sight of the disfigured faces. In spite of the heat, no one thought of covering the bodies with earth.

The village of Guillemont seemed to have disappeared without trace; just a whitish stain on the cratered field indicated where one of the limestone houses had been pulverized. In front of us lay the station, crumpled like a child's toy; further to the rear the woods of Delville, ripped to splinters.

No sooner had day broken than a low-flying RAF plane whirled towards us, and, vulture-like, began drawing its circles overhead, while we fled into our holes and huddled together. The sharp eye of the observer must have noticed something anyway, because before long the plane began to emit a series of low, long-drawn-out siren tones, coming at short intervals. They put one in mind of the cries of a fabulous creature, hanging pitilessly over the desert.

A little later, and the battery seemed to have taken the signals. One heavy, low-arcing shell after the other came barging along with incredible force. We sat helplessly in our refuges, lighting a cigar and then throwing it away again, prepared at any moment to find ourselves buried. Schmidt's sleeve was sliced open by a large shard.

With only the third shell the fellow in the hole next to ours was buried by an enormous explosion. We dug him up again right away; even so, the weight of the masses of earth had left him deathly tired, his face sunken, like a skull. It was Private Simon. His experience had made him wise, because each time anyone moved around in the open while there were aeroplanes about, I could hear his furious voice and a fist waving from the opening of his tarpaulin-covered foxhole.

At three in the afternoon my sentries came to me from the left and stated that they were unable to hold out where they were any longer, as their holes had been shot away. I had to display my full authority to get them back to their stations. What helped me make my case was the fact that I myself was in the place of greatest danger.

A little before ten o'clock at night, a fire-storm was directed at the left flank of the regiment, which, twenty minutes later, had moved over to us. Soon we were completely wrapped in smoke and dust, but most of the shells came down just behind or just in front of our trench, if one can use that word for our smashed hollow. As the storm raged around us, I walked up and down my sector. The men had fixed bayonets. They stood stony and motionless, rifle in hand, on the front edge of the dip, gazing into the field. Now and then, by the light of a flare, I saw steel helmet by steel helmet, blade by glinting blade, and I was overcome by a feeling of invulnerability. We might be crushed, but surely we could not be conquered.

In the platoon to the left of us, Sergeant Hock, the unfortunate rat-catcher of Monchy, aimed to discharge a white flare, picked up the wrong flare, and instead sent up a red barrage light, which was taken up in all quarters. Straight away our own artillery opened up, and it was a joy to behold. One shell after another came yowling down out of the sky and showered the field ahead of us in a fountain of shards and sparks on impact. A mixture of dust, stale gases and the reek of flung carcasses brewed up from the craters.

mistakes

After this orgy of destruction, the shelling quickly flooded back to its previous levels. One man's slip of the hand had got the whole titanic machinery of war rolling.

Hock was and remained an unlucky fellow; that same night, as he was loading his pistol, he shot a flare into his bootleg, and had to be carried back with grave burns.

rain

The following day, it rained hard, which was no bad thing so far as we were concerned, as once the dust turned to mud the feeling of dryness in our mouths wasn't so tormenting, and the great clumps of monstrous blue-black flies basking in the sun – they were like velvet cushions to look at – were finally dispersed. I spent almost the whole day sitting on the ground in front of my foxhole, smoking and eating, in spite of the surroundings, with a healthy appetite.

The following morning, Fusilier Knicke in my platoon got a rifle shot from somewhere through the chest and against his spine, so that he lost the use of his legs. When I went to see how he was, he was lying soberly in a hole in the ground, looking like a man who had come to terms with his own death. That evening

medics @ front

he was carried back through the bombardment, in the course of which, when the stretcher-bearers suddenly had to dive for cover, he suffered an additional broken leg. He died at the dressing-station.

That afternoon one of my men had me come over and look in the direction of Guillemont station, from behind a torn-off British leg. Hundreds of British soldiers were running forward through a flat communication trench, little troubled by the weak gunfire we were able to direct at them. The scene was indicative of the inequality of the resources with which we had to fight. Had we essayed the same thing, our units would have been shot to pieces in a matter of minutes. While on our side there wasn't a single captive balloon to be seen anywhere, the British had about thirty clustered into one vast luminous-yellow bunch, watching with Argus eyes for the least movement to show itself any-

48 hrs @ front before relief arrives

where in the crumpled landscape, to have a hail of steel directed against it.

luck

In the evening, as I gave out the password, a large shell fragment came buzzing into my stomach. Fortunately, it was almost spent, and so merely struck my belt buckle hard and fell to the ground. I was so astonished that it took the concerned cries of my men, and their offers of water from their canteens, to show me that I'd had a near thing.

No POWs her

At dusk, two members of a British ration party lost their way, and blundered up to the sector of the line that was held by the first platoon. They approached perfectly serenely; one of them was carrying a large round container of food, the other a longish tea kettle. They were shot down at point-blank range; one of them landing with his upper body in the defile, while his legs remained on the slope. It was hardly possible to take prisoners in this inferno, and how could we have brought them back through the barrage in any case?

It was almost one o'clock in the morning when I was roused by Schmidt from my half-sleep. Instantly I leaped up, and reached for my rifle. Our relief had come. We handed over what there was to be handed over, and as quickly as possible made our way out of this fiendish place.

But no sooner had we reached the shallow communication trench than a first clutch of shrapnels blew up in our midst. One ball smashed the wrist of the man in front of me, sending the arterial blood spurting everywhere. He reeled, and made to lie down on his side. I took him by the arm, pulled him to his feet in spite of his complaints, and only let go of him when we'd reached the dressing-station next to battle headquarters.

Things were pretty 'hot' along both the defiles, and we were panting for breath. The worst place was a valley we ended up in, where shrapnels and light shells seemed to go up uninterruptedly. Prruch! Prruch! went the spinning iron, sending a rain of sparks into the night. Whee! Another volley! I gasped because, seconds in advance, I knew from the increasing noise that the arc of the next projectile was heading almost exactly for me. An instant later, there was a heavy crash at my feet, and soft scraps of clay flipped into the air. It was a dud!

Everywhere groups of men, either relieving or being relieved, were hurrying through the night and the bombardment, some of them utterly lost, and groaning with tension and exhaustion; shouts fell, and orders, and in monotonous repetition the long-drawn-out cries for help from the abandoned and the wounded. As we raced on, I gave directions to the lost, pulled some men out of shell-holes, threatened others who wanted to lie down, kept shouting my name, and so brought my platoon, as if by a miracle, back to Combles.

Then we needed to march via Sailly and Gouvernements-Ferme to Hennois woods, where we would bivouac. It was only now that the degree of our exhaustion became fully clear. Heads brutishly down, we slunk along the road, often forced off it by cars or munitions columns. In my unhealthy irritation, I couldn't help but think that these vehicles followed no other purpose than to annoy us as they sliced past us, and more than once I caught myself reaching for my pistol.

After our march we had to put up tents, and only then could we throw ourselves on the hard ground. During our stay in the forest camp, we endured great storms of rain. The straw in the tents started to moulder, and many men got sick. We five company officers were not much put out by this external wetness, spending our evenings sitting on our cases in our tent, with a few goodly bottles that had been magicked up from somewhere. In such situations, red wine is the best medicine.

On one of these evenings, our Guards counter-attacked and captured the village of Maurepas. While the two sets of artillery were raging against each other over a wide area, a violent storm broke loose overhead, so that, as in the Homeric battle of gods and men, the disturbance below seemed to be vying with that on high.

Three days later, we moved back to Combles, where my platoon this time occupied four smallish basements. These basements were hewn from blocks of chalk, long and narrow and with arched ceilings; they promised security. They seemed to have belonged to a vintner – or that, at any rate, was my explanation for the fact that they afforded small fireplaces broken into the walls. After I'd posted sentries, we stretched out on the many mattresses that our predecessors had lugged into place here.

The first morning, things were relatively calm; I took a walk through the ravaged gardens, and looted delicious peaches from their espaliered boughs. On my wanderings I happened into a house surrounded by tall hedges, which must have belonged to a lover of antiques. On the walls of the rooms hung a collection of painted plates, holy water basins, etchings and wooden carvings of saints. Old china sat in piles in large cupboards, ornate leather-bound volumes were scattered about the floor, among them an exquisite old edition of *Don Quixote*. I would have loved to pick up a memento, but I felt like Robinson Crusoe and the lump of gold; none of these things were of any value here. So great bales of beautiful silks rotted away in a workshop, without anyone paying them any attention. You had only to think of the glowing barrage at Frémicourt-Ferme, which cut off this landscape, and you soon thought better of picking up any extra baggage.

When I reached my lodgings, the men were back from foraging trips of their own through the gardens, and had boiled up a soup in which you could stand your spoon out of bully beef, potatoes, peas, carrots, artichokes and various other vegetables. While we were eating, a shell landed on the house, and three others came down near by, without us lifting our heads. We had seen and been through too much already to care. The house must have seen some bloody happenings already, because on a pile of rubble

wounded

in the middle room there was a rough cross with a list of names scratched into it. The next day at lunchtime I went back to the china collector's house and picked up a volume of the illustrated supplements to *Le Petit Journal*; then I sat myself down in a reasonably well-preserved room, made a little fire in the hearth with some sticks of furniture, and settled down to read. I had frequent occasion to shake my head, because I had picked up those issues that had appeared at the time of the Fashoda* affair. The time I spent reading was punctuated by four bombs hitting the house. At just about seven o'clock I turned the last page, and went down to the passage outside the basement, where the men were preparing supper at a small stove.

No sooner was I standing with them than there was a sharp report outside the front door, and, in the same moment, I felt a piercing blow low down on my left calf. With the immemorial warrior's refrain 'I've been hit!' I took off, pipe of shag tobacco in my mouth, down the stairs.

Quickly someone brought light, and the thing was examined. As ever in these affairs, I had someone tell me about it, while I stared at the ceiling; in case it wasn't a pretty sight. There was a jagged hole in my putties, out of which a fine spray of blood ran down to the floor. On the opposite side of the leg there was the round bulge of a shrapnel ball under the skin.

The diagnosis was straightforward enough – a typical ticket home: nothing very bad, but nothing too light either. Admittedly, I'd left it to the latest possible moment to get 'a puncture' if I wasn't to miss the bus to Germany. There was something deeply improbable about that hit, because the shrapnel had burst on the ground on the other side of the brick wall that surrounded the courtyard. A shell had previously knocked a little round hole in

---

* Town in the Sudan, and site of an Anglo-French colonial standoff in 1898 involving General Kitchener. The French climb-down paved the way for the *Entente Cordiale*. Rueful reading matter for a German officer in World War I.

this wall, and a tub with an oleander plant stood in front of it. The ball must therefore have gone through the shell-hole, then through the oleander's leaves, crossed the yard and the open door, and, of the many legs in front of it, had picked precisely this one of mine.

After my comrades had bandaged up the wound, they carried me across the street – needless to say, through fire – to the catacombs, and there laid me on the operating table. While a breathless Lieutenant Wetje held my head, our medical major cut out the shrapnel ball with scissors and knife, and told me I was a lucky man, because the ball had passed between shinbone and fibula without harming either. 'Habent sua fata libelli et balli,'* the old corps student observed, while he left a medical orderly to bandage up the wound.

While I lay on a stretcher in a niche in the catacombs waiting for nightfall, I was pleased that a lot of my men came to say goodbye to me. They had a heavy ordeal ahead of them. My revered Colonel von Oppen managed to pay me a short visit.

In the evening I was carried along with the other casualties to the edge of town, and there loaded on to an ambulance. Paying no attention to the cries and screams of his passengers, the driver raced over the craters and other hindrances along the road, heavily bombarded as ever around Frégicourt-Ferme, and finally passed us on to a car that delivered us to the village church at Fins. The switch of cars took place in the middle of the night outside an isolated group of houses, where a doctor examined the bandages and decided our destiny. Half feverish as I was, I had an impression of a young man whose hair had turned completely white, but who tended our wounds with unimaginable care.

The church at Fins was full of hundreds of wounded men. A nurse told me that in the course of the last few weeks, more than thirty thousand casualties had been tended and bandaged here.

* 'Books and bullets have their own destinies.'

wanded

Faced with numbers of that order, I felt pretty insignificant with my silly leg wound.

From Fins, I was taken along with four other officers to a hospital that had been set up in an affluent house in St-Quentin. When we were unloaded, all the window-panes were jangling; it was exactly the moment when the British, with maximal help from their artillery, were taking Guillemont.

When the stretcher next to mine was lifted out of the car, I heard one of those toneless voices that have remained with me:

'Take me to the doctor right away, if you will – I'm very poorly – I have a gas phlegmon.'

That was the term for a horrible form of blood poisoning that often sets in after a man has been wounded, and kills him.

I was carried into a room, where twelve beds stood so close together that one had the impression of a room entirely filled with snow-white pillows. Most of the wounds were grave, and there was a commotion in which, in my feverish state, I dreamily participated. Soon after my arrival, for instance, a young man with a bandage wrapped round his head like a turban, leaped up from his bed and addressed us all. I thought it was some rather extravagant sort of joke, only to see him collapse as suddenly as he'd leaped up. His bed was rolled out through a dark little door, amid a rather grim silence.

Next to me lay a pioneer officer. He had trodden on an explosive in the trench, and the contact had caused a long tongue of flame to leap up. His mutilated foot had been placed under a translucent gauze wrapper. He seemed to be in a good humour, and was happy to have found a listener in me. On my left, a very young ensign was on a diet of claret and egg yolks; he was in the very last stages of emaciation. When the sister wanted to make his bed, she picked him up like a feather; through his skin, you could see all the bones in his body. When the sister asked him at night whether he wouldn't like to write his parents a nice letter,

I guessed it was all up with him, and, indeed, later that night, his bed too was rolled through the dark door to the dying ward.

By noon the next day I was lying in a hospital train that was taking me to Gera, where I was extremely well looked after in the garrison hospital there. A week later, and I was already skipping out in the evenings, though I had to be careful not to run into the head doctor.

It was here that I signed away the three thousand marks that were my entire fortune at the time as a war loan. I never saw them again. As I held the form in my hand, I thought of the beautiful fireworks that the wrong-coloured flare had sparked off – a spectacle that surely couldn't have cost less than a million.

no communication

I return now to the dreadful defile, to view the final act of the drama. My sources are the reports of the few men who were wounded and survived, in particular my orderly, Otto Schmidt.

Following my wounding, my subordinate, Sergeant Heister-mann, took over the command of the platoon, and it was he who a few minutes later led the men to the cratered field at Guillemont. With barely a handful of exceptions – those men who were hit during the march, and were fit enough to get back to Combles – the outfit disappeared without trace in the fiery labyrinths of the battle.

The platoon relieved their predecessors, and settled into the now familiar foxholes. The gap on the right flank had now widened, thanks to the incessant withering fire, so that there was no longer any visual communication. On the left side as well, there were now spaces, so that the position resembled a little island adrift in titanic streams of fire. The whole sector was made up of nothing more than similar islands, greater and lesser, but all of them dwindling. The attacker found himself confronting a net whose meshes had grown too wide to catch anything.

And so the night passed, with increasing disquiet. Towards

morning, a two-man patrol from the 76th showed up, having groped their way through with incredible difficulty. They went away again into the sea of fire, and that was the last the platoon saw of the outside world. The fire concentrated with ever-growing force on the right flank, and slowly worked to widen the gap, knocking out one pocket of resistance after another.

Towards six in the morning, Schmidt reached for the cooking tin that he kept outside our old foxhole, to get some breakfast, but all he found was a piece of flattened and riddled aluminium. Soon the shelling started up again, and slowly raised itself to a crescendo that was inevitably interpreted as the sign of an imminent attack. Aeroplanes appeared, and, like jabbing vultures, began circling low over the ground.

Heistermann and Schmidt, the only occupants of the tiny hole in the ground that had miraculously survived so long, knew that the moment had come for their stand. As they stepped out into the smoke- and dust-filled defile, they saw they were utterly alone. In the course of the night, the bombardment had smashed the last sparse bits of cover between themselves and the right flank, and buried their occupants under quantities of earth. But to the left of them as well, the rim of the defile turned out to be devoid of defenders. The last remnants of the platoon, among them a machine-gun unit, had withdrawn to a narrow shelter, covered over with planks and a thin layer of soil, half-way along the defile, and in its rear slope, with an entrance at either end of it. Heistermann and Schmidt now made for this refuge. On the way there, however, the sergeant, whose birthday it happened to be that day, disappeared. He was following Schmidt, coming up to a bend, and was never seen again.

The only man who made it to the little group in the shelter from the right flank was a lance-corporal, with a bandaged face, who suddenly stripped off his bandage, spewed a torrent of blood over the men and their weapons, and lay down to die. All this time, the power and intensity of the bombardment was still waxing; at any moment, the overcrowded shelter, in which no one now could speak, could reckon on being hit.

Further left, a few soldiers from No. 3 Platoon were still tenaciously defending their crater, and it seems that the position was crushed from the right, where the breach had been forced, which was by now a huge cavity. These soldiers must have been the first to have become aware of an incursion of British storm troops following one final inferno of bombing. At any rate, it seems the occupants of the shelter were alerted to the presence of the enemy by a shouted warning from the left.

Schmidt, the last man to have reached the shelter, and therefore sitting nearest the entrance, was the first man to emerge into the defile. He leaped into the spurting cone of a shell. As the smoke cleared, he saw to his right, just by the site of the foxhole that had so stoutly sheltered us, some lurking khaki figures. Simultaneously, the enemy broke through in numbers on the left of the position. What was happening beyond the projecting rim of the defile could not be seen, because of its depth.

In this desperate situation, the next occupants of the shelter, in particular Sergeant Sievers, plunged out with the intact machine-gun and its operator. To set it up on the floor of the defile and aim it at the enemy on the right was the work of seconds. But even as the gunner had his fist on the belt and his finger on the trigger, British hand-grenades were bobbling down the front slope. The two men fell beside their weapon, without managing to get off a shot. Anyone else leaping out of the shelter was received with rifle bullets, so that in the space of a few moments there was a cluster of dead round both entrances.

Schmidt was laid out by the first volley of hand-grenades. One splinter hit him in the head, others tore off three of his fingers. With his face down, he remained close to the shelter, where an exchange of rifle fire and hand-grenades continued for some time.

At last there was silence, and the British took over the last part of the position. Schmidt, perhaps the last living soul in the defile, heard footfalls announcing the approach of the attacker. Shortly after, rifle shots rang out, and explosions and gas bombs, as the shelter was pumped clear. Even then, towards evening, a last few survivors came crawling out of the shelter, from some nook at the back. They probably made up the little group of prisoners that fell into the hands of the enemy storm troops. British stretcher-bearers picked them up and took them away.

Shortly afterwards, Combles too fell, once the noose had been drawn tight around Frégicourt-Ferme. Its last defenders, who had taken refuge in the catacombs during the bombardment, were mown down fighting round the ruins of the church.

Then things went quiet in the area, until we retook it in spring 1918.

The Woods of St-Pierre-Vaast

After a fortnight in hospital and another fortnight recuperating, I returned to the regiment, which was positioned at Deuxnouds, hard by the familiar Grande Tranchée. For the first two days after my arrival, it remained there, and then two more days in the old-world hill village of Hattonchâtel. Then we steamed out of Mars-la-Tour station back to the Somme.

We were taken off the train at Bohain, and put up in Brancourt. This area, which we often brushed by later, is arable farmland, but almost every house boasts a loom as well.

I was quartered with a couple and their very beautiful daughter. We shared the two rooms of their little cottage, and at night I had to go through the family's bedroom.

On the very first day, the father asked me to compose a letter of complaint to the local commandant, against a neighbour who had grabbed him by the throat, beaten him and, crying 'Demande pardon!', threatened to kill him.

As I was on my way out of my room to go on duty, the daughter pushed the door shut against me. I took this to be one of her little jokes, pushed back, and our combined efforts were enough to lift the door off its hinges, and we waltzed round the room holding it between us for a few moments. Suddenly it came down, and to our mutual embarrassment, and her mother's great hilarity, I saw she was standing there completely naked.

Never in all my life, incidentally, have I heard anyone swear and scold as volubly as that rose of Brancourt did, when a neighbour accused her of having once worked in a certain street in St-Quentin. 'Ah, cette plure, cette pomme de terre pourrie, jetée sur un fumier, c'est la crème de la crème pourrie,'* she bubbled, as she criss-crossed the room with her hands out in front of her like claws, lacking only a victim for her pent-up rage.

Things in this village had quite a baronial flavour to them altogether. One evening I was on my way to call on a comrade, who was quartered with the aforementioned neighbour, a rather coarse Flemish beauty, who went by the name of Madame Louise. I went the back way through the gardens of the two houses, and saw Madame Louise through the kitchen window, sitting at the table helping herself from a large pot of coffee. Suddenly, the door opened and in strode the man who had been given such a cosy billet, with the full self-confidence of a sleepwalker and about as fully dressed as one too. Without saying a word, he picked up the coffee pot, and poured a goodly jet of it through the spout straight into his mouth. Then, every bit as laconically, he walked out again. Feeling I would only get in the way of such an idyllic set-up, I quietly went back the way I had come.

There was a relaxed tone in this area, which was in odd contrast to its agricultural character. I think it must have been something to do with the weaving, because in towns and regions where the spindle rules, there seems to be a different spirit to those where, say, there are a lot of blacksmiths.

As we had been settled in various villages and hamlets by the company, there was only a small group of us in the evenings. Our clique normally consisted of Lieutenant Boje, who commanded the 2nd Company, Lieutenant Heilmann, a dogged warrior who had lost an eye, Ensign Gornick, later to join the Paris airmen, and me. Every night we dined on boiled potatoes with tinned

* This affair of honour is conducted in almost literally 'earthy' language, in which the essential item is a 'mouldy potato'.

Scaring

goulash, and afterwards the playing cards came out and the odd
bottle of 'Polish Rider' or Bénédictine. The dominant personality
was Heilmann, who was one of those people who are resolutely
unimpressed by anything. He was staying in quite a nice billet,
had had quite a bad wound, had witnessed quite a sizeable
funeral. The only exception was anything relating to his native
Upper Silesia, where you could find the biggest village, the biggest goods station and the deepest mineshaft anywhere in the
world.

I was now to be used as a scouting officer, and had been
assigned to the division with a scout troop and two NCOs.
Special assignments like that were really not my line, because to
me the company was like a family, and I was loath to leave it
before a battle.

On 8 November, the battalion travelled through streaming
rain to the now entirely depopulated village of Gonnelieu. From
there, the scout troop was detailed to Liéramont and put under
the command of the divisional intelligence officer, Captain Böckelmann. Along with four of us troop leaders, a couple of observation officers, and his personal adjutant, the captain occupied a
priest's spacious house, whose rooms we divided among ourselves. On one of our first evenings there, there was a long
conversation in the library about the German peace proposals,
which had just been made known. Böckelmann put an end to it
by remarking that during a war no soldier should be permitted
to say the word 'peace'.

Our predecessors familiarized us with the position of the division. Every night, we had to go to the front. Our task was to
reconnoitre the situation, test the communications between the
units, and make a picture of everything, so as to put in reinforcements if need be and perform special duties. My own allotted
area was just left of the woods of St-Pierre-Vaast, and against
another 'nameless' wood.

The scene at night was muddy and wild, often with heavy

Gas attack

exchanges of artillery. Frequently, yellow rockets were shot off that blew up in the air, and sent a rain of fire cascading down, of a colour that somehow reminded me of the tone of a viola.

That very first night, I lost my way in the pitch black and almost drowned in the swamps of the Tortille stream. It was a place of unfathomable mystery; only the night before, a munitions cart had disappeared without trace in a vast shell-crater hidden under a crust of mud.

Having made good my escape from this wilderness, I tried to make my way to the 'nameless woods', where there was a low-level, but unremitting shelling going on. I headed for it pretty insouciantly, because the dull sound of the detonations suggested that the British were shooting off some rather veteran ammunitions. Suddenly, a little puff of wind brought up a sweetish, oniony smell, and at the same time I heard the shout go up in the wood: 'Gas, gas, gas!' From a distance, the cry sounded oddly small and plaintive, not unlike a chorus of crickets.

As I heard the next morning, in that hour in the woods a lot of our men died of poisoning from the clouds of heavy phosgene nestling in the undergrowth.

With weeping eyes, I stumbled back to the Vaux woods, plunging from one crater into the next, as I was unable to see anything through the misted visor of my gas mask. With the extent and inhospitableness of its spaces, it was a night of eerie solitude. Each time I blundered into sentries or troops who had lost their way, I had the icy sensation of conversing not with people, but with demons. We were all roving around in an enormous dump somewhere off the edge of the charted world.

On 12 November, hoping for better luck, I undertook my second mission, which was to test the communications between units in our crater positions. A chain of relays concealed in foxholes led me to my destination.

The term 'crater positions' was accurate. On a ridge outside the village of Rancourt, there were numerous craters scattered, some occupied by a few soldiers here and there. The dark plain, criss-crossed by shells, was barren and intimidating.

It wasn't long before I had lost communication with the chain of craters, and so I headed back, in case I fell into the hands of the French. I encountered an officer I knew from the 164th, who warned me not to hang around as it got lighter. Therefore, I strode rapidly through the nameless woods, staggering through deep pits, over felled trees and an almost impenetrable tangle of branches.

By the time I emerged from the woods, it was day. The cratered field stretched out ahead of me, apparently endlessly, with no sign of life. I paused, because unoccupied terrain is always a sinister thing in a war.

Suddenly a shot rang out, and I was hit in both legs by a sniper's bullet. I threw myself into the nearest crater, and tied up the wounds with my handkerchief, having of course forgotten my field dressing. A bullet had drilled through my right calf and brushed the left.

Extremely carefully, I crawled back into the woods, and hobbled from there through the heavily shelled terrain towards the dressing-station.

Just before I reached it, there was an instance of the way tiny imponderables can determine one's fate in a war. I was roughly a hundred yards from a crossroads when the commander of a digging detail I'd been with in the 9th Company called out to me. We had been speaking for barely a minute when a shell landed on the crossroads, which, but for this chance meeting, would probably have cost me my life. It is hard to see these things as completely random.

After dark, I was carried on a stretcher as far as Nurlu, from where the captain picked me up in a car. On the road lit up by enemy searchlights, the driver suddenly braked. There was a dark obstacle in the way. 'Don't look!' said Böckelmann, who had his arm around me. It was a group of infantry with their leader, who had just been killed by a direct hit. The comrades looked like peaceful sleepers as they lay together in death.

In the priest's house I was given some supper, at least inasmuch as I lay on the sofa in the common room, enjoying a glass of wine. But this cosiness was quickly interrupted by Liéramont's evening blessing. Bombardments of towns and buildings are especially disagreeable, and so we hurriedly moved down to the cellar, having heard a few times the hissing song with which the iron messengers announced themselves, before they finished in the gardens or among the roofbeams of neighbouring houses.

I was rolled up in a blanket and carried downstairs first. That same night, I was brought to the field hospital at Villeret, and then on to the military hospital in Valenciennes.

The military hospital had been set up in a school building close to the station, and it was presently housing four hundred severe cases. Day after day, a procession of corpses left its portals to a leaden thump of drums. Doctors did their bloody best at a row of operating tables. Here, a limb was amputated, there a skull chipped open, or a bandage that the flesh had grown over was peeled away. Whimpers and cries echoed through the harshly lit room, while white-clad sisters bustled efficiently from one table to the next with instruments or bandages.

In the bed next to mine lay a sergeant who had lost a leg, and was fighting a bad case of blood poisoning. Mad periods of fever alternated with cold shivering. His temperature chart performed leaps like a wild mustang. The doctors tried to keep him alive on champagne and camphor, but the needle seemed to be pointing unmistakably to death. What was strange, though, was that, having been delirious for the past few days, at the hour of his death he was once more completely lucid, and made some arrangements for what was to be done afterwards. For instance, he had the sister read him his favourite chapter from the Bible, then he took his leave of us all, by asking our forgiveness for having kept us up at night so often with his fever attacks. At the end, he whispered in a voice to which he tried to give a humorous inflection: 'Ey, Fritz, have yer got a bit of bread for me?' and, a few minutes later, he was dead. That last sentence was a reference to our male nurse, Fritz, an elderly man, whose accent we sometimes imitated, and we were profoundly moved by it because it showed the dying man's wish to cheer us up.

It was during this stay in hospital that I suffered an attack of the glooms, a contributing factor in which was surely the memory of the cold, slimy landscape where I had been wounded. Every afternoon, I would hobble along the banks of a bleak-looking canal under bare poplars. I was especially upset not to have been able to participate in the regiment's attack on the woods of St-Pierre-Vaast – a shining effort that won us several hundred prisoners.

After two weeks, when my wounds had pretty much closed, I returned to my troop. The division was still based where I had left it. As my train rolled into Epéhy, there was a series of explosions outside. The twisted wreckage of freight wagons lying by the rails showed that the attack was in earnest.

'What's going on here?' asked a captain who appeared to be fresh out of Germany. Without stopping to give him an answer, I tore open the door of the compartment and took cover behind the railway embankment, while the train rolled on a little. None of the passengers had been hurt; but a few bleeding horses were led out of the cattle car.

Since I wasn't able to march properly yet, I was given the job of observation officer. The observation post was on a downhill slope between Nurlu and Moislains. It was nothing more than a periscope through which I could view the familiar front line. If the bombing was stepped up, or there were coloured flares or anything else out of the ordinary, I was to inform the divisional command by telephone. For days I perched shivering on a little stool behind the two layers of glass, and the only variety on offer was if the line broke down. If the wire had been shot through, I had to get it repaired by my breakdown squad. In these men, of whose activity I had been all but unaware hitherto, I now found a special type of unappreciated worker in the most perilous conditions. While most others strained to leave a shelled zone, the breakdown squad had to enter it calmly and professionally. Day and night, they went into still-warm shell-holes to tie together the ends of two severed wires; their job was as dangerous as it was unglamorous.

The observation post was well camouflaged in the landscape. All that could be seen from outside was a narrow slit half hidden behind a grassy knoll. Only chance shells ended up there, and, from my safe hiding-place, I was able to follow the activities of individuals and units that I hadn't paid that much attention to when I myself had also been under fire. At times, and most of all at dawn and dusk, the landscape was not unlike a wide steppe inhabited by animals. Especially when floods of new arrivals were making for certain points that were regularly shelled, only suddenly to hurl themselves to the ground, or run away as fast as they could, I was put in mind of a natural scene. Such an impression was so strong because my function was a little like that of an antenna, I was a sort of advance sensory organ, detailed to observe calmly all that was happening before me, and inform the leadership. I really had little more to do than wait for the hour of the attack.

Every twenty-four hours, I was relieved by another officer, and I recovered in Nurlu, where there were relatively comfortable quarters set up in a large wine cellar. I still remember long, pensive November evenings, smoking my pipe by the stove in the little vaulted space, while outside in the ravaged park, the fog dripped from the bare chestnut trees and the occasional echoing blast of a shell broke the stillness.

On 18 December, the division was relieved, and I rejoined my regiment, now on rest in the village of Fresnoy-le-Grand. There, I took over the command of the 2nd Company from Lieutenant

Boje, who had a spell of leave. In Fresnoy, the regiment had four
weeks of uninterrupted rest, and everyone tried to make the most
of it. Christmas and New Year were marked by company parties,
at which the beer and grog flowed. Only five men were left of the
2nd Company with whom I had celebrated Christmas in the
trenches at Monchy, a year ago.

With Ensign Gornick and my brother Fritz, who had joined
the regiment for six weeks as cadets, I occupied the living room
and two bedrooms of a French *rentier*. There I started to relax
again a little, and frequently only got home when it was light.

One morning, as I lay half asleep in bed, a comrade came in to
escort me to duty. We were chatting, and he was toying with my
pistol, which as usual was on my bedside table, when he fired a
shot that narrowly missed my skull. I have witnessed several
fatal accidents in war that were caused by careless handling of
weapons; cases like that are always especially irritating.

In the first week, there was an inspection by General Sontag,
at which the regiment was praised for its deeds in the assault on
the woods of St-Pierre-Vaast, and numerous medals were given
out. As I led the 2nd Company forward on parade, I caught a
glimpse of Colonel von Oppen leaning across and talking to the
general about me. A few hours later, I was ordered to divisional
HQ, where the general awarded me the Iron Cross First Class. I
was all the more delighted, as I had followed the order half
thinking I was going to be carpeted for something. 'It seems you
have a habit of getting yourself wounded,' the General said, 'well,
I've got a little plaster for you.'

On 17 January 1917, I was ordered to leave Fresnoy for
four weeks, to take a company-command course at the French
manœuvring ground of Sissonne near Laon. The work was
rendered very agreeable by the head of our section, Captain Funk,
who had the gift of distilling the great plethora of regulations
into a small number of basic principles; it is a method that always
works, no matter where it is applied.

At the same time, the victualling left something to be desired. Potatoes seemed to have become a thing of the past; day after day, when we lifted the lids of our dishes in the vast mess hall, we found nothing but watery swedes. Before long, we couldn't stand the sight of them. Even though they're better than they're cracked up to be – so long as they're roasted with a nice piece of pork, and plenty of black pepper. Which these weren't.

Retreat from the Somme

At the end of February 1917, I returned to the regiment, which had now for some days been in position near the ruins of Villers-Carbonnel, and there I took over command of the 8th Company.

The approach route to the front line snaked through the eerie and devastated area of the Somme Valley; an old and already badly damaged bridge led across the river. Other approach paths were on log-roads laid over the swampy flats; here we had to walk in Indian file, crashing through the wide, rustling reed beds, and striding over the silent oil-black expanses of water. When shells came down on these stretches, and sent up great liquescent columns of mud and water, or when sprays of machine-gun bullets erred over the swampy surface, all you could do was grit your teeth, because it was like walking on a tightrope, there was nowhere for you to go on either side. Hence, the sight of several fantastically shot-up locomotives that had been stopped in their tracks on the high bank on the other side, roughly level with our destination, was each time greeted with relief that otherwise might have been hard to account for.

In the flats lay the villages of Brie and St-Christ. Towers, of which only one slender wall remained, and in whose window openings the moonlight flittered, dark piles of rubble, topped off by smashed beamwork, and isolated trees despoiled of their twigs on the wide snowy plain scarred by black shell-holes accompanied the path like a mechanical scenery, behind which the ghostly quality of the landscape still seemed to lurk.

The firing trenches had been tidied up slightly following a bad, muddy stretch. The platoon commanders told me that, for a while, relief had only been possible with the use of flares; otherwise there would have been every chance of men drowning. A flare shot diagonally over the trench signified: 'I'm going off watch,' and another, coming the other way, confirmed: 'I've taken over.'

My dugout was in a cross trench about fifty yards behind the front line. It housed my small staff and myself, and also a platoon that was under my personal command. It was dry and quite extensive. At each of its entrances, which were draped with tarpaulins, were little iron stoves with long pipes; during heavy bombardments, clumps of earth often came down them with an awful rumble. At right angles to the principal shelter were a number of little blind passages that were used as dormitories. I had one of these to myself. Apart from a narrow cot, a table and a few hand-grenade chests, the only amenities were a few trusty items, such as a spirit stove, a candle-holder, cooking equipment and my personal effects.

This was also the place where we sat together cosily of an evening, each of us perched on twenty-five live hand-grenades. My companions were the two company officers, Hambrock and Eisen, and it seemed to me that these subterranean sessions of ours, three hundred yards from the enemy lines, were pretty curious affairs.

Hambrock, astronomer by vocation, and a great devotee of E. T. A. Hoffmann, liked to hold forth about Venus, contending that it was impossible to do justice to the pure light of this astral body from anywhere on earth. He was a tiny chap, thin and spidery and red-haired, and he had a face dotted with yellow and green freckles that had got him the nickname 'The Marquess of Gorgonzola'. Over the course of the war, he had fallen into some

eccentric habits; thus, he tended to sleep in the daytime and only
came to life as it got dark, occasionally wandering around all
alone in front of our trenches, or the British ones, it seemed to
make little difference to him. Also, he had the worrying habit of
creeping up to a sentry and firing off a flare right by his ear, 'to
test the man's courage'. Unfortunately, his constitution was really
far too weak for a war, and so it happened that he died of a
relatively trivial wound he suffered shortly afterwards at Fresnoy.

Eisen was no taller, but plump, and, having grown up in the
warmer climes of Portugal as the son of an emigrant, he was
perpetually shivering. That was why he swore by a large red-
chequered handkerchief that he tied round his helmet, knotted
under his chin, claiming it kept his head warm. Also, he liked
going around festooned with weapons – apart from his rifle, from
which he was inseparable, he wore numerous daggers, pistols,
hand-grenades and a torch tucked into his belt. Encountering
him in the trench was like suddenly coming upon an Armenian
or somesuch. For a while he used to carry hand-grenades loose
in his pockets as well, till that habit gave him a very nasty turn,
which he related to us one evening. He had been digging around
in his pocket, trying to pull out his pipe, when it got caught in
the loop of a hand-grenade and accidentally pulled it off. He was
startled by the sudden unmistakable little click, which usually
serves as the introduction to a soft hiss, lasting for three seconds,
while the priming explosive burns. In his appalled efforts to pull
the thing out and hurl it away from him, he had got so tangled
up in his trouser pocket that it would have long since blown him
to smithereens, had it not been that, by a fairy-tale stroke of luck,
this particular hand-grenade had been a dud. Half paralysed and
sweating with fear, he saw himself, after all, restored to life.

It was only temporary, though, because a few months later
he too died in the battle at Langemarck. In his case, too, will-
power had to come to the aid of his body; he was both shortsighted and hard of hearing, so that, as we were to see on the

occasion of a little skirmish, he had to be pointed in the right direction by his men if he was to participate in the action in a meaningful way.

Even so, brave puny men are always to be preferred to strong cowards, as was shown over and over in the course of the few weeks we spent in this position.

If our sector of the front could be described as quiet, mighty poundings of artillery that sometimes came hammering down on our lines proved there was no shortage of fire-power in the area. Also, the British were full of curiosity and enterprise here, and not a week passed without some attempt by little exploratory groups to gain information about us, either by cunning or by main force. There were already rumours of some vast impending 'matériel battle' in the spring, which would make last year's Battle of the Somme appear like a picnic. To dampen the impetus of the assault, we were engaged in an extensive tactical withdrawal. There follow a few incidents taken from this phase:

1 March 1917. Hefty exchanges of fire, to take advantage of the good visibility. One heavy battery in particular – with the help of an observation balloon – practically levelled the No. 3 Platoon's section. In an effort to fill in my map of the position, I spent the afternoon splashing about in the completely inundated 'Trench with no name'. On my way, I saw a huge yellow sun slowly sinking, leaving a black plume of smoke after it. A German aeroplane had approached the pesky balloon and shot it in flames. Followed by furious fire from the ground, it made off happily in steeply banking curves.

In the evening, Lance-Corporal Schnau came to me and reported that for four days now there had been chipping sounds heard below his unit's shelter. I passed on the observation, and was sent a pioneer commando with listening apparatus, which registered no suspicious activity. It later transpired that the whole position was undermined.

In the early hours of 5 March, a patrol approached our position and began to cut at our barbed wire. Alerted by the sentry, Eisen hurried over with a few men and threw bombs, whereupon the attackers turned to flee, leaving two casualties behind. One, a young lieutenant, died shortly after; the other, a sergeant, was badly wounded in the arm and leg. From the officer's papers, it appears his name was Stokes, and that he was with the Royal Munster Fusiliers. He was extremely well dressed, and his features, though a little twisted in death, were intelligent and energetic. In his notebook, I came upon a lot of addresses of girls in London, and was rather moved. We buried him behind our lines, putting up a simple cross, in which I had his name set in hobnails. This experience taught me that not every sally ends as harmlessly as mine have to date.

The next morning, after brief preliminary bombardment, the British with fifty men attacked the adjacent section, under the command of Lieutenant Reinhardt. The attackers had crept up to our wires, and after one of them had given a light signal to their own machine-gunners, by means of a striking surface attached to his sleeve, they had charged our lines as the last of the shells were falling. All had blackened faces, so as not to show against the dark.

Our men had arranged such a consummate reception for them, that only one made it into our trenches, running straight through to the second line, where, ignoring calls to surrender, he was shot down. The only ones to get across the wires were a lieutenant and a sergeant. The lieutenant fell, in spite of the fact that he was wearing body armour, because a pistol bullet, fired into him by Reinhardt point-blank, drove one of its plates into his body. The sergeant practically had both legs sheared off by hand-grenade splinters; even so, with stoical calm, he kept his pipe clenched between his teeth to the end. This incident, like all our other encounters with the Britishers, left us pleasantly impressed with their bravery and manliness.

Later that morning, I was strolling along my line when I saw

Lieutenant Pfaffendorf at a sentry post, directing the fire of a trench mortar by means of a periscope. Stepping up beside him, I spotted a British soldier breaking cover behind the third enemy line, the khaki uniform clearly visible against the sky. I grabbed the nearest sentry's rifle, set the sights to six hundred, aimed quickly, just in front of the man's head, and fired. He took another three steps, then collapsed on to his back, as though his legs had been taken away from him, flapped his arms once or twice, and rolled into a shell-crater, where through the binoculars we could see his brown sleeves shining for a long time yet.

On 9 March, the British once again slathered our sector with everything they had. Early in the morning I was awakened by a noisy barrage, reached for my pistol and staggered outside, still half asleep. Pulling aside the tarpaulin in front of my shelter entrance, I saw it was still pitch black. The lurid flaming of the shells and the whooshing dirt woke me in no time. I ran along the trench without encountering anyone at all, until I came to a deep dugout, where a leaderless bunch of men were cowering together on the step like chickens in the rain. I took them with me, and soon livened up the trench. To my satisfaction, I could hear Hambrock's squeaky voice in another sector, also galvanizing.

After the shelling abated somewhat, I went irritably back to my shelter, only for my temper to be further exacerbated by a call from the command:

'What in God's name is going on here? Why does it take you so long to answer the bloody telephone?'

After breakfast, the bombardment resumed. This time, the British were nailing our position slowly but systematically with heavy bombs. Finally, it got a bit boring; I went down an underground passage to pay a call on little Hambrock, see what he had to drink, and play a few rounds of cards. Then we were disturbed by a gigantic noise; clumps of earth clattered through the door and down the stove-pipe. The entrance had collapsed, the wooden revetment was crushed like a matchbox. Sometimes an

communication

cards + drinks

oily bitter-almond smell seemed to waft through the passage –
were they hitting us with Prussic acid now? Well, cheers anyway!
Once, I needed to answer the call; because of the continual
interruptions from heavy shells, I did it in four separate instalments. Then the batman rushed in with the news that the latrine
had been blown to smithereens, prompting Hambrock to com-
ment approvingly on my dilatoriness. I replied: 'If I'd stayed out
there, I'd probably have as many freckles as you do.'

Towards evening, the shelling stopped. In the mood that always
befell me after heavy bombardments, and which I can only compare to the feeling of relief after a storm, I inspected the line. The
trench looked awful; whole stretches had caved in, five dugout
shafts had been crushed. Several men had been wounded; I visited
them, and found them relatively cheerful. A body lay in the
trench, covered by a tarpaulin. His left hip had been ripped
away by a shell fragment as he stood right at the bottom of the
dugout steps.

In the evening, we were relieved.

On 13 March, I was assigned by Colonel von Oppen to hold
the company front with a patrol of two platoons until the regiment had withdrawn across the Somme. Each one of the four sectors was to be held by one such patrol, under the command of its
own officer. From right to left, the sectors were to be under the
command of Lieutenants Reinhardt, Fischer, Lorek and myself.

The villages we passed through on our way had the look of
vast lunatic asylums. Whole companies were set to knocking or
pulling down walls, or sitting on rooftops, uprooting the tiles.
Trees were cut down, windows smashed; wherever you looked,
clouds of smoke and dust rose from vast piles of debris. We saw
men dashing about wearing suits and dresses left behind by
the inhabitants, with top hats on their heads. With destructive
cunning, they found the roof-trees of the houses, fixed ropes to
them, and, with concerted shouts, pulled till they all came tum-
bling down. Others were swinging pile-driving hammers, and

Booby traps

went around smashing everything that got in their way, from the flowerpots on the window-sills to whole ornate conservatories.

As far back as the Siegfried Line, every village was reduced to rubble, every tree chopped down, every road undermined, every well poisoned, every basement blown up or booby-trapped, every rail unscrewed, every telephone wire rolled up, everything burnable burned; in a word, we were turning the country that our advancing opponents would occupy into a wasteland.

As I say, the scenes were reminiscent of a madhouse, and the effect of them was similar: half funny, half repellent. They were also, we could see right away, bad for the men's morale and honour. Here, for the first time, I witnessed wanton destruction that I was later in life to see to excess; this is something that is unhealthily bound up with the economic thinking of our age, but it does more harm than good to the destroyer, and dishonours the soldier.

Among the surprises we'd prepared for our successors were some truly malicious inventions. Very fine wires, almost invisible, were stretched across the entrances of buildings and shelters, which set off explosive charges at the faintest touch. In some places, narrow ditches were dug across roads, and shells hidden in them; they were covered over by an oak plank, and had earth strewn over them. A nail had been driven into the plank, only just above the shell-fuse. The space was measured so that marching troops could pass over the spot safely, but the moment the first lorry or field gun rumbled up, the board would give, and the nail would touch off the shell. Or there were spiteful time bombs that were buried in the basements of undamaged buildings. They consisted of two sections, with a metal partition going down the middle. In one part was explosive, in the other acid. After these devil's eggs had been primed and hidden, the acid slowly, over weeks, eroded the metal partition, and then set off the bomb. One such device blew up the town hall of Bapaume just as the authorities had assembled to celebrate victory.

On 13 March, then, the 2nd Company left the position, and I took it over with my two platoons. That night, a man by the name of Kirchhof was killed by a shot in the head. Oddly, that one fatal shot was the only one fired by our enemy in the space of several hours.

I arranged all sorts of things to deceive the enemy about our strength. Shovelfuls of earth were flung over the ramparts up and down the trench, and our solitary machine-gun was to fire off bursts now from one flank, now from the other. Even so, our fire-power couldn't help sounding rather thin when low-flying aeroplanes buzzed the position, or a digging party was seen crossing the enemy hinterland. It was inevitable that patrols were sent out every night to different points, to attack our wire entanglements.

On our second-to-last day, I had a close shave. A dud shell from an anti-balloon gun came plummeting down from the sky, and exploded on the traverse where I happened to be leaning. The air pressure picked me up and hurled me across the trench, fortunately into the mouth of a shelter, where I picked myself up, feeling rather confused.

On the morning of the 17th, we sensed that an attack was imminent. From the advanced English trench, which was very muddy and usually unoccupied, we heard the splashing of many boots. The sounds of laughter and shouts from a strong detachment of men suggested they were nicely lubricated inside and out. Dark forms approached our wires, and were driven back by rifle fire; one of them collapsed wailing, and lay there. I withdrew my groups in hedgehog formation to the mouth of one communication trench, and tried to keep the field ahead lit up by flares, as artillery and mortar fire suddenly commenced. We soon ran out of white lights, and moved on to coloured; it was a veritable firework display that we put on. As the designated hour of five o'clock rolled round, we quickly blew up our foxholes with bombs, those of them at any rate that hadn't already been fitted with fiendish contraptions of one sort or another, on which we expended the last of our munitions. It was several hours now since I'd last laid hands on a chest, a door or a water-bucket, for fear of blowing myself up.

At the appointed time, the patrols, some of them already involved in hand-grenade battles with the enemy, withdrew towards the Somme. We were the last to cross the river, before the bridges were blown up by a sapper detachment. Our position was still coming in for drumfire. It wasn't for another few hours that the first enemy outposts reached the Somme. We withdrew behind the Siegfried Line, then still in the process of construction; the battalion took up quarters in the village of Lehaucourt, on the St-Quentin Canal. With my batman, I moved into a cosy little house, whose cupboards and chests were still well supplied. My faithful Knigge would not be persuaded by anything to set up his bed in the warm living room, insisting, as ever, on the chilly kitchen – typical of the restraint of our Lower Saxons.

Our first evening off, I invited my friends round for mulled wine, using all the spices left behind by the previous occupants of the house, because, in addition to praise from our superiors, our patrol had won us all a fortnight's furlough.

In the Village of Fresnoy

On this occasion, the furlough, which I took up a few days later, was to remain uninterrupted. In my journal, I find the brief but eloquent sentence: 'Spent my furlough very well, in the event of my death I shall have no complaints.' On 9 April 1917, I was back with the 2nd Company, who were quartered in the village of Merignies, not far from Douai. What took the edge off my pleasure at the reunion was consternation at being required to accompany the baggage train to Beaumont. Through showers of rain and driving snow, I rode at the head of a crawling column of vehicles, till we finally reached our destination at one in the morning.

After men and horses had variously been found shelter, I went looking for quarters for myself, but could find nowhere that wasn't already taken. Finally, a commissariat orderly had the clever idea of offering me his own bed, seeing as he was manning the telephone exchange anyway. Even as I flopped on to it, still booted and spurred, he told me that the British had taken Vimy Ridge from the Bavarians, and quite a bit of land around. Kindly as he was to me, I could tell he was secretly resentful of the way his quiet village in the back area was being adapted to a meeting-point for front-line forces.

The following morning, the battalion marched off into the direction of heavy firing, to the village of Fresnoy. There I received orders to establish an observation post. With a few men, I found

food looting

a little house on the western edge of the village, and we knocked through the roof to make a viewing-place. We set up residence in the cellar of the same building. As we were clearing it, we made the welcome discovery of a sack of potatoes, to supplement our extremely meagre supplies. Thereafter, I had Knigge make me boiled potatoes with salt every evening. Also, Gornick, now occupying the deserted village of Villerwal with his platoon, sent me a few bottles of claret and a large tin of liver sausage – a comradely gift raised from the suddenly abandoned supplies in a foodstore. A booty expedition thereupon immediately dispatched by me, with baby carriages and similar conveyances to recover further treasures, was forced to return empty-handed, as the British lines had already reached the edge of the village. Gornick told me later that following the discovery of the cache of wine a spontaneous drinking session had ensued, even as the village was being bombarded, and that it had been difficult to reimpose control. In similar situations later, we were simply to shoot holes in barrels and carboys and other containers of alcohol.

On 14 April, I was given instructions to set up an intelligence-clearing station in the village. To that end, I had dispatch-riders, bicyclists, telephone- and light-signal stations and underground telegraph wires, carrier pigeons and a chain of flare positions all put at my disposal. In the evening, I looked out a suitable basement with annexes, and then returned for the last time to my old lodgings on the west of the village. There had been a lot to do that day, and I was pretty tired.

I had the impression, that night, of hearing a few dull crashing sounds and of Knigge calling to me, but I was so fast asleep that I merely mumbled, 'Oh, let them shoot!' and turned over on my side, even though the room was as thick with dust as a chalk mill. In the morning I was woken by little Schultz, Colonel von Oppen's nephew, shouting: 'Good God, do you mean to tell me you slept through that?' When I got up and surveyed the debris, I quickly realized that a heavy shell had exploded on the roof, and smashed all the rooms, including our observation post. The fuse would only have had to be a little bigger, and they could have scraped off our remains with a spoon, and buried us in our mess-tins, as the grunts were given to saying. Schultz told me his runner had taken one look at the wreckage and said: 'There was a lieutenant quartered in there yesterday, better see if he's still there.' Knigge was terribly impressed by my deep sleep.

In the morning, we moved to our new basement. As we were about that, we were almost crushed by the debris of the church tower, which was quite unceremoniously – and without any prior notification – blown up by our engineers, to make it harder for the enemy artillery to get their bearings. In one of the neighbouring villages, no one had troubled to warn a couple of lookouts who had been posted up their church. Miraculously, the men were pulled out of the wreckage alive and unhurt. That one morning saw over a dozen church towers in the area bite the dust.

We settled into our spacious cellar, and furnished it pretty much as we pleased, helping ourselves equally to items from the rich man's castle and the poor man's hovel. Whatever we ended up not liking, fed the fire.

Airplane dogfights

Also during these days, there was a whole series of dogfights, which almost invariably ended with defeat for the British, since it was Richthofen's squadron they were up against. Often five or six planes in succession would be chased away or shot down in flames. Once we saw a pilot tumble out in a great arc, and come down separately from his plane, no more than a little black dot. Admittedly, looking up to watch was not without its attendant dangers; one soldier in the 4th Company was fatally wounded in the throat by a falling splinter.

On 18 April I visited the 2nd Company in their position in an oxbow around the village of Arleux. Boje told me that so far he'd only had a single man wounded, since the pedantic preliminary bombardments of the British left ample time to vacate the target area.

After wishing him luck, I left the village at a gallop, as heavy shells had begun to fall. When I was about three hundred yards away, I stopped to watch the clouds thrown up by the spurting explosions, red or black, depending on whether they'd struck brickwork or garden soil, and mingled with the soft white of bursting shrapnels. When a few clusters of small shells began to fall on the narrow footpaths linking Arleux and Fresnoy, I decided I'd seen enough, and cleared the field to avoid being 'a little bit killed', as the current expression in the 2nd Company had it.

Such excursions, sometimes as far as the little town of Henin-Liétard, were pretty frequent in the first fortnight because, in spite of my large staff and resources, I was given no intelligence whatsoever to clear.

Beginning on 20 April, Fresnoy came under fire from a ship's cannon, whose shells came whining up with a hellish hiss. Following every explosion, the village was wrapped in a vast reddish-brown cloud of picric acid gas, which mushroomed out. Even the dud shells were enough to cause a minor earthquake. One soldier in the 9th Company, who was caught by a shell like that while in the castle grounds, was launched high over the trees and broke every bone in his body when he hit the deck.

One evening, I was on my bicycle, heading back down to the village from a local vantage-point, when I saw the familiar reddish-brown cloud go up. I dismounted and stood in a field to wait for the bombardment to finish. About three seconds after each explosion I heard the gigantic crash, followed by a vast twittering and whistling, as if a dense flock of birds were approaching. Then hundreds of splinters would come dusting the dry fields around. This happened several times, and each time I waited feeling half embarrassed, half simply nosy, for the relatively slow arrival of the splinters.

In the afternoons, the village was under bombardment from all sorts of weapons and calibres. In spite of the danger, I was always loath to leave the attic window of the house, because it was an exciting sight, watching units and individual messengers hurrying across the field of fire, often hurling themselves to the ground, while the earth whirled and spat to the left and right of them. Peeping over Destiny's shoulder like that to see her hand, it's easy to become negligent and risk one's own life.

As I entered the village at the end of one of these ordeals by fire – as that's what they were – I saw a basement flattened. All we could recover from the scorched space were the three bodies. Next to the entrance one man lay on his belly in a shredded uniform; his head was off, and the blood had flowed into a puddle. When an ambulanceman turned him over to check him for valuables, I saw as in a nightmare that his thumb was still hanging from the remains of his arm.

With each day, the bombardment became more intensive, and it soon seemed all but certain that an attack must follow. On the 27th, at midnight, I had the following telegraph message: '67 beginning 5 a.m.', which in our code meant that from five o'clock tomorrow we were to be on a heightened state of alert.

I promptly lay down right away, so as to be up to the anticipated exertions, but as I was on the point of sleep, a shell struck the house, smashed the wall against the basement steps, and filled our room with rubble. We leaped up and hurried into the shelter.

As we sat on the steps, by the light of a candle, tired and sullen, the leader of my light-signalling troop, whose station had been destroyed that afternoon, including two valuable signalling lamps, dashed in to report: 'Lieutenant, the basement of No. 11 has taken a direct hit, there are some men buried in the rubble!' Since I had two bicyclists and three telephonists among them, I hurried over with some of my men.

In the shelter, I found one lance-corporal and one wounded man, and received the following report: As the first shells began to land ominously close, four of the five inhabitants decided to take to the shelter. One of them ran down right away, one of them stayed in his bed imperturbably, and the other three sat down to pull their boots on. The most cautious man and the most carefree, as so often in the war, survived, one of them being quite uninjured, the sleeper receiving a splinter in the thigh, while the other three were torn apart by the shell that flew through the basement wall and blew up in the far corner.

Following this account, I lit a cigar and entered the smoky room, in the middle of which was piled almost to the ceiling a bolus of straw sacks, smashed bedsteads, and other furniture. After we had set down a few candles in niches in the wall, we set about the sorry task. We seized hold of the limbs sticking out from the wreckage, and pulled out the corpses. One man had lost his head, and the end of his torso was like a great sponge of blood. Splintered bones stuck out of the arm stump of the second, and his uniform was drenched with blood from a great wound in his chest. The intestines of the third were spilling out of his opened belly. As we pulled him out, a splintered piece of board caught in the wound with a hideous noise. One orderly passed a remark, and was rebuked by Knigge with the words: 'Shut up, man, you don't waste words over something like this!'

I made an inventory of their personal belongings. It was a ghastly job. The candles flickered reddishly in the dusty air, while the men handed me wallets and rings and watches, as if we were a bunch of gangsters. Fine yellow brick-dust had settled on the dead men's faces, and gave them the rigid appearance of waxen effigies. We draped blankets over them, and hurried out of the basement, having first wrapped the wounded man in a tarpaulin. With the stoical advice 'Better grit your teeth, comrade!' we dragged him through wild shrapnel fire to the dressing-station.

Once back in my lodging, I first of all took some cherry brandy to recover. Before long, the firing got worse again, and we hurriedly gathered in the shelter, having just been given a vivid demonstration of the effects of artillery on cellars.

At precisely fourteen minutes past five, the bombardment, in

IN THE VILLAGE OF FRESNOY

the space of a few seconds, reached an extraordinary pitch. Our intelligence service had been dead right. The shelter was shaking and trembling like a ship in a storm, while all around came the sounds of crashing walls and the splintering of the houses near by collapsing.

At seven o'clock I received a light signal addressed to the 2nd Battalion: 'Brigade requires immediate report on the situation.' An hour later, a deathly tired runner came back with the news: 'Enemy occupying Arleux and Arleux Park. 8th Company ordered to counter-attack. No news as yet. Rocholl, Captain.'

That was the single, albeit crucial, item of news that I was able to pass on with my big staff in the course of my three-week stay in Fresnoy. Now, when my being there was of the utmost value, the artillery had put almost all my means of communication out of commission. I myself was caught like a rat in a trap. The setting up of this intelligence post had proved mistaken; it was a case of over-centralization.

This surprising bit of news now explained to me why rifle bullets had been rattling against the walls for some time and from fairly close.

No sooner had we grasped the extent of the regiment's losses, than the bombardment recommenced with full power. Knigge was the last man standing on the shelter stairs when a thunderous crash told us that the British had at last managed to score a direct hit on our cellar. The stolid Knigge caught a lump of rock on the back, but was otherwise unhurt. Above, everything was in pieces. Daylight reached us through a couple of bicycles that had been crushed into the shelter entrance. We retreated to the bottom step, while the continuing thud and rattle of masonry reminded us of the uncertainty even of this refuge of ours.

As if by a miracle, the telephone was still working; I informed the divisional chief of intelligence of our situation, and was given orders to withdraw with my men to the nearby dressing-station dugout.

So we packed up our few essentials, and set off towards the shelter's alternative exit, which was at least still intact. Even though I didn't stint with threats and orders, the rather un-battle-hardened telephonists took such a long time to leave the relative protection of the shelter and expose themselves to direct fire that that entrance was hit by a heavy shell and collapsed with a great crash. It was fortunate that no one was hit, only our little dog set up a howl, and was never seen again.

Now we had to heave aside the bicycles that were blocking the cellar exit, creep on all fours over the debris, and slip through a crack in the wall into the open. Without stopping to take in the unbelievable change that had come over the place, we headed out of the village as fast as we could. No sooner had the last man of us got past the front gate, than the house took one more huge hit, and that was the *coup de grâce*.

The terrain between the edge of the village and the dressing-station was receiving a total artillery barrage. Light and heavy shells with impact-, fire- and time-delay fuses, duds, empty cases and shrapnels all participated in a kind of madness that was too much for our eyes and ears. In amongst it all, going either side of the witches' cauldron of the village, support troops were advancing.

Fresnoy was one towering fountain of earth after another. Each second seemed to want to outdo the last. As if by some magical power, one house after another subsided into the earth; walls broke, gables fell, and bare sets of beams and joists were sent flying through the air, cutting down the roofs of other houses. Clouds of splinters danced over whitish wraiths of steam. Eyes and ears were utterly compelled by this maelstrom of devastation.

We spent the next two days in the dressing-station dugout, in conditions of great overcrowding, because in addition to my men it housed the staffs of two battalions, two relief detachments, and the inevitable odds and sods. The coming and going around the entrances, where there was a continual buzz of activity as

around a beehive, of course didn't go unnoticed by our opponents. Soon wickedly aimed shells landed at one-minute intervals
on the footpaths outside, and the calls for the ambulancemen
were never-ending. To this unpleasant bit of target-practice I lost
four bicycles, which I had left next to the entrance. They were
comprehensively remodelled and cast to the four winds.

At the entrance, stiff and silent, rolled in a tarpaulin, his big
hornrims still on his face, lay Lieutenant Lemière, the commander
of the 8th Company, who had been brought here by his men. He
had received a shot in the mouth. His younger brother was to fall
only a few months later, hit in the same way.

On 30 April my successor took over from me with the relief
regiment, the 25th, and we moved to Flers, the rendezvous
for the 1st Battalion. Leaving the heavily shelled limekiln,
'Chezbontemps', on our left, we strolled blissfully across the
fields to Beaumont in the balmy afternoon. Our eyes once more
appreciated the beauty of the earth, relieved to have escaped the
unbearable constriction of the shelter hole, and our lungs drew
in the intoxicating spring air. With the rumble of guns behind us,
we were able to say with the poet:

> A day that God the maker of the world
> Made for sweeter things than fighting.

In Flers, I found my designated quarters had been occupied by
several staff sergeant-majors, who, claiming they had to guard
the room on behalf of a certain Baron von X, refused to make
room, but hadn't reckoned on the short temper of an irritated
and tired front-line officer. I had my men knock the door down,
and, following a short scuffle in front of the peacetime occupants
of the house, who had hurried along in their nightgowns to see
what the matter was, the gentlemen, or gentleman's gentlemen,
were sent flying down the stairs. Knigge was sufficiently gracious
to throw their boots out after them. After this successful attack,

I climbed into my nicely warmed-up bed, offering half of it to my friend Kius, who was still wandering around looking for an abode. The sleep in this long-missed fixture did us so much good that the following morning we woke, as they say, fully refreshed.

Since the 1st Battalion had not lost many men during the recent fighting, the mood was pretty cheerful as we marched to the station at Douai. Our destination was the village of Serain, where we were to rest and recuperate for a few days. We had a friendly welcome and good accommodation from the villagers, and already on our first evening the happy sounds of reunited comrades could be heard from many of the dwellings.

Such libations after a successfully endured engagement are among the fondest memories an old warrior may have. Even if ten out of twelve men had fallen, the two survivors would surely meet over a glass on their first evening off, and drink a silent toast to their comrades, and jestingly talk over their shared experiences. There was in these men a quality that both emphasized the savagery of war and transfigured it at the same time: an objective relish for danger, the chevalieresque urge to prevail in battle. Over four years, the fire smelted an ever-purer, ever-bolder warriorhood.

The next morning, Knigge appeared and read out some orders, from which I understood that I was to take over the command of the 4th Company at around noon. This was the company in which the Lower Saxon poet Hermann Löns fell in the autumn of 1914 outside Rheims, a volunteer at the age of almost fifty.

Against Indian Opposition

The 6th of May 1917 already found us back on the march, heading once more for the familiar destination of Brancourt, and on the following day we moved, via Montbréhain, Ramicourt and Joncourt, to the Siegfried Line that we had left only a month before.

The first evening was stormy; heavy rain clattered down on the already flooded terrain. Soon, though, a succession of fine warm days reconciled us to our new place. I enjoyed the splendid landscape, untroubled by the white balls of shrapnel and the jumping cones of shells; in fact, barely noticing them. Each spring marked the beginning of a new year's fighting; intimations of a big offensive were as much part of the season as primroses and pussy-willows.

Our sector was a semi-circular bulge in front of the St-Quentin Canal, at our rear we had the famous Siegfried Line. I confess I am at a loss to understand why we had to take our place in these tight, undeveloped limestone trenches, when we had that enormously strong bulwark just behind us.

The front line wound its way through meadowland shaded by little clumps of trees, wearing the fresh green of early spring. It was possible to walk safely in front of and behind the trenches, as many advance positions secured the line. These posts were a thorn in the enemy's side, and some weeks not a night would pass without an attempt to remove the sentries, either by guile or by brute force.

But our first period in position passed pleasantly quietly; the weather was so beautiful that we spent the nights lying on the grass. On 14 May, we were relieved by the 8th Company, and moved, the fires of St-Quentin on our right, to our resting-place, Montbréhain, a large village that had as yet taken little harm from the war and afforded very agreeable accommodation. On the 20th, as the reserve company, we occupied the Siegfried Line. It was summer holidays; we spent the days sitting in little summer huts erected on the slopes, or swimming and rowing on the canal. I spent the time lying stretched out on the grass reading the whole of Ariosto to my great enjoyment.

These idyllic positions have the one drawback that one's superior officers like to visit them, which is a great dampener to the cosiness of trench life. That said, my left flank, posted against the already 'nibbled at' village of Bellenglise, had no shortage of fire to complain of. On the very first day, one man was hit by a shrapnel in the right buttock. On hearing the news, I rushed to the scene of the misfortune, and there he was, happily sitting up on his left, waiting for the ambulancemen to arrive, drinking coffee and munching on a vast slice of bread and jam.

On 25 May, we relieved the 12th Company at Riqueval-Ferme. This farm, formerly a great landed estate, served each of the four companies in the position alternately as base. From there, units went out to man three machine-gun nests positioned in the hinterland. These diagonally positioned support-points, covering each other like chess pieces, represented the first attempts in this war at a more supple, variable form of defence.

The farm was a mile at the most behind the front line; even so, its various buildings, dotted about in a rather overgrown park, were still completely unscathed. It was also densely populated – dugouts had yet to be created. The blooming hawthorn avenues in the park and the attractive surroundings gave our existence here an intimation of the leisurely country idyll that the French are so expert at creating – and that, so close to the front. A pair of swallows had made their nest in my bedroom, and were busy from very early in the morning with the noisy feeding of their insatiable young.

In the evenings, I took a stick out of the corner and strolled along narrow footpaths that went winding through the hilly landscape. The neglected fields were full of flowers, and the smell grew headier and wilder by the day. Occasional trees stood beside the paths, under which a farmworker might have taken his ease in peacetime, bearing white or pink or deep-red blossoms, magical apparitions in the solitude. Nature seemed to be pleasantly intact, and yet the war had given it a suggestion of heroism and melancholy; its almost excessive blooming was even more radiant and narcotic than usual.

It's easier to go into battle against such a setting than in a cold and wintry scene. The simple soul is convinced here that his life is deeply embedded in nature, and that his death is no end.

On 30 May, this idyll was over for me, because that was the day Lieutenant Vogeley was released from hospital, and resumed command of the 4th Company. I returned to my old 2nd, on the front line.

Two platoons manned our sector from the Roman road to the so-called Artillery Trench; a third was at company headquarters, some two hundred yards back, behind a little slope. There Kius and I shared a tiny plank lean-to together, trusting to the incompetence of the British artillery. One side was built into the downhill slope – the direction the shells would be coming from – while the other three offered their flanks to the enemy. Every day as the morning greetings were wafted up to us, one might have heard a conversation between the occupants of the top and bottom bunks that went roughly like this:

'I say, Ernst, are you awake?'

'Hm?'

'I think they're shooting!'

'Oh, I don't want to get up yet; I'm sure they'll be finished soon.'

A quarter of an hour later:

'I say, Oskar!'

'Hm?'

'They seem to be going on for ever today; I thought I heard a shrapnel ball come flying through the wall just now. I think we'd better get up after all. The artillery observer next door seems to have scarpered ages ago!'

We were unwise enough always to take our boots off. By the time we were finished, the British usually were too, and we could sit down at the ridiculously small table, drink our sour, stewed coffee, and light a morning cigar. In the afternoons, we mocked the British gunners by lying out on a tarpaulin and doing some sunbathing.

In other respects, too, our shack was an entertaining place to be. As we lay idly on our wire-sprung beds, enormous earthworms would come nosing out of the earthen wall; if we interfered with them, they would show a surprising turn of speed, disappearing back into their holes. A gloomy mole occasionally came snuffling out of his warren; his appearances always greatly enlivened our siesta time.

On 12 June, I was told to take a troop of twenty men and invest an outpost on the company front. It was late when we left the trench and headed along a footpath winding through the hilly countryside, into the pleasant evening. Dusk was so far advanced that the poppies in the abandoned fields seemed to merge with the bright-green grass. In the declining light, I saw more and more of my favourite colour, that red which shades into black that is at once sombre and stimulating.

Whatever thoughts we might have had we kept to ourselves as we walked silently over the flowery slopes, with our rifles over our shoulders, and twenty minutes later we had reached our destination. In whispers the post was taken over, a guard was mounted, and then the men who had been relieved slipped off into the dark.

new movement

The outpost leaned against a steep little slope, with a line of hurriedly dug foxholes. Behind it, a hundred yards or so back, a small tangle of woodland merged with the night. In front and to the right rose two hills across which ran the British lines. One of them was crested by the ruins of the auspiciously named 'Ascension Farm'. A little path led between the hills, in the general direction of the enemy.

That was where, while inspecting my sentries, I ran into Sergeant-Major Hackmann and a few men from the 7th; they were just about to go out on patrol. Even though I wasn't supposed to leave the outpost, I decided to join them for the hell of it.

Adopting a type of movement of my own devising (of which more later), we had crossed two entanglements, and crested the hill, strangely without encountering any sentries, when we heard the sounds of the British digging to the right and left of us. Later on, I realized that the enemy must have withdrawn his sentries to have them out of the way for the ambush I will go on to describe.

The movement that I alluded to a moment ago consisted in letting members of a patrol go forward one at a time when there was a chance that we might encounter the enemy at any moment. So there was never more than one man in front, taking it in turn to risk being the one shot by a hidden sentry, while the others were all at his back ready to lend support at a moment's notice. I took my turn with the rest, even though my presence with the rest of the patrol might have mattered more; but there is more to war than such tactical considerations.

We crawled around several digging parties, as there were unfortunately large wire obstacles between them and ourselves. After quickly rejecting the rather eccentric sergeant-major's suggestion that he might pretend to be a deserter, and keep the enemy distracted until we had gone around the first enemy sentries, we crept back to the outpost.

There is something stimulating about such excursions; the

senses on high alert.

heart beats a little faster, and one is bombarded by fresh ideas. I resolved to dream away the mild night, and rigged up a nest for myself in the tall grass on the slope, lining it with my coat. Then I lit my pipe as discreetly as I could, and drifted off on the wings of my imagination.

In the middle of my 'pipe dreams', I was startled by a distinct rustling coming from the woods and the meadow. In the presence of the enemy, one's senses are always on the qui vive, and it's a strange thing that one can feel sure, even on the basis of rather ordinary sounds: This is it!

Straight away the nearest sentry came rushing up to me: 'Lieutenant, sir, there are seventy British soldiers advancing on the edge of the wood!'

Though somewhat surprised at such a precise count, I hid in the tall grass on the slope, along with four riflemen, to wait and see what happened next. A few seconds later, I saw a group of men flitting across the meadow. As my men levelled their rifles at them, I called down a soft: 'Who goes there?' It was NCO Teilengerdes, an experienced warrior from the 2nd, collecting up his excited unit.

The other units quickly arrived. I had them form into a line stretching from the slope to the wood. A minute later, they were standing ready, with fixed bayonets. It couldn't hurt to check the alignment; in such situations, you can't be too pedantic. As I was upbraiding a man who was standing a little back, he replied: 'I'm a stretcher-bearer, sir.' He had his own rules to follow. Relieved, I ordered the men to advance.

As we strode across the strip of meadow, a hail of shrapnel flew over our heads. The enemy was laying down a dense fire in an attempt to disrupt our communications. Involuntarily, we slipped into a jogtrot, to reach the lee of the hill in front of us.

Suddenly, a dark form arose out of the grass. I tore off a hand-grenade and hurled it in the direction of the figure, with a shout. To my consternation, I saw by the flash of the explosion that it was Teilengerdes, who, unnoticed by me, had somehow run on ahead, and tripped over a wire. Fortunately, he was unhurt. Simultaneously, we heard the sharper reports of British grenades, and the shrapnel fire became unpleasantly concentrated.

Our line melted away, in the direction of the steep slope, which was experiencing heavy fire, while Teilengerdes and I and three men stayed put. Suddenly one of them jogged me: 'Look, the British!'

Like a vision in a dream, the sight, lit only by falling sparks, of a double line of kneeling figures at the instant in which they rose to advance, etched itself into my eye. I could clearly make out the figure of an officer on the right of the line, giving the command to advance. Friend and foe were paralysed by this sudden, unexpected meeting. Then we turned to flee – the only thing we could do – the enemy, it seemed, still too paralysed to fire at us.

We leaped up and ran towards the slope. Even though I tripped over a wire laid treacherously in the tall grass and flew head over heels, I made it safely, and ordered my excited troops into a compressed line.

Our situation was now such that we were sitting under the bowl of fire, as under a tightly woven basket. What appeared to have happened was that in our advance we had disturbed the enemy's flanking manœuvre. We were at the foot of the slope, on a somewhat worn path. The wheel-ruts were enough to afford us some minimal protection against their rifles, because one's instinctive response to danger is to press oneself as close as possible to mother earth. We kept our guns pointed at the wood, which meant that the British lines were behind us. This one circumstance unsettled me more than anything that might be going on in the wood, so, during the ensuing action, I took care to send occasional lookouts up the slope.

Suddenly the shelling ceased; we needed to steel ourselves for an attack. No sooner had our ears grown used to the surprising silence, than sounds of crackling and rustling were heard coming from the wood.

'Halt! Who goes there? Password!'

We must have shouted for about five minutes, including the old 1st Battalion watchword 'Lüttje Lage' – an expression for beer and a short, familiar to all Hanoverians; but all we got back was a muddle of voices. Finally I decided to give the order to shoot, even though there were some of us who felt certain they had heard some words of German. My twenty rifles discharged their bullets into the wood, bolts rattled, and soon we heard the wailing of wounded from the brush. I had an uneasy feeling, because I thought it was within the bounds of possibility that we were firing at a detachment sent to help us.

I was relieved, therefore, to see little yellow tongues of flame flash back, although they soon stopped. One man was hit in the shoulder, and the stretcher-bearer tended to him.

'Hold your fire!'

Slowly the order took effect, and the shooting stopped. The tension in any case had been broken by our taking some action.

Further calls for the password. I scraped together what little English I had, and shouted a few (I hoped, persuasive) words of encouragement: 'Come here, you are prisoners, hands up!'

Thereupon, more confused shouting, which sounded to us like the German word 'Rache, Rache!' ['Revenge, revenge!']. A single man emerged from the edge of the wood and came towards us. One of the men made the mistake of shouting 'Password!' to him, causing him to stop irresolutely and turn back. Obviously a scout.

'Shoot him down!'

A volley of a dozen shots; the figure subsided into the tall grass.

The little episode filled us with satisfaction. From the edge of the wood, once more there was the strange jabbering; it sounded as though the attackers were encouraging one another to advance against the mysterious defenders.

We stared intently at the dark line of wood. It began to get light, and a thin morning fog rose off the meadow.

Then we saw something that was a rarity in this war of long-range weapons. Out of the dark brush, a line of figures emerged and stepped on to the open meadow. Five, ten, fifteen, a whole line. Trembling fingers took off safety-catches. A distance of fifty yards, thirty, fifteen . . . Fire! The rifles barked for several minutes. Sparks flew as spurts of lead struck weapons and steel helmets.

Suddenly a shout: 'Watch out, left!' A mob of attackers was running towards us from the left, headed by an enormous figure with an outstretched revolver, and swinging a white club.

'Left section! Left front!'

The men spun round, and welcomed the new arrivals in a standing posture. A few of the enemy, among them their leader, collapsed under the hurriedly fired-off shots, the others vanished as quickly as they had appeared.

Now was our moment to charge. With fixed bayonets and loud hurrahs, we surged into the little wood. Hand-grenades flew into the tangled undergrowth, and in no time at all we were back in control of our outpost, although admittedly without having come to grips with our elusive foe.

We assembled in an adjacent cornfield and gazed at each other's pale and exhausted faces. The sun had risen radiantly. A lark was ascending, getting on our wicks with its trilling. It was all unreal after that feverishly intent night.

While we handed round our canteens and lit cigarettes, we heard the enemy leaving along the path, with a few loudly lamenting wounded in tow. We even caught a glimpse of them, but not long enough to chase after and finish them off.

I went off to survey the battlefield. From the meadow arose exotic calls and cries for help. The voices were like the noise that frogs make in the grass after a rainstorm. In the tall grass we discovered a line of dead and three wounded who threw

themselves at our feet and begged us for mercy. They seemed to
be convinced that we would massacre them.

In answer to my question 'Quelle nation?' one replied: 'Pauvre
Rajput!'

So these were Indians we had confronted, who had travelled
thousands of miles across the sea, only to give themselves a
bloody nose on this god-forsaken piece of earth against the
Hanoverian Rifles.

They were delicate, and in a bad way. At such short range, an
infantry bullet has an explosive effect. Some of them had been
hit a second time as they lay there, and in such a way that the
bullets had passed longitudinally, down the length of their bodies.
All of them had been hit twice, and a few more than that. We
picked them up, and dragged them towards our lines. Since they
were screaming like banshees, my men tried to hold their mouths
shut and brandished their fists at them, which terrified them still
more. One died on the way, but he was still taken along, because
there was a reward for every prisoner taken, whether alive or
dead. The other two tried to ingratiate themselves with us by
calling out repeatedly: 'Anglais pas bon!' Why these people spoke
French I couldn't quite understand. The whole scene – the mixture
of the prisoners' laments and our jubilation – had something
primordial about it. This wasn't war; it was ancient history.

Returned to the line, we were received in triumph by the
company, who had heard the sounds of fighting, and had been
pegged back by a heavy artillery barrage, and our captives were
much gawped at. Here I was able to set the minds of our captives
at rest – they seemed to have been told the direst things about
us. They thawed a little, and told me their names; one of them
was Amar Singh. Their outfit was the First Hariana Lancers, a
good regiment, I'm told. Then I retired with Kius, who took
half a dozen photographs, to our hut, and had him treat me to
celebratory fried eggs.

Our little skirmish was mentioned in the divisional orders for

Propaganda

the day. With only twenty men we had seen off a detachment several times larger, and attacking us from more than one side, and in spite of the fact that we had orders to withdraw if we were outnumbered. It was precisely an engagement like this that I'd been dreaming of during the *longueurs* of positional warfare.

It turned out, by the way, that we lost a man in addition to the one who was wounded, and that in mysterious circumstances. The fellow in question was barely fit for active service any longer, because an earlier wound had left him morbidly fearful. We only noticed he was missing the next day; I assumed that in a fit of panic he ran off into one of the cornfields, and there met his end.

The following evening, I received orders to occupy the outpost again. As the enemy might have dug himself in there by now, I took the wood in a pincer movement; I led one detachment, Kius the other. Here, for the first time, I adopted a particular mode of approaching a dangerous site, which consisted of having one man after another going around it. If the place was in fact occupied, a simple left- or rightward movement created a possibility for flanking fire. After the war, I included this manœuvre in the *Infantry Engagement Manual*, under the name of 'flanking file'.

The two detachments met up without incident at the slope – aside from the fact that Kius barely missed shooting me as he cocked his pistol.

There was no sign of the enemy, it was only on the path between the two hills that I had reconnoitred with Sergeant-Major Hackmann that a sentry challenged us, fired a flare and some live rounds. We made a note of the noisy young man for another time.

In the place where the night before we had beaten back the flank attack we found three bodies. They were two Indians and a white officer with two gold stars on his shoulder-straps – a first lieutenant. He had been shot in the eye. The bullet had exited through his temple and shattered the rim of his steel helmet,

which I kept as a souvenir. In his right hand he still held the club
– reddened with his own blood – and in his left a heavy Colt
revolver, whose magazine had only two bullets left in it. He had
evidently had serious intentions towards us.

In the course of the following days, more bodies were discovered in the undergrowth – evidence of the attackers' heavy
losses, which added to the gloomy atmosphere that prevailed
there. As I was making my way through a thicket once, on my
own, I was dismayed by a quiet hissing and burbling sound. I
stepped closer and encountered two bodies, which the heat had
awakened to a ghostly type of life. The night was silent and
humid; I stopped a long time before the eerie scene.

On 18 June, the outpost was again attacked; on this occasion,
things didn't go so well for us. Panic developed; the men fled in
all directions, and couldn't be brought together again. In the
confusion, one of them, Corporal Erdelt, ran straight towards
the slope, tumbled down it, and found himself in the midst of a
group of lurking Indians. He flung hand-grenades around, but
was seized by the collar by an Indian officer, and hit in the face
with a wire whip. Then his watch was taken off him. He was
kicked and punched to make him march; but he successfully
escaped when the Indians once lay down to avoid some machine-
gun fire. After wandering around for a long time behind the
enemy lines, he came back with nothing worse than a few bloody
welts across his face.

On the evening of 19 June, I set off with little Schultz, ten men
and a light machine-gun on a patrol from the now distinctly
morbid-feeling place, to pay a call on the sentry on the path who
had reacted so noisily to our presence there a few days ago.
Schultz and his men went right, and I went left, to meet at the
path, promising to come to one another's aid if there was any
trouble. We worked our way forward on our bellies through the
grass and furze, stopping to listen every so often.

Suddenly, we heard the sharp rattle of a rifle bolt. We lay

completely riveted to the ground. Anyone who's been on a patrol will be familiar with the rapid succession of disagreeable feelings that flooded us in the next few seconds. You've at least temporarily lost the freedom of action, and you have to wait and see what the enemy will do.

A shot rang out through the oppressive silence. I was lying behind a clump of furze; the man on my right was dropping hand-grenades down on to the path. Then a line of bullets spurted in front of our faces. The sharp sound of the reports told us the marksmen were only a few feet away. I saw that we had fallen into a trap, and ordered retreat. We leaped up and ran back like crazy, while I saw that rifle fire had engaged my left-hand troop as well. In the middle of all this clatter, I gave up all hope of a safe return. Every moment I was expecting to be hit. Death was at our heels.

From the left, we were attacked with shrill hurrahs. Little Schultz admitted to me later he'd had a vision of a long tall Indian behind him with a knife, reaching out to grab him by the scruff of the neck.

Once, I fell and brought down Corporal Teilengerdes in the process. I lost steel helmet, pistol and hand-grenades. On, on! At last we reached the protective slope, and charged down it. Little Schultz and his people came round the corner at about the same time. He reported to me breathlessly that at least he'd given the cheeky sentry a stiff rebuke in the form of a few hand-grenades. A man was dragged in who had been shot in both legs. All the others were unhurt. The worst thing was that the man who'd been carrying the machine-gun, a recruit, had fallen over the wounded man, and had left the machine-gun behind.

While we were still arguing the toss, and planning a follow-up expedition, an artillery bombardment began that reminded me of the one we'd had on the 12th, down to the hopeless confusion it started. I found myself with no weapon, alone on the slope with the wounded man, who dragged himself forward on both hands, creeping up to me, and wailed: 'Please, Lieutenant, sir, don't leave me!'

I had to, though, to go and organize our defences. The wounded man was at least taken in later the same night.

We occupied a row of shallow firing positions on the edge of the wood, feeling heartily relieved to see day break without further incident.

The following evening found us in the same place, with the aim of getting our machine-gun back, but suspicious noises we heard as we approached suggested there was once again a welcoming committee waiting for us, and we turned back.

We were therefore ordered to get the gun back by main force. At twelve o'clock the next night, following three minutes' preliminary bombardment, we were to attack the enemy sentries and look for our gun. I had privately feared that its loss would make difficulties for us, but I put on a brave face and fired some ranging shots with some of the batteries myself in the afternoon.

At eleven o'clock, therefore, my companion in misfortune, Schultz, and I found ourselves back at that eerie spot where we had already had so many adventures and scrapes. The smell of decomposition in the humid air was too much. We had brought a few sacks of quicklime with us, and now sprinkled that on the bodies. The white stains loomed like shrouds out of the blackness.

Tonight's other 'undertaking' began with our own machine-gun bullets whistling round our legs, and smacking into the slope. I had a furious argument with Schultz, who had given the machine-gunners their range. We made it up again, though, when Schultz discovered me behind a bush with a bottle of Burgundy, which I had brought along to strengthen me for the dubious venture.

At the agreed time, the first shell went up. It landed fully fifty yards behind us. Before we could wonder at this peculiar gunnery, a second had come down right next to us on the slope, and dusted us with earth. This time, I wasn't even allowed to curse, as the artillery had been my responsibility.

After this somewhat discouraging overture, we went ahead, more for the sake of honour and duty than with any particular hope of success. We were lucky the sentries seemed to have quit their posts, otherwise we should have been accorded a rough welcome this time too. Unfortunately, we didn't manage to find the machine-gun; admittedly, we didn't spend that much time looking for it either. It was probably long since safe in British hands.

On the way back, Schultz and I gave each other a piece of our minds: I over his instructions to the machine-gunners, he over the artillery targeting. And yet I had done my work so scrupulously I couldn't understand what had gone wrong. It wasn't till later that I learned that guns always shoot short at night, and that I should therefore have added another hundred yards to the range. Then we discussed the most important aspect of the affair: the report. We wrote it in such a way that we were both satisfied.

As we were relieved the next day by troops from another division, there was no more argy-bargy. We were returned for the time being to Montbréhain, and marched from there to Cambrai, where we spent almost the entire month of July.

The outpost was finally lost the night after our departure.

Langemarck

Cambrai is a sleepy little town in the Artois, with a name full of historical associations. Its narrow old streets wind their way round an imposing town hall, ancient town gates, and many churches where the great Archbishop Fénelon once preached his sermons. Hefty towers rise out of a mass of pointed gables. Wide avenues lead to the well-kept town park, which is graced by a memorial to the aviator Blériot.

The inhabitants are quiet, friendly people, who lead comfortable lives in their large, plain but well-furnished houses. A lot of pensioners spend their declining years there. The little town is justifiably known as 'La ville des millionnaires', because shortly before the war it could boast no fewer than forty such.

The Great War pulled the place out of its enchanted sleep, and turned it into the focal point of enormous battles. Brisk new life went clattering over the cobbles, and jangled the little windows, behind which anxious faces peeped out to try and see what on earth was going on. Strangers drank lovingly maintained cellars dry, jumped into mighty mahogany beds, and in their continual succession disturbed the contemplative ease of the people, who now stood huddled together on corners and in doorways of their unrecognizable little town, telling each other – not too loudly – horror stories about the occupation, and the certain prospects for the ultimate victory of their own.

The men lived in barracks, the officers were accommodated

along the Rue des Liniers. During our time there, that street came to resemble a street of student digs; wide-ranging conversations out of windows, bouts of nocturnal singing, and various scrapes and adventures were the things with which we largely concerned ourselves.

Every morning, we moved out to exercise on the large square by the subsequently renowned village of Fontaine. I had the sort of task that was congenial to me, as Colonel von Oppen had entrusted me with assembling and training a body of storm troops. I had plenty of volunteers for this body, but found I preferred to stick to the tried-and-tested associates from my various patrols and missions. And since this was a new unit, I devised the rules and training myself.

My billet was most agreeable; my hosts, a kindly jewellers' couple by the name of Plancot-Bourlon, rarely let me eat my lunch without sending up some delicacy or other. And in the evenings we often sat up over a cup of tea, played cards and chatted. The perennial question came up a lot, of course: Why does mankind have wars?

In these hours together, Monsieur Plancot often related tricks and pranks played upon one another by the idle and witty folk of Cambrai, who in peacetime had caused the streets and bars and markets to ring with laughter, and reminded me of my dear 'Uncle Benjamin'.

For example, one particular joker had sent a letter to all the hunchbacks of the area, summoning them to appear before a certain notary over an important matter of an inheritance. Then, hiding behind a curtain in a house across the way at the hour in question with a few friends, he enjoyed the spectacle of seventeen furious rowdy goblins, assailing the poor notary.

There was another good story about an old spinster who lived opposite, who had a strange long and skew neck. Twenty years before, she had been known as a girl who was in a rush to get married. Six young fellows presented themselves, and to each she gladly gave permission to speak to her father. The following Sunday, a substantial coach drew up with the six suitors inside, each one with a bouquet of flowers. In her alarm and confusion, the girl locked the door and hid herself, while the young fellows delighted the street with their larking about.

Or this one: one day at the market, a notorious young man of Cambrai goes up to a farmer's wife and, pointing to a soft white cheese prettily sprinkled with herbs, asks her:

'How much do you want for that cheese?'

'Twenty sous, monsieur!'

He gives her the twenty sous.

'So the cheese belongs to me now, is that right?'

'Of course, monsieur!'

'So I can do whatever I want with it?'

'But of course!'

Splat! he throws the cheese in her face, and leaves her standing there.

On 25 July, we left our pleasant temporary home, and travelled north to Flanders. We had read in the newspapers that an artillery battle had been raging there for weeks already, outdoing the Battle of the Somme, if not in intensity then in range.

In Staden, we detrained to the distant roar of cannon, and marched through the unfamiliar landscape towards the camp at Ohndank. Either side of the dead-straight military road were green, fertile, elevated beet fields and juicy pastures surrounded by hedges. Tidy farmhouses lay scattered about, with low overhanging thatched or tiled roofs, and bunches of tobacco hung on the walls to dry in the sun. The country people we passed were Flemish, and spoke in that rough tongue that we almost thought we understood. We spent the afternoon in farm gardens, where the enemy aviators could not see us. Occasional ships' ordnance would fly over our heads, with a gurgling sound we could hear from far off, and hit near by. One dived into one of the many little streams in the area, and killed several men of the 91st, who happened to be bathing in it.

As evening approached, I went up to the front line with an advance detachment, to prepare the relief. We passed through the forest of Houthulst and the village of Koekuit to the reserve battalion, and on the way were forced to break stride by a few heavy shells. In the dark I could hear the voice of one recruit who was still unversed in our ways: 'That lieutenant never seems to take cover.'

'He knows what's what,' he was told by a member of the storm troop. 'If there's one on its way, then he's the first to lie down.'

We only took cover now when it was necessary, but then we didn't hang around. The degree of necessity is something that only an experienced man can determine, who can sense the course of the shell before the new soldier can hear the light fluttering of its approach. To hear better when things got hot, I would even exchange my steel helmet for a forage cap.

Our guides, who didn't inspire complete confidence, advanced along endless box trenches. That's the term for passages that are not dug into the ground, because they would instantly fill with water, but are built up between lines of sandbags and fascines. After that we brushed an amazingly dishevelled-looking wood, out of which, our guides told us, a regimental staff had been pushed back a few days ago by the small matter of a thousand ten-inch shells. 'Such prodigality,' I thought to myself.

After traipsing this way and that through the thick brush, we were finally left standing completely lost, and abandoned by our guides, on a rush-covered spot, surrounded by marshy pools of black water that gave back the moonlight. Shells plunged into the soft soil, sending up great sprays of mud that splattered down. At last our unhappy guide, with whom we were now pretty incensed, came back, claiming to have remembered the way. Then he proceeded to lead us astray again, as far as a dressing-station, over which, in short, regular intervals, shrapnels broke up, sending their balls and empty casings clattering through the boughs. The doctor on duty provided us with a better guide, who escorted us to the Mauseburg, the headquarters of the reserve line.

I straight away went on to the company of the 225th Regiment, which was to be relieved by our 2nd, and after a long search found a few houses in the cratered landscape that had been discreetly toughened on the inside with reinforced concrete. One of these had been smashed in the day before by a direct hit, and its inhabitants crushed as in a mousetrap by the collapsing roof plate.

For the rest of the night, I squeezed into the overcrowded concrete box of the company commander, a decent grunt, who whiled away the time with his servant over a bottle of schnapps and a large tin of salt pork, stopping often to shake his head and listen to the steadily increasing roar of the artillery. Then he would sigh for the good old days on the Russian front, and curse the way his regiment had been pumped out. In the end, my eyes simply fell shut.

My sleep was heavy and troubled; the high explosive shells falling all round the house in the impenetrable dark evoked extraordinary feelings of solitude and abandon in me. I pressed myself unconsciously against a man lying beside me on the pallet. Once, I was startled awake by a powerful impact. We lit the walls to check if the house had been breached. It turned out to have been a small shell that had exploded against the outer wall.

The following afternoon I spent with the battalion commander in the Mauseburg. In rapid sequence, the six-inch shells came down close to the command centre, while the captain, his adjutant and the orderly played unending rounds of skat, and handed round a soda bottle full of rotgut. Sometimes he would put down his cards to attend to a messenger, or, with concerned expression, wonder about the safety of our concrete blockhouse against the bombardment. In spite of his loyal conviction to the contrary, we finally convinced him that it wouldn't stand up to a direct hit from above.

In the evening, the shelling waxed to a demented fury. Ahead of us, coloured flares went up in a continual stream. Dust-covered runners reported that the enemy was attacking. After weeks of drumming, the infantry battle was about to begin; we had come at the right time.

I returned to company headquarters, and waited for the company to arrive. They finally got in at four in the morning, during a vehement shelling session. I took charge of my platoon, and led it to its place, a concrete construction disguised by the ruins of a demolished house, in the middle of a huge cratered field of desperate horror.

At six in the morning, the dense Flanders fog lifted, and permitted us to view our situation in its full hideousness. Straight away, a swarm of enemy aeroplanes flew in low over our heads, surveying the battered terrain, and giving siren signals, while isolated infantrymen jumped for cover in shell-holes.

Half an hour later, the shelling commenced, washing over our little refuge like a typhoon. The forest of explosions gradually thickened into a solid whirling wall. We squatted together, every second expecting the annihilating hit that would blow us and our concrete blocks away, and leave our strongpoint level with the pitted desert all around.

And so the day passed, with mighty outbursts of shelling, and momentary quieter phases during which we sat and gritted our teeth.

In the evening, an exhausted runner turned up, and gave me an order from which I understood that the 1st, 3rd and 4th Companies would commence a counter-attack at ten to eleven in the morning, and the 2nd should wait to be relieved and then swarm into the front line. To gain strength for the hours ahead, I lay down, never guessing that my brother Fritz, whom I had

dead

supposed to be still in Hanover, was even now hurrying forward with a platoon from the 3rd Company, through the fire-storm close by our hut.

I was long kept from sleep by the cries of a wounded man whom a couple of Saxons had brought in. They had lost their way and had fallen asleep, completely exhausted. When they woke up the following morning, their comrade was dead. They carted him to the nearest shell-hole, scooped a couple of shovelfuls of earth over him, and mooched off, leaving behind them another of the countless unknown and unmarked graves of this war.

unmarked graves

I didn't wake from my deep sleep until eleven o'clock, washed myself in my steel helmet, and sent for further instructions to the company commander, who, to my consternation, had moved off without leaving word where. That's war for you; things happen in a way you wouldn't have thought possible on the exercise ground.

While I was still sitting on my pallet, cursing and wondering what to do, a runner arrived from Battalion HQ and told me to take over the 8th Company.

I learned that the 1st Battalion's counter-attack last night had collapsed with heavy casualties, and that the survivors were defending themselves in a small wood ahead of us, the Dobschutz woods, and either side of it. The 8th Company had been given the task of swarming forward to the wood to give support, but had been roughed up on open ground before even getting there by a heavy barrage, taking bad losses. Since their commander, First Lieutenant Budingen, was among those wounded, I should take them along myself.

After taking leave of my orphaned platoon, I set off with the orderly across the shrapnel-strewn wastes. A despairing voice stopped us on our stooping, scurrying progress. In the distance, a figure half out of his shell-hole was waving a bloodied stump at us. We pointed to the blockhouse we'd just left, and hastened on.

The 8th, when I found them, were a despondent little bunch, clustered behind a row of blockhouses.

'Platoon commanders!'

Three NCOs came forward and declared that a second advance in the direction of the Dobschutz woods could not be undertaken. True, heavy explosions reared up in front of us like a wall of fire. First, then, I had the platoons assemble behind three huts; each one numbered fifteen or twenty men. Just then, the shelling turned to us. The confusion was indescribable. By the left blockhouse, a whole section went up in the air, then the right took a direct hit and buried Lieutenant Budingen, still lying there wounded, under several tonnes of rubble. It was like being pounded in a mortar and pestle. Deathly pale faces stared at each other, as the wounded wailed all round.

By now it probably didn't matter whether we stayed put, took to our heels, or advanced. So I gave the order to follow me, and leaped into the midst of the shelling. After no more than a couple of bounds, a shell covered me with earth, and hurled me back into the last crater. I couldn't think why I hadn't been hit, because the shells were coming so thick and fast they practically brushed my head and shoulders, and they scoured open the ground under my feet like huge beasts. The fact that I ran through them without being touched could only be due to the way the ploughed earth gulped the shells down, before its resistance caused them to detonate. The plumes of the explosions didn't travel laterally like bushes, but steeply up in a spear shape, like poplars. Others only brought up a little bell. Also, I began to notice that further forward the force of the shelling was lesser. After I had worked my way through the worst of it, I looked about me. The terrain was empty.

At last, two men emerged from clouds of dust and smoke, then another, then two more. With these five, I succeeded in reaching my objective.

In a half-exploded blockhouse sat the commander of the 3rd

BROTHER

Company, Lieutenant Sandvoss, and little Schultz, with three heavy machine-guns. I was welcomed with loud hellos and a gulp of cognac, then they explained the situation to me, and a very disagreeable one it was too. The British were right up against us, and we had no contact with troops to the left or right. We could see that this corner was one fit only for warriors grizzled in powder fumes.

Out of the blue, Sandvoss asked me if I'd heard about my brother. The reader may imagine my consternation when I learned that he'd taken part in the night attack, and had been reported missing. He was the dearest to my heart; a feeling of appalling, irreplaceable loss opened up in front of me.

Then in walked a soldier, who told me that my brother was lying wounded in a nearby shelter. He pointed at a desolate-looking blockhouse, covered over by uprooted trees, that had already been vacated by its defenders. I dashed through sniper fire, across a clearing, and walked in. What a reunion! My brother lay in a room full of the stink of death, surrounded by the groans of gravely wounded men. I found him in poor shape. As he'd advanced, he'd been hit by a couple of shrapnel balls, one of them had penetrated his lung, the other shattered his right shoulder. There was a gleam of fever in his eyes; an opened-out gas mask was perched on his chest. It was only with great difficulty that he could move, speak, breathe. We squeezed each other's hands, and said what had to be said.

It was clear to me that he couldn't remain where he was, because at any moment the British might attack, or a shell might crush the already badly damaged hut. The best thing I could do for my brother was get him taken back right away. Even though Sandvoss was opposed to any further weakening of our numbers, I told the five men who had come with me to take Fritz to the medical shelter, 'Columbus's Egg', and there pick up some men to collect the other casualties. We tied him up in a tarpaulin, slid a long pole through it, and two of the men shouldered it. One more handshake, and the sorry procession set off.

I watched the swaying burden being taken off through a forest of towering shell bursts. With each explosion I winced, till the little group had vanished into the haze of battle. I felt both that I was representing my mother, and that I would have to account to her for whatever happened to my brother.

After bandying a little with the slowly advancing British from the shell-holes at the front edge of the wood, I spent the night with my men, who had grown a little more numerous by now, and a machine-gun crew among the wreckage of the block-house. High-explosive shells of quite exceptional ferocity were coming down all the time, one of which just missed killing me that evening.

Towards morning, the machine-gun suddenly started rattling away, as some dark figures were approaching. It was a patrol from the 76th Regiment come to get in touch with us, and one of them was left dead. Mistakes like that happened quite frequently at that time, and one didn't spend too much time anguishing over them.

At six in the morning, we were relieved by a detachment of the 9th, who gave me orders to occupy the Rattenburg with my men. On the way there, I had a cadet disabled by shrapnel.

The Rattenburg [Rats' castle or fortress] turned out to be a shot-up shell of a building reinforced with concrete slabs, close to the swampy course of the Steenbach. The name fitted. We made our way in, feeling pretty shattered, and threw ourselves down on straw-covered pallets till a plentiful lunch and a revivifying pipe afterwards more or less restored us. *no real rat*

In the early afternoon, shelling with large and very large calibres began. Between six o'clock and eight, it was simply one explosion after the next; often the building was shaking and threatening to collapse from the horrible jolts of duds impacting near by. There were the usual conversations about the safety or otherwise of the structure. We thought the concrete ceiling was fairly trustworthy; but as the 'castle' was close to the steep bank of the stream, we thought there was a chance that a shell with a low trajectory might undermine us, and send us, concrete and all, skittering down into the stream bed.

When the firing died down in the evening, I clambered over a slope, which was being buzzed around by a hornets' nest of shrapnel, to the hospital shelter, 'Columbus's Egg', to ask the doctor, who was just then examining the horribly mutilated leg of a man who was about to die, about my brother. I was overjoyed to learn that he had been shipped back in reasonably good shape.

Later on, the ration party appeared, bringing the company, now reduced to just twenty men, hot soup, canned beef, coffee, bread, tobacco and schnapps. We ate heartily, and handed the bottle of '98 proof' round. Then we settled off to sleep, disturbed only by the swarming mosquitoes that bred along the stream, shelling, and occasional bombardments with gas.

At the end of that restless night, I was so fast asleep that my men had to wake me when the fire intensified to – in their eyes – an alarming degree. They reported that men were drifting back from the front line all the time, saying the line had been given up and the enemy was advancing.

Following the old soldier's watchword that a good breakfast will hold body and soul together, I took some nourishment, lit a pipe, and then took a look around outside.

My view was somewhat restricted because we were swathed in thick smoke. The shelling grew more imposing by the minute, and soon reached that climactic stage that was so thrilling as to produce an almost amused indifference. The earth showered on to our roof incessantly; twice the building itself was hit. Incendiaries threw up heavy milk-white clouds, out of which fiery streaks dribbled to the ground. A piece of that phosphoric mass smacked down on to a stone at my feet, and I was able to watch it burn for minutes. Later on, we were told that men it had landed on had rolled around on the ground, without being able to quench the flames. Delay shells drilled themselves into the ground with a roar, throwing up flat casts of earth. Swathes of gas and fog crept slowly across the terrain. Rifle and machine-gun fire rang out from just ahead of us, a sign that the enemy must already be very near.

Down on the bed of the Steenbach, a group of men were wading through the constantly changing scenery of leaping geysers of mud. I saw among them the battalion commander, Captain von Brixen, with a bandaged arm, being supported by two ambulancemen, and I hurried down to him. He called to warn me that the enemy were pressing forward, and I should see that I found cover quickly.

Before long the first infantry bullets were smacking into the surrounding craters or bursting against masonry debris. More and more fleeing figures were disappearing into the haze behind us, while furious rifle fire spoke for the implacable defence of those holding on further forward.

The hour was at hand. We had to defend the Rattenburg, and I told the men, some of whom looked troubled, that we were not about to run away. They were allotted various loopholes, and our one and only machine-gun was set up in a window-opening. A crater was designated as a dressing-station, and a stretcher-bearer, who before long found himself with plenty of work on his hands, sat in it. I picked up a rifle off the floor, and hung a belt of cartridges round my neck.

As our band was very small, I tried to bolster it from the numbers of those who were drifting around leaderless. Most of them heard our appeal willingly enough, glad of the chance to join in somewhere, while others hurried on their way, having stopped in disbelief and seen what poor prospects we offered. It was no time for niceties. I ordered my men to aim at them.

Magnetically drawn by the barrels of the rifles, they slowly

The guns fall silent

came nearer, even though one could see from their expressions that they were really most reluctant to keep us company. There were various excuses, prevarications, more or less compelling arguments.

'But I don't even have a gun!'

'Then wait till someone gets shot, and use his!'

In the course of one last, massive intensification of the shelling, during which the ruins of the house were struck several times, and the pieces of brick came hurtling down on to our helmets, I was thrown to the ground by a fearful blow. To the amazement of the men, I picked myself up, unhurt.

After that titanic final drumroll, things got quieter. The shelling now passed over our heads, on to the Langemarck–Bixschoote road. We weren't even that happy to see it. So far we hadn't seen the wood for the trees; danger had come down at us on such a massive scale and in so many guises that we couldn't really begin to cope with it. After the storm had passed over our heads, everyone had time to prepare themselves for what inevitably must come.

And come it did. The guns ahead of us fell silent. The defenders had been finished off. Out of the haze, a dense line of men began to approach. My men shot, concealed behind the ruins, the machine-gun was clicking away. As though smeared away, the attackers disappeared into the craters, and tied us down by their return of fire. On either flank, strong detachments began to march forward. Before long, we were surrounded by rifles.

The situation was hopeless; there was no point in merely sacrificing the soldiers. I gave the order for withdrawal. Now it was difficult to get the committed and tenacious soldiers to stop.

Taking advantage of a long cloud of smoke that hung down near the water, we made good our escape, partly wading through streams whose water went up to our hips. Although the noose around us was all but drawn tight, we still squirmed our way out. I was the last man out of our little strongpoint, supporting

Lieutenant Hohlemann, who was bleeding badly from a wound to the head, but was still making jokes at his own expense.

As we crossed the road, we ran into the 2nd Company. Kius had heard of our situation, from wounded men going back, and had come, not at his own prompting, but in response to the urging of his men, to get us out.

It was a spontaneous initiative. We were moved, and it created in us a kind of happy euphoria, the sort of mood in which you want to pull up trees by the roots.

After a short discussion, we decided to stop and allow the enemy to catch us up. Here, too, there were artillerymen present, signallers, telephonists, and various stray bits and bobs, who could only be persuaded by force that, given the particular circumstances, they too were required to lie down with a rifle in the front line. By means of cajoling, ordering and rifle butts, we established a new defensive line.

Then we sat down in a trench that was more imagination than reality, and breakfasted. Kius pulled out his inevitable camera and took pictures. On our left there was a sudden commotion, coming from the outskirts of Langemarck. Our men fired at various figures who were running around, until I called a halt. Unhappily, an NCO came up and reported that a company of Fusilier Guards had dug in by the road, and had suffered casualties from our fire.

Thereupon I ordered us to advance, through dense rifle fire, to join them. We lost a few men, and Lieutenant Bartmer of the 2nd Company was gravely wounded. Kius stayed at my side, munching what was left of his bread and butter as he advanced. When we had occupied the road from where the terrain fell away down into the Steenbach, we saw that the British had purposed exactly the same thing. The nearest khaki-clad figures were only twenty yards away. The field was full of lines of men and marching columns, as far as the eye could see. Even the Rattenburg was already being swarmed all over.

They were completely unconcerned, so engrossed were they in what they were doing. One man had a roll of wire on his back, which he was slowly unspooling. Obviously they had seen hardly any fire, and were just cheerfully advancing. Even though they were in vastly superior numbers, we thought we would put a spoke in their wheel. There was a good deal of shooting, but aimed shooting. I saw a stout corporal from the 8th Company calmly rest his rifle on a splintered tree trunk; with every shot an attacker fell. The enemy were bewildered, and started hopping about this way and that, like rabbits, while clouds of dust were whirled up between them. Some were hit, the rest crept into shell-craters, to lie low until it got dark. The wheels had come off their advance; they had paid for it dearly.

At around eleven o'clock, rosette-decorated aircraft circled down towards us, and were driven away by fierce fire. In the middle of that crazy banging away, I had to laugh at one soldier who came up to me and wanted me to confirm that it was he with his rifle who had brought down one plane in flames.

Right after I'd occupied the roadway, I'd reported to regimental headquarters and called in support. In the afternoon, infantry columns, engineers and machine-gunners came to reinforce us. Taking a leaf from Old Fritz's [Frederick the Great] tactical handbook, they were all stuffed into our already over-full front line. From time to time, the British snipers managed to kill one or two men who crossed the road without looking.

Almost four, and a very nasty bout of shrapnel ensued. The loads were flung right at the road. There was no doubt about it, the flyers had identified our new position, and it looked as if we were going to be in for some rough times.

And soon a violent bombardment followed, with light and heavy shells. We lay pressed together in the overcrowded, dead-straight roadside ditch. The fire danced before our eyes, twigs and clumps of clay whistled down upon us. To the left of me, a bolt of lightning flared up, leaving white, acrid steam. I crept

Dealing w/ imminent death

over to my neighbour on all fours. He was motionless. Blood trickled from little jagged splinter wounds too numerous to count. Further right there were more heavy losses.

After a half-hour of this, there was quiet. Quickly we dug deep holes in the flat sides of the ditch, so as to have at least some protection against splinters in the event of a second attack. As we dug, our shovels encountered guns, ammunition belts and cartridges from 1914 – proof that this wasn't the first time this ground had drunk blood. Our predecessors here had been the volunteers of Langemarck.

As dusk was falling, we were treated to a second helping. I squatted next to Kius in a little sitz-shelter, that had cost us a fair few digging blisters. The ground was being tossed around like a ship's plank under the close and very close explosions. We thought this might well be it.

My steel helmet pulled down over my brow, staring at the road, whose stones shot sparks when iron fragments flew off them, I chewed my pipe and tried to talk myself into feeling brave. Curious thoughts flashed through my brain. For instance, I thought hard about a French popular novel called *Le vautour de la Sierra* that had fallen into my hands in Cambrai. Several times I murmured a phrase of Ariosto's: 'A great heart feels no dread of approaching death, whenever it may come, so long as it be honourable.' That produced a pleasant kind of intoxication, of the sort that one experiences, maybe, on a rollercoaster. When the shells briefly abated, I heard fragments of the lovely song of 'The Black Whale at Askalon' coming from the man next to me, and I thought my friend Kius must have gone mad. But everyone has his own particular idiosyncratic method.

At the end of the shelling, a large splinter hit me in the hand. Kius flashed his torch at it, and saw it was only a flesh wound.

After midnight, it started to rain gently; patrols from a supporting regiment that had advanced as far as the Steenbach found only craters full of mud. The British had retreated behind the stream.

Exhausted by the strains of this momentous day, we settled down in our holes, except for the sentries. I pulled the ragged coat of my dead neighbour up over my head, and fell into an unquiet slumber. Towards dawn, I woke up shivering, and discovered my situation was sorry indeed. It was bucketing down, and the little rivulets on the road were all emptying themselves into my foxhole. I rigged up a dam, and baled out my resting-place with the lid of my mess-tin. As the rivulets deepened, I put up successive parapets on my earthworks, until in the end the weak construction gave way to the growing pressure, and, with a grateful gurgle, a dirty rush of water filled my foxhole up to the top. While I was busy fishing my pistol and helmet out of the mire, I watched my bread and tobacco go bobbing along the ditch, whose other denizens had suffered similar misfortunes to mine. Shivering and trembling, without a dry stitch on our bodies, we stood there knowing the next bombardment would find us utterly helpless, on the muddy road. It was a wretched morning. Once again, I learned that no artillery bombardment is as capable of breaking resistance in the same measure as the elemental forces of wet and cold.

In the wider scheme of the battle, however, that downpour was a real godsend for us, because it doomed the English push to bog down in its first, crucial days. The enemy had to get his artillery through the swampy cratered landscape, while we could trundle our ammunition along intact roads.

At eleven in the morning, as we were in the pit of despair, a saving angel appeared to us in the guise of a dispatch-rider who brought the order for the regiment to assemble in Koekuit.

On our march back, we saw just how difficult forward communications and supply must have been on the day of the attack. The roads were thick with soldiers and horses. Alongside a few limbers sieved with holes, twelve gruesomely shot-up horses blocked the road.

On a rain-slicked pasture, over which the milk-white balls of a few shrapnels hung like clouds, the rest of the regiment came together. It was a little band of men, of about company strength, and a couple of officers in the middle. The losses! Almost the entire complement of two battalions in officers and men. Grimly the survivors stood in the teeming rain, and waited to be assigned quarters. Then we got dried in a wooden hut, huddled round a burning stove, and, over a hearty breakfast, we once more felt courage flow back into our limbs.

In the early evening, the first shells hit the village. One of the huts was hit, and several men from the 3rd Company killed. In spite of the bombardment, we lay down betimes with the desperate hope that we wouldn't be called upon to counter-attack or reinforce or otherwise be thrown out into the rain.

At three in the morning, the order came to move out. We marched down the corpse- and wreckage-strewn road to Staden. The shelling had come this far; we came upon an isolated crater ringed by twelve bodies. Staden, which at our arrival had seemed such a lively place, already had quite a few bombed houses to show. The bleak market-place was littered with domestic rubble. A family left the little town at the same time as us, driving ahead of them their only possession: a cow. They were simple people; the man had a wooden leg, the woman was leading the crying children by the hand. The wild sounds behind us cast a further pall over the sad scene.

The remnants of the 2nd Battalion were housed in an isolated farmyard, in the midst of juicy high pastures, behind tall hedges. There I was put in command of the 7th Company, with whom I was to share sorrow and joy until the end of the war.

In the evening, we sat in front of the old tiled stove, sipping a stiff grog, and listening to the renewed thunder of the battle.

A sentence caught my eye from a military communiqué in a newspaper: 'The enemy was held along the line of the Steenbach.'

It was an odd thing that our apparently confused actions in the depths of the night had had such pronounced and public consequences. We had done our part towards bringing the attack, which had begun with such mighty force, to a halt. However colossal the quantities of men and *matériel*, the work at decisive points had been done by no more than a few handfuls of men.

Before long, we went up to the hayloft to lie down. In spite of our nightcaps, most of the sleepers still had vivid dreams, and tossed and rolled, as though the Battle of Flanders had to be fought all over again.

On 3 August, weighed down with the meat and fruits of this deserted province, we marched off to the station of the nearby town of Gits. In the station canteen, the reduced battalion, once more in fine fettle, drank coffee together, spiced by the earthy language of a couple of heavy Flemish beauties as waitresses. What especially tickled the men was the way that, following the regional custom, they addressed everyone, officers included, as 'Du'.

After a few days, I got a letter from my brother Fritz, by now in hospital in Gelsenkirchen. He wrote that he would probably have a stiff arm and a rattling lung till the day he died.

From his account I excerpted the following passage, to complement my own narrative. It gives a vivid sense of how it felt to be an inexperienced soldier, dropped into the hurricane of the *matériel* battle.

'"Fall in for the attack!" My platoon commander's face peered down into our little foxhole. The three men with me ended their conversation and, cursing, got to their feet. I stood up, tightened my steel helmet, and stepped out into the gloaming.

'The scene had changed; it had grown foggy now, and cool. The bombardment had moved off and its dull thunder was now assailing other parts of the vast battlefield. Planes were droning through the air, calming the anxiously raised eye by displaying large Maltese crosses painted on the undersides of their wings.

'I went one more time to the spring, which still looked remarkably clean and pure amidst all the rubble and debris, and filled my water-bottle.

'The company formed up by platoons. Quickly I clipped four hand-grenades on to my belt, and went to my section, from which two men were missing. There was barely time to take down their names before the whole thing was set in motion. The platoons proceeded in single file through the cratered landscape, skirted around bits of timber, pressed against hedges, and jangling and thumping made their way towards the enemy.

'The attack was to be carried out by two battalions; ours and one battalion from the regiment next to ours. Our orders were short and sharp. British units who had got across the canal were to be repulsed. My role in this undertaking was to remain with my section far forward, to be in position for a British counter-attack.

'We reached the ruins of a village. Out of the hideously scarred soil of Flanders rose black, splintered trunks of trees, all that was left of what had once been a large forest. Vast swathes of smoke hung around, and dimmed the evening with their heavy, gloomy clouds. Over the naked earth, which had been so pitilessly and repeatedly ripped open, hovered choking yellow or brown gases that drifted sluggishly about.

'We were ordered to prepare for a gas attack. At that moment, a huge bombardment set in – the British must have been made aware of our advance. The earth leaped up in hissing fountains, and a hail of splinters swept over the land like a shower of rain. For an instant, each man froze motionless, then they started running in all directions. I heard the voice of our battalion commander, Captain Böckelmann, shouting some command at the top of his voice, but I was unable to understand.

'My men had vanished. I found myself with some other platoon, and together we pressed towards the ruins of a village that the implacable shells had levelled. We broke out our gas masks.

'Everyone threw themselves to the ground. Next to me on the left knelt Lieutenant Ehlert, an officer whom I'd come across first at the Somme. Next to him was an NCO, lying down, peering into the distance. The force of the barrage was terrific; I confess it exceeded my wildest notions. It was a wall of yellow flame flickering in front of us; a hail of clods of earth, bricks and iron splinters that battered down on our heads, striking sparks from our steel helmets. I had the sensation that it had become harder to breathe, and that whatever air was left in this iron-charged atmosphere was no longer quite sufficient for my lungs.

'For a long time I stared into that glowing witches' cauldron, the furthest point of which was the jabbing fire from the mouth of a British machine-gun. The thousandfold bee-swarm of these shells that flowed over us was past hearing. I realized that our attack, which had been prepared by a mere half-hour's drumfire, was already smashed before it could properly begin by this immense defensive shelling. Twice in quick succession, an incredible din seemed to swallow up all the other noise. Shells of the very largest calibre exploded. Whole fields of rubble took off, revolved in the air and smashed to the ground with an infernal racket.

'In response to a yell from Ehlert, I looked right. He raised his left hand, gestured to people behind him, and leaped up. I got to my feet cumbersomely, and took off after him. My feet still felt as if they were burning, but the stabbing pain had relented somewhat.

'I had covered barely twenty yards before, cresting a shell-crater, I was dazzled by a flaring shrapnel that exploded less than ten paces away from me, and about ten feet off the ground. I felt two blows against my chest and shoulder. I let go of my rifle, and staggered backwards, before rolling back into the crater. I could dimly hear Ehlert calling out as he rushed past: "He's hit!"

'He was not to see another day. The attack failed, and on his way back, he and all his surviving comrades were killed. A shot through the back of the head ended the life of this brave officer.

'When I woke up after being unconscious for I don't know how long, things had quietened down. I tried to pull myself up, as I was lying head down in the crater, but felt violent pain in my shoulder with every move. My breathing was shallow and sporadic, my lungs couldn't take in enough air for me. Hit in lung and shoulder, I thought, remembering the two buffets I'd received (they hadn't hurt at all) earlier. I abandoned my pack and belt and, in an access of utter indifference, even my gas mask. I kept my steel helmet on, and hung my water-bottle off a loop on my tunic.

'I managed to get out of the crater. After no more than about five steps of a laborious crawl, I broke down in another crater. After another hour, I made another attempt, since the battlefield was once more being shaken by light drumfire. That attempt also got me nowhere. I lost my precious water-bottle, and sank into a state of total exhaustion, from which I was woken, much later, by a burning thirst.

'It started raining gently. I managed to collect some dirty water in my helmet. I was utterly disorientated, with no notion of where the German lines were running. It was one crater next to another, one wider and deeper than the one before, and from the bottom of these deep pits all you could see were clay walls and a grey sky. A storm drew up, its thunders rather stolen by the onset of a new drumfire. I pressed myself tight against the wall of my crater. A lump of clay struck my shoulder; heavy splinters passed over my head. Gradually, I lost all sense of time as well; I didn't know if it was morning or evening.

'Two men appeared, crossing the field in great bounds. I shouted out to them in German and English; they vanished into the mist like shadows, without appearing to have heard me. At last, three other men came towards me. I recognized one of them as the NCO who had lain next to me the previous day. They took me with them to a little hut near by – it was full of wounded men, who were being tended by a couple of medical orderlies. I had lain thirteen hours in the crater.

'The huge bombardment of the battle was working away like a monstrous hammering and rolling mill. Shell after shell smacked down next to us, often drenching the roof with sand and earth. I was bandaged up, and given a fresh gas mask, a piece of bread and red jam, and a little water. The orderly looked after me as though I'd been his own son.

'The British were beginning to press forward. They approached with little leaps and bounds, then ducked away in the craters. Shouts and calls were heard from outside.

'Suddenly, bespattered with mud from his boots to his helmet, a young officer burst in. It was my brother Ernst, who at regimental HQ the day before had been feared dead. We greeted one another and smiled, a little stiffly, with the emotion. He looked about him and then looked at me with concern. His eyes filled with tears. We might both be members of the same regiment, true, but even then this reunion on the battlefield had something rare and wonderful about it, and the recollection of it has remained precious to me. After just a few minutes, he left me, and brought in the last five members of his company. I was laid on a tarpaulin, they stuck a sapling through the straps, and shouldered me off the battlefield.

'My carriers took it in turn to carry me. Our little sedan-chair veered now right, now left, zigzagging to avoid the frequent shells. Forced on occasion to take cover abruptly, they dropped me a few times, sending me bashing into shell-holes.

'At last we reached the tin- and concrete-cladded shelter that went by the odd name of "Columbus's Egg". I was dragged down the stairs and laid on a wooden pallet. With me in the room were a couple of officers I didn't know, sitting and listening in silence to the hurricane concert of the artillery. One, I later heard, was Lieutenant Bartmer, the other a medical orderly by the name of Helms. Never have I enjoyed a drink more than the mixture of rainwater and red wine that he gave me to sip. I was burning up with fever. I struggled for breath, and felt oppressed by the notion that the concrete ceiling of the shelter was on my chest, and that with each breath I had to heave it up.

'The assistant surgeon Köppen came in, himself quite out of breath. He had run across the battlefield, shells following him at every step. He recognized me, bent over me, and I saw his face contort to a soothingly smiling grimace. After him came my battalion commander, and when, strict man that he was, he patted me kindly on the back, I had to smile because I got the idea that the Kaiser himself would appear any moment, and ask how I was doing.

'The four of them sat together, drinking out of tin cups and whispering among themselves. I realized that they must have been talking about me at one stage, and then I heard odd words like "brothers", "lung" and "wound", which I couldn't quite make sense of. Then they went back to talking aloud, about the state of the battle.

'Mortally tired as I was, a feeling of happiness now sneaked in that grew stronger and stronger, and which stayed with me throughout the ensuing weeks. I thought of death, and the thought did not disturb me. Everything within me and around me seemed stunningly simple, and, with the feeling "You're all right," I slid away into sleep.'

Regniéville

On 4 August, we left the train at the famous station of Mars-la-Tour. The 7th and 8th Companies were billeted at Doncourt, where we led a life of calm contemplation for a few days. The only thing that made difficulties for me were the short rations. It was strictly forbidden to go foraging; and, even so, every morning the military police brought me the names of men they'd caught lifting potatoes, and whom I had no option but to punish – 'for being stupid enough to get yourselves caught' was my own, unofficial, reason.

That it doesn't do to steal was brought home to me as well in those days. Tebbe and I had snaffled a glass coach from an abandoned Flemish mansion and managed to get it on the transport, away from prying eyes. Now, we wanted to undertake a jaunt to Metz, to live life at the full once more. So we harnessed up one afternoon, and drove off. Unfortunately, the carriage, constructed for the plains of Flanders rather than the hills of Lorraine, had no brakes. We left the village already doing quite a lick, and before long we were on a wild ride that could only end badly. First to go was the coachman, then Tebbe, who made a hard landing on a pile of agricultural implements. I stayed behind on the silken upholstery, feeling rather unhappy. A door sprang open, and was knocked off by a passing telegraph mast. At last the carriage raced down a steep slope, and smashed against a wall at the bottom. Leaving the wrecked conveyance by a window, I was to my astonishment unhurt.

On 9 August, the company was inspected by the divisional commander, Major-General von Busse, who praised the men for the way they had comported themselves in the recent battle. The following afternoon, we were put on trains and taken up towards Thiaucourt. From there we marched straight to our new position, which was on the wooded hills of the Côte Lorraine, facing the much-shelled village of Regniéville, a name familiar from dispatches.

On the first morning, I took a look at my sector, which seemed rather long for one company, and consisted of a confused mass of half-collapsed trenches. The firing trench had been flattened in quite a few places by a type of heavy mortar-bomb much in favour in these parts. My dugout was a hundred yards back, down the so-called Commercial Trench, close to the main road out of Regniéville. It was the first time in quite a while that we were up against the French.

A geologist would have enjoyed the posting. The approach trenches cut through six distinct types of rock, from coral rag to the Gravelotte marl that the firing trench had been cut into. The yellow-brown rock was full of fossils, especially of a flattish, bun-shaped sea urchin, which one could see literally thousands of along the trench walls. Each time I walked along the sector, I returned to my dugout with my pockets full of shells, sea urchins and ammonites. It was a pleasant feature of the marl that it stood up to bad weather much better than the clay we were used to. In places the trench was even carefully bricked up, and the floor concreted, so that even quite large amounts of water drained away easily.

My dugout was deep and drippy. It did have one quality I didn't much care for: instead of the lice we were used to, this area offered their more mobile cousins. The two sorts apparently stand in much the same adversarial relationship to one another as black rats and *Rattus norvegicus*. In this instance, even the usual complete change of undergarments didn't help, as the thoughtful parasites would stay behind in the straw bedding. The sleeper on the brink of despair would be driven to unmake his bed, and have a thorough hunt.

The food also left quite a bit to be desired. Aside from a rather watery soup at lunchtime, there was just a third of a loaf of bread with an offensively small quantity of 'spread', which usually consisted of half-off jam. And half of my portion was invariably stolen by a fat rat, which I often vainly tried to catch.

The companies in reserve and on rest lived in curious villages of blockhouses hidden deep in the forest. I was particularly fond of my quarters in reserve, which were glued on to the steep slope of a wooded ravine, in a blind corner. There I lived in a tiny hut that was half bedded into the slope, surrounded by rampant hazel and cornel-cherry bushes. The window looked out on to a wooded facing slope, and a narrow strip of meadow at the bottom, which a stream flowed through. Here, I amused myself by feeding innumerable garden spiders, who had set up their huge webs across the bushes. A collection of bottles of all sorts against the back wall of the hut suggested that my eremitic predecessors must have spent some contemplative times here, and I endeavoured to keep up the proud tradition of the place. In the evening, when the mists rose off the stream bed, and mingled with the heavy white smoke of my wood fire, and I sat in the gloaming with the door open, between the chill autumnal air and the warmth of the fire, I thought I had come up with just the right peaceful sort of drink: a fifty-fifty mixture of red wine and advocaat in a big-bellied glass. I would sip the mixture, and read or keep my diary. These quiet soirées helped me to get over the fact that a gentleman from the depot who had seniority over me had popped up to claim command of my company from me, and that, as a platoon commander, I was relegated to boring trench duty. I tried to vary the endless sentry spells as before, with regular jaunts 'up-country'.

On 24 August, the gallant Captain Böckelmann was wounded by a shell splinter – the third commanding officer the battalion had lost in a very short space of time.

In the course of trench duty, I struck up a friendship with Kloppmann, an NCO, an older, married man who distinguished himself by his great zest for battle. He was one of those men in whom, in respect of courage, there isn't the slightest deficiency anywhere; a man among hundreds. We agreed we should like to visit the French in their trenches, and decided to make a date for our first call on 29 August.

Cutting wire

We crawled towards a gap in the enemy wires, which Kloppmann had cut the night before. We were unpleasantly surprised, then, to find it had been patched up; therefore we cut it again, rather noisily, and climbed down into the trench. After lurking for a long time behind the nearest traverse, we crept on, following a telephone wire to its end in a bayonet stuck in the ground. We found the position blocked off several times by wire, and once by a heavy gate, but all of it unoccupied. After taking a good look at it all, we went back the same way, and patched the wire to conceal the fact that we'd been.

The following evening, Kloppmann went snuffling around the place again, only this time to be received by rifle fire and those lemon-shaped hand-grenades also known as 'duck's eggs', one of which landed perilously close to his head as he pressed it into the ground, but failed to detonate. He needed to show a turn of speed. The evening after, we were both out there again, and found the front trench occupied. We listened to the sentries and identified their positions. One of them was whistling a pretty tune. At last, they started firing at us and we crept back.

When I was back in the trench, my comrades Voigt and Haverkamp suddenly appeared. They had obviously been celebrating, and had had the bizarre idea of leaving our cosy reserve camp behind, walking through the pitch-black wood to the front line, and, as they said, go on patrol. It's always been a principle of mine that a man should be responsible for himself, and so I let them climb out of the trench, even though our opponents were still agitated about something. Their patrol, admittedly, consisted of nothing beyond looking for the silk parachutes of French rockets, and swinging these about their heads, chasing one another back and forth under the enemy's noses. Of course, they were fired at, but after a long time they returned happily enough. Bacchus looks after his own.

On 10 September, I went from the reserve camp to regimental headquarters to ask for leave. 'You've been on my mind,' the colonel gave back, 'but the regiment needs to embark on some clearing action, and I want to entrust that to you. Pick a few men, and go and practise with them in the Souslœuvre camp.'

We were to enter the enemy trench in two places and try to take prisoners. The patrol was divided into three, a couple of storm units and one detachment that was to sit in the enemy trench and guard our rear. I was in overall command, and led the left-hand group, the right I entrusted to Lieutenant von Kienitz.

When I called for volunteers, to my surprise – it was, after all, late in 1917 – about three fourths of the men in all companies of the battalion stepped forward. I chose the participants in my wonted way, passing them in review, and choosing the 'good faces'. A few of those that didn't make it were almost in tears over their rejection.

Myself included, my party consisted of fourteen men, including Ensign von Zglinitzky, the NCOs Kloppmann, Mevius, Dujesiefken, and a couple of pioneers. All the free spirits of the 2nd Battalion were there.

For ten days, we practised throwing hand-grenades, and rehearsed the undertaking on a piece of trench that was made in the image of the original. It was astonishing that with so much realism, I only had three men hurt by splinters. We were excused all other duties, so that on 22 September when I returned to the company position for the night, I was in charge of a semi-wild but useful band of men.

In the evening, Kienitz and I walked through the wood to the regimental headquarters, where Captain Schumacher had invited us for a farewell dinner. Then we lay down in our dugouts for a few hours' rest. It's a strange feeling, knowing that the next day you'll be risking your life, and before falling asleep you examine your conscience.

At three in the morning we were woken, got up, washed, and had breakfast prepared for us. I had a scene right away with my servant, who had used too much salt and ruined the fried eggs I had ordered especially to give me strength for the occasion; not a good beginning.

We pushed away our plates and went over all the possible contingencies. We passed around the cherry brandy, and Kienitz told us some fine old jokes. At twenty to five, we gathered up the men and led them to the jumping-off point in the firing trench. Gaps had already been cut in the wire, and long arrows whitened with lime pointed us to our objectives. We said goodbye with a handshake and waited for whatever was to pass.

I had got together some kit appropriate to the sort of work I meant to be doing: across my chest, two sandbags, each containing four stick-bombs, impact fuses on the left, delay on the right, in my right tunic pocket an 08 revolver on a long cord, in my right trouser pocket a little Mauser pistol, in my left tunic pocket five egg hand-grenades, in the left trouser pocket luminous compass and whistle, in my belt spring hooks for pulling out the pins, plus bowie knife and wire-cutters. In my inside tunic pocket I carried a full wallet with my home address, in my right back pocket, a flat flask of cherry brandy. We had removed shoulder straps and Gibraltar badges, so as to give our opponents no clue as to our regiment. For identification, we had a white band round each arm.

At four minutes to five, the division on our left started a little diversionary fire. On the dot of five, the sky opened up behind our front, and the shells arced and whooshed over our heads. I stood with Kloppmann outside the dugout, smoking one last cigar; then, because a number of the shells were falling short, we were forced to take cover within. Watch in hand, we counted off the minutes.

At precisely five past five, we were out of the dugout and on to the prepared paths through the enemy wires. I ran ahead, a hand-grenade in my raised hand, and saw the right-hand party rushing out through the first glimmer of dawn. The enemy entanglement was feeble; I cleared it in a couple of bounds, then stumbled over a trip-wire and plunged into a crater from which Kloppmann and Mevius had to pull me out.

'In!' We leaped into the first trench, encountering no resistance, while to our right we heard the crash of a hand-grenade battle commence. Paying no attention to it, we crossed a line of sandbags, ducked into more craters, and surfaced again in front of a line of knife-rests in the second line. Since that too was completely shot up, and offered no prospect of prisoners, we hurried on along a communication trench. Finding it blocked, I first sent our pioneers forward to deal with it; but then, as they seemed to be making no progress, I took up a pickaxe myself. This was no time for fiddling about.

As we entered the third trench, we made a discovery that gave us pause: a burning cigarette end on the ground told us the enemy were in the immediate vicinity. I made a sign to my men, clutched my grenade a little harder, and crept through well-constructed trenches, with many rifles leaning against their walls. In situations like this, your memory latches on to the tiniest thing. Here, it was the image – as in a dream – of a mess-tin with a spoon standing in it. In twenty minutes' time, that piece of observation was to save my life.

Suddenly we saw shadowy figures disappear in front of us. We gave chase, and found ourselves in a dead end, with the entrance to a dugout in one wall. I stood there and called out: 'Montez!' A tossed-out hand-grenade was the only reply. Evidently, it was a timed fuse; I heard the little snap, and had time to leap back. It tore out part of the opposite wall at head height, ripped my silk cap, gave me several lacerations on my left hand, and took off the tip of the little finger. The pioneer officer next to me had his nose pierced. We took a few steps back, and bombed the dangerous place with hand-grenades. One enthusiast threw in a smoke stick, thereby making any further attack on the place impossible. We doubled back, and followed the third line in the opposite direction, looking for enemy. Everywhere we saw discarded weapons and bits of equipment. The question, where were the owners of all these rifles and what did they have in mind for us, kept putting itself ever-more insistently, but with primed grenade and pistol at the ready, we went grimly on, ever deeper into the bare, gunpowdery trench.

It was only thinking about it later that I understood our subsequent course. Without realizing it, we had turned into a third communication trench, and – well into the middle of our own barrage – were approaching the fourth line. From time to time, we ripped open one of the boxes built into the trench walls, and popped a hand-grenade into our pockets as a souvenir.

After running down a series of cross and parallel trenches, no one knew where we were, or where the German lines were. Gradually we were getting flustered. The needles of our luminous compasses danced in our unsteady hands, and as we scanned the heavens for the Pole Star, all our school lore suddenly left us. The sound of voices in a nearby trench indicated that the enemy had got over his initial surprise. Soon they would be on to us.

After turning back yet again, I found myself the last in line, and suddenly saw the mouth of a machine-gun swinging to and fro over a sandbag traverse. I leaped towards it, stumbling as I did so over a French corpse, and saw NCO Kloppmann and

Ensign von Zglinitzky busying themselves with it, while Fusilier Haller was going through a blood-stained corpse for papers. We struggled with the gun, barely conscious of where we were, obsessed with the idea of bagging some booty. I tried to undo the screws; another man severed the loading belt with his wire-cutters; finally we plucked up the thing, tripod and all, and dragged it away with us entire. At that instant, from a parallel trench, in the direction where we thought our own lines were to be found, came an excited but threatening enemy voice: 'Qu'est-ce qu'il y a?' and a black ball, dimly visible against the still-dark sky, came flying towards us in a high arc. 'Watch it!' There was a flash between Mevius and me; a splinter drove into Mevius's hand. We dispersed, getting further and further tangled up in the mesh of trenches. The only men I still had with me at this stage were the pioneer NCO, blood pouring from his nose, and Mevius, with his damaged hand. The only thing that delayed our end was the confusion of the French, who still hadn't dared to come out of their holes. Even so, it could only be a matter of minutes till we encountered some detachment of sufficient strength and resolve, who would happily put us out of our misery. Mercy wasn't exactly in the air.

I had already given up hope of getting out of this hornets' nest in one piece, when I suddenly gave a shout for joy. My eye had lit on the mess-tin with the spoon standing in it; now I got the picture. As it was already quite light, there wasn't a second to lose. We raced across the open field, the first rifle bullets whistling past us, towards our own lines. In the furthest French trench, we ran into Lieutenant von Kienitz's patrol. As the cry of 'Lüttje Lage!' came back, we knew we were over the worst. Unfortunately, I dropped on to a badly wounded man. Kienitz hurriedly told me he'd driven off French sappers in the first trench with hand-grenades, and, going on, had taken some losses, dead and wounded, from our own artillery fire.

After a longish wait, two more of my men appeared, NCO

Soldier vs. general

Dujesiefken and Fusilier Haller, who at least had some comforting news for me. As he'd wandered around, he had ended up in a remote sap, and had found three machine-guns, one of which he had taken off its mount and picked up with him. As it was getting lighter all the time, we raced over no man's land back to our own front line.

Of the fourteen who had set out, only four returned, and Kienitz's patrol had suffered heavy losses as well. My dejection was a little helped by the words of the stout Oldenburger Dujesiefken, who, while I was getting my hand bandaged up in the dugout, was outside telling his comrades what had befallen, finishing with the sentence: 'I must say, though, that Lieutenant Jünger is really something else: my word, the sight of him vaulting over those barricades!'

Then, almost all of us with bandaged heads or hands, we marched through the woods to the regimental headquarters. Colonel von Oppen welcomed us, and sat us down to coffee. He was disappointed at our lack of success, but still told us we'd done our best. We felt comforted. Then I was put in a car, and taken to divisional command, who wanted a full report. A few hours before, I had had enemy hand-grenades exploding in my ears; now I was enjoying sitting back in a powerful car, being whisked along the highway, eating up the miles.

The general staff officer received me in his office. He was pretty cut up, and I saw to my irritation that he was trying to leave the blame for the failure of our mission at my door. When he jabbed his finger at the map and asked questions like: 'Don't you think you should have turned right into this communication trench instead?' I realized that the kind of confusion where notions like right and left just go out the window was quite outside his experience. For him the whole thing had been a plan; for us an intensely experienced reality.

The divisional commander greeted me kindly, and soon improved my mood. I sat next to him at lunch with my ragged tunic and bandaged hand, and tried, without false modesty, to make him see this morning's action in the best way, in which I think I succeeded.

The next day, Colonel von Oppen summoned the members of the patrol once more, and gave out Iron Crosses and two weeks' furlough apiece. In the afternoon, those of the fallen who were brought in were buried in the military cemetery at Thiaucourt. In among the fallen of this war, there were also fighters from 1870. One of those old graves was marked by a mossy stone with the inscription: 'Distant to the eye, but to the heart forever nigh!' A large stone slab was etched with the lines:

> Heroes' deeds and heroes' graves,
> Old and new you here may see.
> How the Empire was created,
> How the Empire was preserved.

That evening I read in a French communiqué: 'A German attack at Regniéville was foiled; prisoners were taken.' Wolves had broken into the sheep-pen, but lost their bearings – nothing more. At any rate, the short item told me that among our lost comrades there were some who had survived.

Some months later, I got a letter from one of the missing men, Fusilier Meyer, who had lost a leg in the hand-grenade battle; after wandering around a long time he, with three companions, had been engaged in a fight, and, heavily wounded, had been taken prisoner, after the others, NCO Kloppmann among them, had died. Kloppmann was one of those men you couldn't imagine being taken alive.

I experienced quite a few adventures in the course of the war, but none was quite as eerie as this. It still makes me feel a cold sweat when I think of us wandering around among those unfamiliar trenches by the cold early light. It was like the dream of a labyrinth.

REGNIÉVILLE

A few days later, after some preliminary shrapnel fire, Lieutenants Domeyer and Zürn with several companions leaped into the enemy firing trench. Domeyer ran into a heavily bearded French reservist who, when called upon to 'Rendez-vous!' replied with an irascible 'Ah non!' and threw himself at him. In the course of a bitter tussle, Domeyer shot him through the throat with his pistol, and was forced to return, as I had done, *sans* captives. In our mission alone we had used enough munitions to have furnished forth a whole battle in 1870.

Flanders Again

The day I returned from my furlough, we were relieved by Bavarian troops, and billeted at first in the nearby village of Labry.

On 17 October we were entrained, and after travelling for a day and a half found ourselves back on Flemish soil, having last left it barely two months previously. We spent the night in the small town of Izegem, and the following morning marched to Roulers, or, to give it its Flemish name, Roeselare. The town was in the early stages of destruction. There were still shops with goods in them, but the inhabitants were already living in their cellars, and the ties of bourgeois existence were being loosened by frequent bombardment. With the war raging on all sides, a shop window opposite my quarters containing, of all things, ladies' hats, seemed the height of absurd irrelevance. At night, looters broke into the abandoned houses.

I was the only person in my billet on the Ooststraat to be living above ground. The building belonged to a draper, who had fled at the beginning of the war, leaving an old housekeeper and her daughter to look after it. The two of them were also minding a little orphan girl whom they had found wandering the streets as we were marching in, and of whom they knew nothing, not even her name or her age. They all were terrified of bombs, and begged me, practically on their knees, not to leave light on upstairs for the wicked aeroplanes. I have to say, I laughed on the other side

of my face when I was standing in the window with my friend
Reinhardt, watching an English plane flitting over the rooftops
in the beam of a searchlight, a huge bomb came down near by,
and the air pressure wrapped the window-panes about our ears.

For the next round of fighting, I had been designated as an
intelligence officer, and sent to regimental staff. To learn a little
more, I looked up the 10th Bavarian Regiment, whom we were
to relieve, ahead of time. I found their commander to be friendly
enough, even though he chided me over the non-regulation 'red
ribbon' on my cap, which ought really to have been covered over
with grey, so as not to draw any gunfire to the spot.

Two orderlies took me to the clearing-station, which was said
to have a very good view of the front. No sooner had we left
headquarters than a shell stirred up the meadow. My guides were
quite adept at avoiding the shelling – which towards noon turned
into an uninterrupted rumble – by taking byways through the
poplar woods that were dotted about. They worked through
the gold-gleaming autumnal landscape with the instincts of the
experienced modern warrior, who, even in the densest bombardment, can hit on a path that offers at least reasonable odds of
getting through.

On the doorstep of an isolated farmyard that appeared to have
been freshly bombed, we saw a man lying face down on the
ground. 'He's stopped one!' said the stolid Bavarian. 'Air's got a
high iron content,' said his companion, looking around apprais-
ingly, and strode quickly on. The clearing-station lay the other
side of the heavily shelled Passchendaele–Westroosebeke road.
It was rather like the one I had commanded in Fresnoy, having
been installed next to a building that had been reduced to a pile
of rubble, and having so little cover that the first half-accurate
shell would knock it for six. I was briefed by three officers, who
seemed to be leading a very companionable cave-life in the place
and were pleased that they were to be relieved, about the enemy,
the position and how to approach, and then went by way of

Roodkruis-Oostnieuwkerke, back to Roulers, where I reported to the colonel.

As I passed through the streets of the little town, I kept an eye out for the cosy names of the numerous little pubs that are such an apt expression of whatever the Flemish equivalent for *dolce vita* is. Who wouldn't feel tempted by a pub-sign called 'De Zalm' [Salmon], 'De Reeper' [Heron], 'De Nieuwe Trompette', 'De drie Koningen' or 'Den Oliphant'? Even to be welcomed in the intimate 'Du' form in that pithy and guttural language puts one right at ease. May God permit this splendid country, which has so often in its history been the battlefield for warring armies, to rise again from this war with its old quality intact.

admiration for belgium

In the evening, the town was once again bombed. I went down into the cellar, where the women were huddled trembling in a corner, and switched on my torch to settle the nerves of the little girl, who had been screaming ever since an explosion had knocked out the light. Here was proof again of man's need for home. In spite of the huge fear these women had in the face of such danger, yet they clung fast to the ground which at any moment might bury them.

On the morning of 22 October, with my reconnaissance group of four men, I started off for Kalve, where the regimental staff were to be relieved this morning. At the front, there was very heavy fire, whose lightnings tinged the mist blood red. At the entrance to Oostnieuwkerke a building was hit by a heavy shell and collapsed just as we were about to pass it. Lumps of debris trundled across the street. We tried to go around the place, but ended up having to go through it after all, as we weren't sure of the direction to Kalve. As we hurried on, I called out for directions to an NCO who was standing in a doorway. Instead of giving me an answer, he thrust his hands deeper into his pockets, and shrugged his shoulders. As I couldn't stand on ceremony in the midst of this bombardment, I sprang over to him, held my pistol under his nose, and got my information out of him that way.

FLANDERS AGAIN

It was the first time in the war that I'd come across an example of a man acting up, not out of cowardice, but obviously out of complete indifference. Although such indifference was more commonly seen in the last years of the war, its display in action remained very unusual, as battle brings men together, whereas inactivity separates them. In a battle, you stand under external pressures. It was on the march, surrounded by columns of men moving out of the battle, that the erosion of the war ethos showed itself most nakedly.

In Roodkruis, a little farmstead at a fork in the road, things got really worrying. Limbers chased across the shelled road, troops of infantry wended along through the brush either side of the road, and innumerable wounded men dragged themselves back. We encountered one young artilleryman who had a long, jagged splinter sticking out of his shoulder, like a spear. He passed us, wandering like a somnambulist, never once looking up.

Laying wire

We turned right off the road, to the regimental headquarters, which stood in a ring of fire. Near by, a couple of telephonists were laying their wires across a cabbage field. A shell landed right next to one of them; we saw him crumple, and thought he was done for. But then he picked himself up, and calmly continued laying his wire. As the headquarters consisted of a tiny concrete blockhouse that barely had room for the commander, an adjutant and an orderly, I looked for a place near by. I moved in, with intelligence, gas-protection and trench-mortar officers, to a wooden shack that didn't exactly strike me as the embodiment of a bomb-proof abode.

In the afternoon, I went up the line, seeing as news had come in that the enemy had that morning attacked our 5th Company. My route went via the clearing-station to the Nordhof, essentially a former farmhouse, in whose ruins the commander of the battalion in reserve was staying. From there, a path, not always recognizable as such, led to the commander of the fighting troops.

The heavy rains of the past few days had turned the crater field into a morass, deep enough, especially around the Paddelbach, to endanger life. On my wanderings, I would regularly pass solitary and abandoned corpses; often it was just a head or a hand that was left protruding from the dirty level of the crater. Thousands have come to rest in such a way, without a sign put up by a friendly hand to mark the grave.

After the extremely sapping crossing of the Paddelbach, which was only possible after improvising a bridge from fallen poplars, I came across Lieutenant Heins, the commander of the 5th Company, along with a handful of loyal men, in an enormous shell-crater. The crater position was on a hill, and as it wasn't completely inundated, undemanding grunts might find it habitable. Heins told me that that morning a British line had appeared and then disappeared again, when it had come under fire. They in turn had shot a few men from the 164th, who had run off at their approach. Other than that, everything was tiptop; I returned to headquarters, and reported to the colonel.

The following day, our lunch was rudely interrupted by some shells landing hard by our wooden walls, sending up spurts of dirt that slowly spiralled down on to our tar-paper roof. Everyone streamed out of the hut; I fled to a nearby farmhouse, and, because it was raining, went inside. That evening, precisely the same chain of events, only this time I stayed in the open, as the rain had stopped. The next shell flew into the middle of the collapsing farmhouse. That's the role of chance in war. More than elsewhere, small causes can have a vast effect.

On 25 October, we had already been driven out of our shacks by eight o'clock, one of them being nailed by only the second shell to be fired. Further shells flew into the damp pastures. They gave the impression of just expiring there, but they tore up considerable craters. Alerted by my experience of the day before, I sought out an isolated and confidence-inspiring crater in the large cabbage field behind headquarters, and didn't leave it for

quite some time afterwards. It was on that day that I got to hear
the bad news of the death of Lieutenant Brecht, who had fallen
in battle as a divisional observation officer in the crater field just
right of the Nordhof farm. He was one of those few who, even
in this war of *matériel*, always had a particular aura of calm
about him, and whom we supposed to be invulnerable. It's
always easy to spot people like that in a crowd of others – they
were the ones who laughed when there were orders to attack.
Hearing of such a man's death inexorably led to thoughts of my
own mortality.

The morning hours of 26 October were filled by drumfire of
unusual severity. Our artillery too redoubled its fury on seeing
the signals for a barrage that were sent up from the front. Every
little piece of wood and every hedge was home to a gun, whose
half-deaf gunners did their business.

As wounded men going back were making exaggerated and
unclear statements about a British advance, I was sent off to
the front at eleven o'clock with four men, for more accurate
information. Our way led through heated fire. We passed numerous wounded, among them Lieutenant Spitz, the commander
of the 12th, with a shot in the chin. Even before we got to the
command dugout we came under aimed machine-gun fire, a sure
sign that the enemy must have forced our line back. My suspicion
was confirmed by Major Dietlein, the commander of the 3rd
Battalion. I found the old gentleman engaged in crawling out of
the doorway of his three-parts inundated blockhouse, and fishing
in the mud for his meerschaum cigar-holder. MAPS

The British had forced a way through our front line, and had
occupied a ridge from where they commanded the Paddelbach
basin and our battalion headquarters. I entered the change in the
position with a couple of red strokes on my map, and then geed
the men up for their next sapping run through the mud. We
bounded across the terrain overlooked by the British, got behind
the crest of the next elevation, and from there, more slowly,

advanced to the Nordhof. To the right and left of us shells splashed down in the swamp and sent up vast mud mushrooms ringed with innumerable lesser splatters. The Nordhof also needed to be got through in a hurry, as it was under fire from high-explosive shells. Those things went off with a peculiarly nasty and stunning bang. They were fired over, a few at a time, with only short intervals between them. Each time, we had to make some rapid ground and then wait for the next round in a shell-hole. In the time between the first distant whine and the very close explosion, one's will to live was painfully challenged, with the body helpless and motionless left to its fate.

Shrapnels were also present in the compound, and one threw its freight of balls in our midst, with a multiple clatter. One of my companions was struck on the back of the helmet, and thrown to the ground. After lying there stunned for some time, he struggled to his feet and ran on. The terrain around the Nordhof was covered with a lot of bodies in frightful condition.

Since we went about our work with some diligence, we often got to see places that until very recently had been strictly no go. It gave us an insight into all the other things that went on in out-of-the-way places. Everywhere we saw traces of death; it was almost as though there wasn't a living soul anywhere in this wasteland. Here, behind a dishevelled hedge, lay a group of men, their bodies covered with the fresh soil that the explosion had dropped on them after killing them; there were two runners lying by a crater, from which the acrid fumes of explosive were still bubbling up. In another place, we found many bodies in a small area: either a group of stretcher-bearers or an errant platoon of reservists that had been found by the centre of a ball of fire, and met their end. We would surface in these deadly places, take in their secrets at a glance, and disappear again into the smoke.

After hurrying unscathed across the heavily bombarded stretch the other side of the Passchendaele–Westroosebeke road, I was able to report to Colonel von Oppen.

The next morning, I was sent to the front at six o'clock with instructions to establish whether, and if so where, the regiment was in touch with the units on its flanks. On my way, I ran into Sergeant-Major Ferchland, who was taking the 8th Company orders to advance to Goudberg, and, in the event of there being a gap between us and the regiment on the left, to close it. In the speedy performance of my duty, I could do nothing better than fall in with him. After searching for some time, we finally found the commander of the 8th, my friend Tebbe, in a rather inhospitable part of the crater landscape close to the clearing-station. He was not pleased with the order to perform such a visible movement in broad daylight. During our laconic conversation, further oppressed by the indescribable dreariness of the craters in the early light, we lit cigars, and waited for the company to collect itself.

After no more than a few paces, we came under carefully aimed infantry fire from the opposing heights, and had to go on alone, each man dodging from crater to crater. Crossing the next ridge, the fire became so intense that Tebbe gave orders to occupy a crater position until nightfall. Puffing on his cigar, he reviewed his line.

I made up my mind to go forward and check on the size of the gap myself, and rested awhile in Tebbe's crater. The enemy's artillery was soon finding its range, to punish the company for its bold advance. A projectile smashing down on the rim of our little refuge and leaving both my face and my map spattered with mud, told me it was time to go. I bade goodbye to Tebbe, and wished him all the best for the hours ahead. He called after me: 'God, just let it be night, the morning will come by itself!'

We picked our way across the Paddelbach basin, where we were within view of the enemy, ducking behind the foliage of shot-over poplars, and using their trunks to balance along. From time to time one of us would disappear up to the hips in mire, and would certainly have drowned but for the presence of his comrades and their helpfully extended rifle butts. I aimed for a blockhouse that had a group of soldiers standing around it. In front of us, a stretcher carried by four bearers was heading in the same direction as we were. Puzzled to see a wounded man being carried towards the front, I took a look through my binoculars, and saw a line of khaki-clad figures with flat steel helmets. At the same instant, the first shots rang out. As there was nowhere to take cover, we had no option but to run back, with the bullets plugging into the mud all round us. The chase through the morass was very fatiguing; but the minute we stopped, completely out of breath, and offered the British a still target, a clutch of high-explosive shells gave us our second wind. The shells had the virtue, moreover, of obscuring us from view with their smoke. The least pleasant aspect of this chase was the prospect that almost any sort of wound was enough to see you to a watery grave. We hurried along the crater rims, as along the narrow walls of a honeycomb. Trickles of blood here and there indicated that some unlucky men must have gone there before us.

Dog tired, we reached the regimental headquarters, where I handed in my sketches, and gave a report on the situation. We had investigated the gap. Tebbe would advance under cover of night to fill it.

On 28 October, we were relieved in turn by the 10th Bavarian reserves, and, prepared to step in if needed, were put up in villages in the back area. The general staff withdrew as far as Most.

At night we sat in the bar of an abandoned public house, and celebrated the promotion and engagement of Lieutenant Zürn, who had just got back from leave. For such behaviour we were duly punished the following morning by being woken at six by a gigantic drumfire, which, though far away, still shattered my windows. The alarm went off immediately. Obviously, the closing of the gap had not gone completely according to plan. The rumour was going around that the British had broken through. I spent the day waiting for orders at the observation point, in an area lying under sparse fire. A light shell drove through the window of one building, sending three wounded artillerymen staggering out, covered in brick dust. Three more lay dead under the rubble.

The next morning, I received the following orders from the Bavarian commander: 'By repeated enemy pressure, the position of the regiment to the left of us has been further pushed back, and the gap between the two regiments greatly widened. In view of the danger that the regiment might be outflanked on the left, yesterday evening the 1st Battalion of the 73rd Fusiliers moved forward to counter-attack, but was apparently dispersed by the barrage, and never reached the enemy. This morning, the 2nd Battalion was sent forward into the gap. We have at present no news of either. Information is required on the position of the 1st and 2nd Battalions.'

I set off on my way, and had only got as far as Nordhof when I met Captain von Brixen, the commanding officer of the 2nd Battalion, who had the position sketched in his pocket. I copied it, and had thereby effectively carried out my task, but I went on anyway to the headquarters of the troops in the line, to effect a personal reconnaissance. The way was littered with dead, their pale faces staring up out of water-filled craters, or already so covered with mud that their human identity was almost completely masked. Many of the sleeves had the blue Gibraltar brassard.

The commanding officer was a Bavarian, Captain Radlmaier. This extremely diligent officer told me in some detail what Captain von Brixen had already told me in hasty outline. Our 2nd Battalion had suffered heavy casualties; among many others, the adjutant and the commander of the brave 7th. The adjutant, Lemière, was the brother of the Lemière who had commanded the 8th Company, and had fallen at Fresnoy. Both were from Liechtenstein, and both had volunteered to fight on the German side. Both died, shot in the mouth.

The captain pointed to a blockhouse a couple of hundred yards away, that had been particularly doggedly defended yesterday. Shortly after the attack had begun, the man in command of it, a sergeant-major, saw a British soldier leading back three German prisoners. He picked him off, and acquired three more men for the defence. When they had used up all their ammunition, they tied a British captive to the door, in order to put a temporary stop to the firing, and were able to retire unobserved after nightfall.

Another blockhouse, this one under a lieutenant, was called upon to surrender; by way of reply, the German leaped out, grabbed the Englishman, and pulled him inside, to the astonishment of his watching troops.

That day, I saw little troops of stretcher-bearers going around the battlefield with raised flags, and not coming under fire. The only time the warrior got to see such scenes in this often subterranean war, was when the need for them had become too dire.

My return was impeded by a nasty irritant gas that smelled of rotten apples from the British shells that had saturated the ground. It made breathing difficult, and caused the eyes to tear up. After I'd made my report to headquarters, I met two officer friends of mine on stretchers outside the dressing-station, both gravely wounded. One was Lieutenant Zürn, in whose honour we had celebrated only two nights before. Now he was lying on a door, half stripped, with the waxy colour that is a sure sign of imminent death, staring up at me with sightless eyes as I stepped out to squeeze his hand. The other, Lieutenant Haverkamp, had had an arm and a leg so badly smashed by shell splinters that a double amputation seemed probable. He lay, deathly pale, on his stretcher, smoking cigarettes which his bearers lit for him and put in his mouth.

Once again, our losses were appalling, especially of young officers. This second Battle of Flanders was a monotonous affair; it was fought on sticky, muddy ground, and it caused immense casualties.

On 3 November, we were put on trains at the station in Gits, still fresh in our memory from the first Flanders Campaign. We saw our two Flemish waitresses again, but they weren't what they had been either. They too seemed to have been through some heavy action.

We were taken to Tourcoing, a pleasant sister town of Lille, for a few days. For the first and last time in the entire war, every man of the 7th Company slept on a feather bed. I was put up in a magnificent room in the house of a rich manufacturer on the Rue de Lille. I greatly enjoyed my first evening on a leather armchair in front of an open fire in a marble fireplace.

Those few days were used by all of us to enjoy the life that we'd had to fight so hard to cling on to. We still couldn't quite grasp that for the time being we'd given death the slip, and we wanted to feel the possession of this new lease of life, by enjoying it in every way possible.

The Double Battle of Cambrai

The delightful days at Tourcoing were soon over. For a short while we were at Villers-au-Tertre, where we were brought up to strength by new drafts, and on 15 November we were put on trains for Lécluse, the resting-place of the battalion in reserve on the new front now assigned to us. Lécluse was a fairly large village in the lake country of the Artois. Extensive reed beds were home to ducks and water-fowl, and the waters were full of fish. Fishing was strictly forbidden, yet even so there were mysterious noises coming from the water at night. One day I was sent the pay-books of men in my company who had been caught by the town commandant fishing with bombs. I refused to make an issue of it, because the good spirits of the men mattered far more to me than the protection of French fishing-rights or the dinner-tables of the military bigwigs. From then on, I found, almost every night, a giant pike anonymously left outside my door. The day after I treated my two company officers to lunch with 'Pike à la Lohengrin' as the *pièce de résistance*.

On 19 November, I took my platoon commanders to see the part of the line where we would be going in a day or two. It was in front of the village of Vis-en-Artois. But then we didn't enter the line as soon as we'd thought, because there was an alarm nearly every night and we were variously sent off to the Wotan Line, the reserve gun positions, or the village of Dury to be in

Plans changing

readiness for an expected British attack. Experienced warriors knew that nothing good could come of this.

And indeed we heard on 29 November from Captain von Brixen that we were to take part in a sweeping counter-offensive against the bulge that the tank battle at Cambrai had made in our front. Even though we were pleased to play the part of the hammer, having so long been the anvil, we wondered whether the troops, still exhausted from Flanders, would be up to the job. That said, I had every confidence in my company; they had never let anyone down yet.

On the night of 30 November to 1 December, we were put on lorries. In the process, we took our first losses, as a soldier dropped a hand-grenade which for some reason exploded, gravely injuring him and another man. Someone else feigned insanity in an attempt to get out of the battle. After a lot of toing and froing, a buffet in the ribs from an NCO seemed to sort him out, and we were able to go. It showed me that that sort of play-acting is difficult to keep up.

We drove, squashed together, almost as far as Baralle, where we were made to stand for hours in a ditch and wait for orders. In spite of the cold, I lay down in a meadow and slept till dawn. Since we had been prepared for the attack, it came as something of a disappointment to learn that the 225th, whom we were to support, had decided to go it alone. We were to stay in readiness in the castle grounds of Baralle.

At nine o'clock in the morning our artillery began a powerful pounding, which from quarter to twelve to ten to twelve achieved the intensity of drumfire. The woods of Bourlon, which were not even under direct attack as they were too heavily defended, simply vanished in a chartreuse fog of gas. At ten to twelve we observed through our binoculars lines of riflemen emerging on to the empty crater landscape, while in the rear the batteries were harnessed up and rushed forward to new positions. A German aeroplane brought down a British barrage balloon in flames; we saw the occupants parachute clear. The fact that he circled round them as they drifted through the air, and fired tracer rounds at them, was further evidence of the growing bitterness of the conflict.

After following the progress of the attack avidly from the elevation of the castle grounds, we emptied a dixie of noodles and lay down for a nap on the frozen ground. At three o'clock we received orders to advance as far as the regimental HQ, which was situated in the lock-chamber of a drained canal bed. We went there by platoons, through a feeble scattered fire. From there the 7th and 8th were sent forward to the officer commanding the troops in reserve, to relieve two companies of the 225th. The five hundred yards of canal that were to be got through lay under a dense barrage. We got there by running in a tight mass, without sustaining any losses. Numerous corpses showed that other companies had been made to suffer heavily. Reserves were squeezed up against the banks, busily trying to dig foxholes in the canal walls. As all the places were taken, and the canal, as a landmark, was a magnet for artillery fire, I led my company to a crater field to the right of it, and left it up to each individual to settle down as they liked. A splinter jangled against my bayonet. Together with Tebbe, who had followed our example with his 8th Company, I looked out a suitable crater, which we covered with a tarpaulin. We lit a candle, ate supper, smoked our pipes, and had a shivering conversation. Tebbe, who even in these insalubrious surroundings always remained something of a dandy, was telling me some long and involved story about a girl who had sat for him once in Rome.

At eleven o'clock, I received orders to advance into the erstwhile front line, and report to the commander of the fighting troops. I gathered up my men and moved forward. Mighty shells were falling only singly now, but then one promptly smashed down at our feet like a greeting from hell, and filled the canal bed with dark smoke. The men fell silent, as if an icy fist had them by the neck, and stumbled along over barbed wire and debris in my wake. It is an eerie feeling to be striding through an unknown position by night, even when the shelling isn't particularly strong; your eyes and ears are subject to all sorts of deceptions. Everything feels cold and alien as in some cursed other world.

At last, we found the spot where the front line met the canal, and wended our way through the crowded trenches to the battalion headquarters. I stepped in, and found a bunch of officers and orderlies standing around in an atmosphere one could have cut with a knife. Then I learned that the attack had not prospered so far, and was to be taken up again in the morning. The feeling in the room was rather doomy. A couple of battalion commanders started on lengthy negotiations with their adjutants. From time to time special weapons' officers tossed an item into the conversation from the height of their bunks, which were swarming like hen-roosts. The cigar smoke was dense. Servants tried to cut bread for their officers in the middle of the bustle; a wounded man charged in, and caused pandemonium by announcing an enemy hand-grenade attack.

Finally, I was able to take down my orders for the attack. At six o'clock in the morning we were to roll up Dragon Alley and as much as possible of the Siegfried Line. The two battalions of the regiment in the line were to commence attacking on our right at seven o'clock. The discrepancy in times made me suspect that our high-ups didn't quite trust this attack, and were giving us the role of guinea-pigs. I objected to the two-phase attack, and our time was duly commuted to seven o'clock. The next morning was to show what a difference that made.

Since I had absolutely no idea where Dragon Alley was, I asked for a map as I was leaving, but was told they had none to spare. I drew my own conclusions, and went out into the fresh air. Other commanders don't often give strange units a cushy time.

After I'd spent a long time wandering around the position with my heavily laden soldiers, one man spotted a sign with the half-effaced writing 'Dragon Alley' on a small sap going forward, which was blocked off by knife-rests. When I went down there, after a few steps, I heard the sound of foreign voices. Silently I crept back. It was evident that I had encountered the spearhead of the British attack, either through over-confidence or, in ignorance of where they were, behaving incautiously. I had the sap blocked off right away by a platoon.

Right next to Dragon Alley was an enormous hole in the ground that I took to be a tank-trap, and there I had the whole company assemble, to explain our orders, and to give the different platoons their places. While speaking, I was several times interrupted by small shells. Once, a dud even plummeted into the back wall of the hole. I was standing up on the rim, and, with every explosion, I could see the steel helmets assembled below me perform a deep and synchronous bow in the moonlight.

In case of the possibility of us all being wiped out by a chance hit, I sent the first and second platoons back into the trench, and settled myself into the pit with the third. Men from another unit, which had been roughed up on Dragon Alley that morning, had a worrying impact on my men, telling them that an English machine-gun fifty yards away was an insurmountable obstacle across the trench. We decided therefore, at the first sign of resistance, to fan out left and right and make a concerted bombing attack.

The endless night hours I spent huddled up against Lieutenant Hopf in a hole in the ground. At six o'clock I got up and, with the curious feeling that precedes any attack, settled a last few details. You have butterflies in the stomach as you talk to the platoon commanders, try to make jokes, run around as if you were facing a parade in front of the commander-in-chief; in a word, you try and make yourself as busy as possible, to avoid any troubling thoughts. A soldier offered me a mug of coffee that he'd warmed up on a paraffin stove, and that had a magical effect on me, spreading warmth and confidence throughout my body.

On the dot of seven, we drew up in the determined order in a long, snaking line. We found Dragon Alley untenanted; a row of empty ammunitions drums behind a barricade attested to the fact that the notorious machine-gun had been withdrawn. That cheered us up no end. After I'd blocked off a well-constructed trench that led off to the right, we entered a defile. It slowly climbed, and before long we found ourselves on the open field just as day was breaking. We turned about and tried the trench off to the right, where we found plenty of signs of yesterday's failed attack. The ground was littered with British corpses and hardware. This was the Siegfried Line. Suddenly, the leader of the shock troops, Lieutenant Hoppenrath, seized the rifle from one of his soldiers, and fired. He had encountered a British sentry, who threw a few hand-grenades and then took to his heels. We went on, and soon encountered further resistance. Hand-grenades were thrown by both sides, and exploded with loud bangs. The shock troops attacked. Bombs were passed from hand to hand; snipers took up position behind traverses to deal with the enemy throwers; the platoon commanders peered over the edge of the trench to see if a counter-attack might be coming; and the light machine-gun units set up their weapons in suitable places. We attacked the trench from the front with grenades, and covered its length with our rifles. Things now started to perk up all around, and swarms of bullets crossed over our heads.

After a short fight, excited voices called out from the other side, and before we understood what was happening, the first British soldiers came out towards us with their hands above their heads. One after another, they rounded the traverse and unbuckled, while our guns and pistols remained levelled at them. They were young, good-looking fellows in new uniforms. I let them go by me, and said 'Hands down!' and summoned a platoon to lead them away. Most of them showed us by their confident smiles that they didn't expect us to do anything too terrible to them. Others tried to propitiate us by holding out cigarette

packets and bars of chocolate. With the waxing joy of the huntsman, I saw we had made a huge catch; the line seemed unending.
We had counted past a hundred and fifty, and more were still
coming out. I stopped an officer and asked him about the rest of
the position, and its defence. He replied very politely; he really
didn't need to stand to attention. He took me to the company
commander, a wounded captain, who was in a nearby foxhole. I
saw myself face to face with a young man of about twenty-six,
with fine features, leaning against the shelter door with a bullet
through his calf. When I introduced myself to him, he lifted his
hand to his cap, I caught a flash of gold at the wrist, he said his
name, and handed over his pistol. His opening words showed me
he was a real man. 'We were surrounded.' He felt obliged to
explain to his opponent why his company had surrendered so
quickly. We talked about various matters in French. He told me
there were quite a few German wounded, whom his men had
bandaged and fed, in a nearby shelter. When I asked him how
strong the rearward defences of the line were, he would give me
no information. After I had promised to have him and the other
wounded men sent back, we parted with a shake of the hand.

Outside the dugout, I ran into Hoppenrath, who told me we'd
taken about two hundred prisoners. For a company that was
eighty strong, that wasn't bad going. After I'd posted sentries,
we took a look around at the captured trench, which was bristling
with weapons and all manner of equipment. In the fire-bays lay
machine-guns, mortars, hand- and rifle-grenades, water-bottles,
sheepskin jerkins, waterproofs, tarpaulins, tins of meat, jam, tea,
coffee, cocoa and tobacco, bottles of cognac, tools, pistols, flare
pistols, undergarments, gloves; in short, pretty much anything
you could think of. Like an old feudal commander, I allowed a
few minutes for taking plunder, to give the men a chance to draw
breath, and to take a look at some of the items. I, for my part,
was unable to resist ordering up a little breakfast for myself in a
dugout entrance and filling my pipe with some fine Navy Cut

tobacco while I scribbled out my report to the commanding officer of the troops in the line. Painstaking man that I am, I also sent a copy to our battalion commander.

Half an hour later, we set off again in euphoric mood – perhaps the British cognac might have contributed a little – and made our way forward along the Siegfried Line, dodging from traverse to traverse.

We were fired on from a pillbox built into the trench, and we therefore climbed out on to the nearest fire-step to have a look around. Whilst we were trading bullets with the occupants, one man was knocked flat as if by an invisible fist. A bullet had drilled through the top of his helmet, and ploughed a furrow along the top of his skull. I could see the brain rise and fall in the wound with every heartbeat, and yet he was capable of going back on his own. I had to remind him to leave his knapsack behind, he had been going to take it, and I implored him to take his time and be careful.

I asked for some volunteers to break the resistance by an attack across the open field. The men eyed each other doubtfully; only an awkward Pole, whom I had always taken for a cretin, climbed out of the trench, and trudged off towards the pillbox. Unfortunately, I've forgotten the name of this simple man, who taught me that you can't say you really know a man if you haven't seen him under conditions of danger. Then Ensign Neupert and his section leaped out of the line, while we continued along the trench at the same time. The British fired off a few shots and fled, leaving the pillbox for us. One of our attackers had collapsed in mid-charge, and was lying on the ground a few steps away from it. He had received one of those shots to the heart that lay a man out as if he were asleep.

As we proceeded, we encountered some stiff resistance from some hand-grenade throwers we couldn't see, and gradually found ourselves pushed back to the pillbox. There we locked ourselves up. In the contested line of trench, both sides sustained losses. Unfortunately, one of ours happened to be NCO Mevius, whom I had discovered to be a bold fighter on the night of Regniéville. He was lying face down in a puddle of blood. When I turned him over, I saw by a large hole in his forehead that it was too late for any help. I had just exchanged a few words with him; suddenly a question I'd asked went unanswered. A few seconds later, when I looked round the traverse to see what was keeping him, he was already dead. It was an eerie feeling.

After our opponents had also pulled back a little, a protracted exchange of fire ensued, with a Lewis gun barely fifty yards away from us forcing us to keep our heads down. We responded with one of our own light machine-guns. For maybe half a minute, the two guns fought it out, with the bullets spraying and bouncing everywhere. Then our gunner, Lance-Corporal Motullo, collapsed with a shot in the head. Even though his brains were dribbling down past his chin, he was still lucid as we carried him into the nearest shelter. Motullo was an older man, one of those who would never have volunteered; but once he was standing behind his machine-gun, I had occasion to observe that, even though he was standing in a hail of bullets, he didn't duck his head by so much as an inch. When I asked him how he was feeling, he was capable of replying in complete sentences. I had the sense that his mortal wound didn't hurt him at all, maybe that he wasn't even aware of it.

Gradually, things calmed down a little, as the British for their part were also busy digging themselves in. At twelve o'clock, Captain von Brixen, Lieutenant Tebbe and Lieutenant Voigt came by; they offered their congratulations on the company's successes. We sat down in the pillbox, lunched off British provisions, and discussed the position. In between times, I was having to negotiate with about two dozen Britishers, whose heads appeared out of the trench a hundred yards away, and who seemed to want to surrender. But as soon as I put my own head over the parapet, I found myself under fire from somewhere further back.

Suddenly, there was some commotion at the British barricade. Hand-grenades flew, rifles banged, machine-guns clattered. 'They're coming! They're coming!' We leaped behind sandbags and started shooting. In the heat of battle, one of my men, Corporal Kimpenhaus, jumped up on to the parapet, and fired down into the trench until he was brought down by two bad wounds in his arms. I took a note of this hero of the hour, and was proud to be able to congratulate him two weeks later, on the award of the Iron Cross, First Class.

No sooner had we got back from this interruption to our lunch than there was more pandemonium. It was one of those curious incidents that can suddenly and unpredictably transform an entire situation. The noise was coming from a subaltern in the regiment on our left who wanted to line up with us, and seemed inflamed by a berserk fury. Drink seemed to have tipped his innate bravery into a towering rage. 'Where are the Tommies? Lemme at 'em! Come on boys, who's coming with me?' In his insensate fury, he knocked over our fine barricade, and plunged forward, clearing a path for himself with hand-grenades. His orderly slipped ahead of him along the trench, shooting down anyone who survived the explosions.

Bravery, fearless risking of one's own life, is always inspiring. We too found ourselves picked up by his wild fury, and scrabbling around to grab a few hand-grenades, rushed to form part of this berserker's progress. Soon I was up alongside him, tearing along the line, and the other officers too, followed by riflemen from my company, weren't slow in coming. Even Captain von Brixen, the battalion commander, was up there in the van, rifle in hand, bringing down enemy grenade-throwers over our heads.

The British resisted manfully. Every traverse had to be fought for. The black balls of Mills bombs crossed in the air with our own long-handled grenades. Behind every traverse we captured, we found corpses or bodies still twitching. We killed each other, sight unseen. We too suffered losses. A piece of iron crashed to

Grenade battle as ballet

the ground next to the orderly, which the fellow was unable to avoid; and he collapsed to the ground, while his blood issued on to the clay from many wounds.

We hurdled over his body, and charged forward. Thunderous crashes pointed us the way. Hundreds of pairs of eyes were lying in wait behind rifles and machine-guns in the dead land. We were already a long way in front of our own lines. From all sides, bullets whistled round our steel helmets or struck the trench parapet with a hard crack. Each time a black iron oval broke the horizon, one's eye sized it up with that instantaneous clarity of which a man is only capable in moments of life and death. During those instants of waiting, you had to try to get to a place where you could see as much of the sky as possible, because it was only against its pale backdrop that it was possible to see the black jagged iron of those deadly balls with sufficient clarity. Then you hurled your own bomb, and leaped forward. One barely glanced at the crumpled body of one's opponent; he was finished, and a new duel was commencing. The exchange of hand-grenades reminded me of fencing with foils; you needed to jump and stretch, almost as in a ballet. It's the deadliest of duels, as it invariably ends with one or other of the participants being blown to smithereens. Or both.

In those moments, I was capable of seeing the dead – I jumped over them with every stride – without horror. They lay there in the relaxed and softly spilled attitude that characterizes those moments in which life takes its leave. During my leaping progress, I had a difference of opinion with the subaltern, who was really quite a card. He wanted to be first, and insisted that I supply him with bombs, rather than throw them myself. In amongst the short terrible shouts that accompany the work, and by which you alert the other to the presence of the enemy, I would sometimes hear him: 'One *man* to throw! And after all I was the instructor at the storm troop training!'

A trench that led off to the right was cleaned up by soldiers of the 225th, who were trailing in our wake. British soldiers caught in a cleft stick tried to flee across the open fields, but were mown down in the fire that straight away was directed at them from all sides.

And those soldiers we were pursuing gradually felt the Siegfried Line becoming too hot for them. They tried to disappear down a communications trench that led off to the right. We jumped up on to the sentry steps, and saw something that made us shout with wild glee: the trench they were trying to escape down doubled back on itself towards ours, like the curved frame of a lyre, and, at the narrowest point, they were only ten paces apart! So they had to pass us again. From our elevated position, we were able to look down on the British helmets as they stumbled in their haste and excitement. I tossed a hand-grenade in front of the first lot, bringing them up short, and after them all the others. Then they were stuck in a frightful jam; hand-grenades flew through the air like snowballs, covering everything in milk-white smoke. Fresh bombs were handed up to us from below. Lightnings flashed between the huddled British, hurling up rags of flesh and uniforms and helmets. There were mingled cries of rage and fear. With fire in our eyes, we jumped on to the very lip of the trench. The rifles of the whole area were pointed at us.

Suddenly, in my delirium, I was knocked to the ground as by a hammer blow. Sober, I pulled off my helmet and saw to my terror that there were two large holes in it. Cadet Mohrmann, leaping up to assist me, assured me that I had a bleeding scratch at the back of my head, nothing more. A bullet shot from some distance had punched through my helmet and only brushed my skull. Half unconscious, I reeled back with a hurriedly applied bandage, to remove myself from the eye of the storm. No sooner had I passed the nearest traverse than a man ran up behind me and told me that Tebbe had just been killed in the same place, by a shot in the head.

That news floored me. A friend of mine with noble qualities, with whom I had shared joy, sorrow and danger for years now, who only a few moments ago had called out some pleasantry to me, taken from life by a tiny piece of lead! I could not grasp the fact; unfortunately, it was all too true.

In this murderous sector of trench, all my NCOs and a third of my company were bleeding to death. Shots in the head rained down. Lieutenant Hopf was another one of the fallen, an older man, a teacher by profession, a German schoolmaster in the best sense of the word. My two ensigns and many others besides were wounded. And yet, the 7th Company held on to the conquered line, under the command of Lieutenant Hoppenrath, the only able-bodied officer remaining, until we were relieved.

Of all the stimulating moments in a war, there is none to compare with the encounter of two storm troop commanders in the narrow clay walls of a line. There is no going back, and no pity. And so everyone knows who has seen one or other of them in their kingdom, the aristocrat of the trench, with hard, determined visage, brave to the point of folly, leaping agilely forward and back, with keen, bloodthirsty eyes, men who answered the demands of the hour, and whose names go down in no chronicle.

On the way back, I stopped with Captain von Brixen for a moment, who with a few troops was shooting at a row of heads over a nearby parallel trench. I stood between him and the other marksmen, and watched the bullets striking home. In the dreamlike mood that followed the shock of my wounding, it never occurred to me that my white turban-like bandage must be visible miles away.

Suddenly a blow to the forehead knocked me to the floor, while my eyes were drenched with blood. The man next to me fell at the same time, and started to moan. Shot in the head through steel helmet and temple. The captain feared he had lost two company commanders on one day, but on inspection could make out only two surface wounds near the hairline. They must have been caused by the bursting bullet, or perhaps splinters from the helmet of the wounded man. This same man, with whom I shared pieces of metal from the same bullet, came to visit me after the war; he worked in a cigarette factory, and, ever since his wound, had been sickly and a little eccentric.

Weakened by further loss of blood, I accompanied the captain, who was returning to his command post. Skirting the heavily shelled village of Mœuvres at a jogtrot, we got back to the dugout in the canal bed, where I was bandaged up and given a tetanus injection.

In the afternoon, I got on a lorry, and had myself driven to Lécluse, where I gave my report to Colonel von Oppen over supper. After sharing a bottle of wine with him, feeling half asleep but in a wonderful mood, I said good-night, and, following this immense day, hurled myself with a meritorious feeling on to the bed that my trusty Vinke had made up for me.

A couple of days after that, the battalion moved into Lécluse. On 4 December, the divisional commander, General von Busse, addressed the battalions involved, singling out the 7th Company. I marched them past, bandaged head held high.

I had every right to be proud of my men. Some eighty men had taken a long stretch of line, capturing a quantity of machine-guns, mortars and other *matériel*, and taken some two hundred prisoners. I had the pleasure of being able to announce a number of promotions and distinctions. Thus, Lieutenant Hoppenrath, the leader of the shock troops, Ensign Neupert, the stormer of the pillbox, and the brave barricade defender, Kimpenhaus, all got to wear the well-earned Iron Cross, First Class, on their breasts.

I didn't bother the hospitals with my fifth double-wounding, but allowed them to heal over the course of my Christmas leave. The scrape to the back of my head got better quickly, the shards in my forehead grew in, to provide company for two others that I'd got at Regniéville, one in my left hand, the other in my earlobe.

At this time, I was surprised by the Knight's Cross of the House of Hohenzollern, which was sent to me at home.

That gold-edged cross and a silver cup bearing the legend 'For the Victor of Mœuvres', which the other three company commanders in the battalion presented to me, are my souvenirs of the double battle of Cambrai, which will enter the history books as the first attempt to break out of the deadly stasis of trench-fighting by new methods.

I also brought back my holed helmet, and keep it as a pendant to the other one that the lieutenant-colonel of the Indian Lancers had worn when leading his men against us.

At the Cojeul River

Even before my furlough, on 9 December 1917, we were called
upon to relieve the 10th Company in the front line after not many
days of rest. The position was, as already mentioned, in front of
the village of Vis-en-Artois. My sector was bordered on the right
by the Arras–Cambrai road, and on the left by the boggy course
of the Cojeul river, across which we stayed in touch with the
neighbouring company by means of nocturnal patrols. The
enemy lines were obscured from sight by a little rise in the ground
between our two positions. Apart from occasional patrols who
fiddled with our wires at night, and the hum of an electricity
generator at Hubertus-Ferme not far off, the enemy infantry gave
few signs of life. Distinctly unpleasant, though, were frequent
attacks by gas shells, which caused quite a few casualties. These
were delivered by several hundred iron pipes fitted into the
ground, torched electrically in a flaming salvo. As soon as it lit,
the cry of gas went up, and whoever didn't have his mask in front
of his face by the time the things landed was in a bad way. In
some places, the gas had such density that even the mask didn't
help, because there was simply no oxygen left in the air to breathe.
And so we incurred losses.

My shelter was dug back into the vertical wall of a gravel pit
that gaped behind the line, and was shelled almost every day.
Behind it rose the blackened iron skeleton of a destroyed sugar
factory.

That gravel pit was an eerie place indeed. In amongst the shell-holes where used weaponry and materials were dumped were the crooked crosses marking graves. At night, you couldn't see your hand in front of your face, and had to wait from the expiry of one flare to the going up of another if you weren't to leave the duckboard path and come to a watery end in the Cojeul.

If I wasn't busy with the construction of the trench, I spent my days in the icy shelter, reading and drumming my feet against the dugout frames to keep them warm. A bottle of *crème de menthe* in a niche in the limestone served the same purpose, and my orderlies and I swore by it.

We were freezing; but if the least little plume of smoke had gone up into the murky December sky from the gravel pit, the place would soon have been rendered uninhabitable, because the enemy seemed to take the sugar factory for our headquarters, and expended most of their powder on that old iron shell. So it was only really after dark that the life came back into our frozen bones. The little stove was lit, and spread a cosy warmth, as well as thick smoke. Before long the ration parties were back from Vis, and came clattering down the steps with their canteens, which were much awaited. And then, if the endless succession of swedes, barley and dried vegetables happened to be interrupted for once by beans or noodles, why then, there was no limit to our contentment. Sometimes, sitting at my little table, I would listen happily to the earthy conversations of the orderlies, as they hunkered, wreathed in tobacco smoke, round the stove, where a pot of grog was steaming headily. War and peace, fighting and home-life, rest-billet and leaves were discussed in great detail, and there were a good few pithy sayings besides. For instance, the orderly went away on leave with the words: 'There's nothing like being in your own bed at home, and your old woman nuzzling you all over.'

On 19 January, we were relieved at four in the morning, and marched off through thick snow to Gouy, where we were to spend some time training for the imminent offensive. From the instructions issued by Ludendorff as far along the chain as company commanders, we concluded that there was a mighty do-or-die offensive in the offing.

We practised the almost-forgotten forms of skirmishing in line and open warfare, also there was a lot of target-practice with rifle and machine-gun. Since every village behind the line was full up to the last attic, every roadside was used for a target, and the bullets sometimes went whizzing around all over the shop, as if in a real battle. A machine-gunner from my company shot the commander of another regiment out of the saddle while he was reviewing some troops. Luckily, it was nothing more than a flesh wound in the leg.

Several times I had the company practise attacks on complicated trench networks, using live hand-grenades, to turn to account the lessons of the Cambrai battle. Here, too, there were casualties.

On 24 January, Colonel von Oppen left to take command of a battalion in Palestine. He had led the regiment, whose history is inextricably bound up with his name, from the autumn of 1914 without interruption. Colonel von Oppen was living proof that there is such a thing as a born leader. He was always surrounded by a nimbus of confidence and authority. The regiment is the largest unit whose members know one another; it's the largest military family, and the stamp of a man like von Oppen shows clearly in thousands of common soldiers. Sad to say, his parting words: 'See you back in Hanover!' were never to come about; he died shortly afterwards of Asiatic cholera. Even after I'd heard the news of his death, I received a letter from him. I owe him a very great deal.

On 6 February, we returned to Lécluse, and on the 22nd, we were accommodated for four days in the cratered field left of the Dury–Hendecourt road, to do digging work in the front line. Viewing the position, which faced the ruined village of Bullecourt,

I realized that part of the huge push which was expected up and down the whole Western Front would take place here.

Everywhere there was feverish building, dugouts were constructed, and new roads laid. The cratered field was plastered with little signs stuck in the middle of nowhere, with ciphered letters and numbers, presumably for the disposition of artillery and command posts. Our aeroplanes were up all the time, to keep the enemy from getting a look. To keep everyone synchronized, on the dot of noon every day a black ball was lowered from the observation balloons, which disappeared at ten past twelve.

At the end of the month, we marched back to our old quarters in Gouy. After several battalion and regimental drills, we twice rehearsed an entire divisional breakthrough, on a large site marked with white ribbons. Afterwards, the commander addressed us, giving us to understand that the storm would be let loose in the next few days.

I have happy memories of the last evening we sat round the table, heatedly discussing the impending war of movement. Even if, in our enthusiasm, we spent our last pennies on wine, what else did we need money for? Before long, we would either be through the enemy lines, or else in the hereafter. It was only by reminding us that the back area still wanted to live that the captain kept us from smashing all the glasses, bottles and plates against the wall.*

We had no doubt but that the great plan would succeed. Certainly, if it didn't, it wouldn't be through any fault of ours. The troops were in fine fettle. If you listened to them speak in their dry Lower Saxon tones of the forthcoming 'Hindenburg Sprint', you knew they would handle themselves as they always did: tough, reliable, and with a minimum of fuss.

On 17 March, after sundown, we left the quarters we had

---

* In accordance with the German proverb 'Scherben bringen Glück', shards or breakages are lucky.

come to love, and marched to Brunemont. The roads were choked with columns of marching men, innumerable guns and an endless supply column. Even so, it was all orderly, following a carefully worked-out plan by the general staff. Woe to the outfit that failed to keep to its allotted time and route; it would find itself elbowed into the gutter and having to wait for hours till another slot fell vacant. On one occasion we did get in a little jam, in the course of which Captain von Brixen's horse impaled itself on a metalled axle and had to be put down.

The Great Battle

The battalion was quartered in the château of Brunemont. We
heard that we were to move up on the night of 19 March, to be
put in reserve in the dugouts in the line near Cagnicourt, and that
the great push was to begin on the morning of 21 March 1918.
The regiment had orders to punch through between the villages
of Ecoust-St-Mein and Noreuil, and to reach Mory on the first
day. We were well acquainted with the terrain; it had been our
back area in the trench-fighting at Monchy.

I dispatched Lieutenant Schmidt, known universally as
'Schmidtchen' as he was such a lovely fellow, on ahead to secure
quarters for the company. At the pre-arranged time, we marched
out of Brunemont. At a crossroads, where we picked up our
guides, the companies fanned out. When we were level with the
second line, where we were to be quartered, it turned out our
guides had lost their way. We found ourselves roving around in
the poorly lit, boggy, cratered landscape, and asking other,
equally uninformed troops for directions. To avoid overtiring the
men, I called a halt, and sent the guides out in different directions.

Sections piled arms and squeezed into a vast crater, while
Lieutenant Sprenger and I perched on the rim of a smaller one,
from which we could see into the big one, as from a box in the
theatre. For some time now, shells had been landing a hundred
paces or so in front of us. A shell landed quite close by; splinters
splattered into the clay sides of the crater. A man yelled and

claimed he'd been hurt in the foot. While I felt the man's muddy boot, looking for a hole, I called to the men to disperse among the surrounding shell-holes.

There was another whistle high up in the air. Everyone had the choking feeling: this one's heading our way! Then there was a huge, stunning explosion – the shell had hit in our midst.

Half stunned I stood up. From the big crater, burning machine-gun belts spilled a coarse pinkish light. It lit the smouldering smoke of the explosion, where a pile of charred bodies were writhing, and the shadows of those still living were fleeing in all directions. Simultaneously, a grisly chorus of pain and cries for help went up. The rolling motion of the dark mass in the bottom of the smoking and glowing cauldron, like a hellish vision, for an instant tore open the extreme abysm of terror.

After a moment of paralysis, of rigid shock, I leaped up, and like all the others, raced blindly into the night. I tumbled head-first into a shell-hole, and only there did I finally grasp what had happened. – Not to see or hear anything any more, out of this place, off into deep darkness! – But the men! I had to tend to them, they were my responsibility. – I forced myself to return to that terrible place. On the way, I saw Fusilier Haller, who had captured the machine-gun at Regniéville, and I took him with me.

The wounded men were still uttering their terrible cries. A few crawled up to me, and when they recognized my voice, wailed: 'Lieutenant, sir, Lieutenant!' One of my best-loved recruits, Jasinski, whose thigh had been crumpled by a splinter, grabbed hold of my legs. Cursing my inability to be of assistance, I patted him feebly on the back. Moments like that are not easily shaken off.

I had to leave the unlucky ones to the one surviving stretcher-bearer in order to lead the handful of unhurt men who had gathered around me from that dreadful place. Half an hour ago at the head of a full battle-strength company, I was now wandering around a labyrinth of trenches with a few, completely demoralized men. One baby-faced fellow, who was mocked a few days ago by his comrades, and on exercises had wept under the weight of the big munitions boxes, was now loyally carrying them on our heavy way, having picked them up unasked in the crater. Seeing that did for me. I threw myself to the ground, and sobbed hysterically, while my men stood grimly about.

After spending several hours, often menaced by shells, running hopelessly up and down trenches, where the mud and water were feet deep, we crept exhausted into a few cubby-holes meant for munitions that were set in the walls of a trench. Vinke covered me with his blanket; even so, I couldn't close my eyes, and smoked cigars while I waited for the dawn, feeling completely apathetic.

First light showed the cratered scene full of unsuspected life. Troops were trying to find their units. Artillerymen were lugging crates of ammunition, trench-mortar men pulled their mortars along; telephonists and light-signallers were rigging up their lines. There were all kinds of chaotic activities going on, barely half a mile from the enemy, who, extraordinarily, seemed to have no idea.

At last, in Lieutenant Fallenstein, the commander of the machine-gun company, an old front officer, I met someone who was able to show me our quarters. He greeted me with: 'Good Christ, man, you look frightful! You look like you've got jaundice.' He pointed out a large dugout that we must have passed a dozen times that night, and there I saw Schmidtchen, who knew nothing of our calamity. The soldiers who had been supposed to guide us were also there. From that day forth, each time we moved into new quarters, I took care to choose the guides myself. In war you learn your lessons, and they stay learned, but the tuition fees are high.

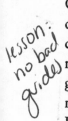

After I had seen my men settled in, I returned to the site of last night's horror. The place looked grisly. Scattered around the scorched site were over twenty blackened bodies, almost all of them burned and flayed beyond recognition. We had to enter some of the dead as 'missing' later, because there was simply nothing left of them.

Soldiers from the adjacent parts of the line were busy pulling the bloodied effects of the dead out of the horrible tangle, and looking through them for booty. I chased them off, and instructed my orderly to take possession of the wallets and valuables to save them for the men's families. As it turned out, we had to leave it all behind the next day, when we went over the top.

To my delight, Sprenger emerged from a nearby dugout with a whole lot of men who had spent the night there. I had the section leaders report to me, and found out that we had sixty-three men. And the previous night, I'd set out in high spirits with a hundred and fifty! I was able to identify over twenty dead and sixty wounded, many of whom later died of their injuries. My inquiries involved a lot of looking around in trenches and craters, but it had the effect of distracting me from the horror.

My one, feeble consolation was that it might have been even worse. Fusilier Rust, for instance, was standing so close to the bomb blast that the straps on his munitions box caught fire. NCO Pregau, who, admittedly, went on to lose his life the next day, was not even scratched as he stood between two comrades who were torn to ribbons.

We spent the rest of the day in pretty low humour, much of it sleeping. I was frequently called away to see the battalion commander, as there were many details of the attack to be settled. Otherwise, lying on a bunk, I conversed with my two officers on all kinds of trivial subjects, all to escape our tormenting thoughts. The refrain was: 'Well, thanks be to God, all that can happen is we get shot.' A few remarks that I addressed to the men gathered on the dugout steps, to try to cheer them up, seemed to have little effect. I was hardly in a cheer-bringing mood.

At ten, a messenger arrived with instructions to go to the front line. A wild animal dragged from its lair, or a sailor feeling the deck sinking under his feet, must have felt like us as we took our leave of the warm, secure dugout and headed out into the inhospitable darkness.

There was already some activity. We dashed down Felix Lane under sharp shrapnel fire, and reached the front line without casualties. While we were wending our way along the trenches, over our heads the artillery was being trundled across bridges into forward positions. The regiment, whose most-advanced battalion we were to be, had been given a very narrow sector of the front. Every dugout was immediately jammed. Those left in the cold dug themselves holes in the trench walls, so as to have at least minimal protection against the artillery barrage that was to be expected before the attack. After a lot of toing and froing, it seemed everyone had some kind of foxhole. Once more Captain von Brixen assembled the company commanders to talk through the plan. For the last time, watches were synchronized, and then we all shook hands and went our separate ways.

I sat down with my two officers on the dugout steps, to wait for five past five, when the preliminary shelling was due to start. The mood had lifted somewhat, as the rain had stopped, and the starry night gave promise of a dry morning. We chatted and smoked. At three o'clock there was breakfast, and a flask went the rounds. During the early morning hours, the enemy artillery was so lively we feared the British might have caught a whiff of something. A few of the numerous munitions dumps dotted around blew up.

Shortly before the show, the following flash signal was circulated: 'His Majesty the Kaiser and Hindenburg are on the scene of operations.' It was greeted with applause.

The watch-hands moved round; we counted off the last few minutes. At last, it was five past five. The tempest was unleashed.

A flaming curtain went up, followed by unprecedentedly brutal roaring. A wild thunder, capable of submerging even the loudest detonations in its rolling, made the earth shake. The gigantic roaring of the innumerable guns behind us was so atrocious that

even the greatest of the battles we had experienced seemed like a tea party by comparison. What we hadn't dared hope for happened: the enemy artillery was silenced; a prodigious blow had laid it out. We felt too restless to stay in the dugout. Standing out on top, we gasped at the colossal wall of flame over the English lines, gradually obscuring itself behind crimson, surging clouds.

The only thing that took the edge off our enjoyment of this spectacle were our watering eyes and inflamed mucous membranes. The clouds of our gas shells, beaten back by a headwind, wrapped us in a powerful aroma of bitter almonds. I looked on in concern as some of the men started coughing and choking, and finally tore the masks off their faces. I was therefore at pains myself to suppress any cough, and breathe slowly and carefully. Finally, the cloud dispersed, and after an hour it was safe to take off our gas masks.

It had become light. At our rear, the massive roaring and surging was still waxing, even though any intensification of the noise had seemed impossible. In front of us an impenetrable wall of smoke, dust and gas had formed. Men ran past, shouting cheerily in our ears. Infantrymen and artillerymen, pioneers and telephonists, Prussians and Bavarians, officers and men, all were overwhelmed by the elemental force of the fire-storm, and all were impatient to go over the top at nine-forty. At twenty-five past eight our heavy mortars, which were standing massed behind our front lines, entered the fray. We watched the daunting two-hundredweight bombs loop high up into the air, and come crashing down with the force of volcanic eruptions on the enemy lines. Their impacts were like a row of spurting craters.

Even the laws of nature appeared to have been suspended. The air swam as on hot summer days, and its variable density caused fixed objects to appear to dance to and fro. Shadows streaked through the clouds. The noise now was a sort of absolute noise – you heard nothing at all. Only dimly were you aware that thousands of machine-guns behind you were slinging their leaden swarms into the blue air.

The last hour of the preparation was more dangerous than all four of its predecessors, during which we had moved around insolently on the parapets. The enemy brought in a heavy battery that hurled shell after shell into our overcrowded lines. To move out of the way, I turned left and met Lieutenant Heins, who asked me if I'd seen Lieutenant Solemacher: 'He's wanted to take over command, Captain von Brixen's fallen.' Shaken by this news, I went back, and sat myself in a deep foxhole. By the time I got there, I had forgotten what I'd been told. I was as in a dream, sleepwalking through this storm.

NCO Dujesiefken, my comrade at Regniéville, was standing in front of my foxhole, begging me to get into the trench as even a light shell bursting anywhere near would cause masses of earth to come down on top of me. An explosion cut him off: he sprawled to the ground, missing a leg. He was past help. I jumped over him, and darted into a foxhole on the right, where a couple of pioneers had already sought shelter. Heavy shells continued to rain down all round us. You suddenly saw black clumps of earth spinning out of a white cloud; the sound of the explosion was engulfed by the noise level. In the sector to our left, three men from my company were torn to pieces. One of the last hits, a dud, killed poor Schmidtchen as he sat on the dugout steps.

I was standing with Sprenger, watch in hand, in front of my foxhole, waiting for the great moment to come. The rest of the company had clustered round. We managed to cheer and distract them with a few crude jokes. Lieutenant Meyer, who briefly stuck his head round the traverse, told me later he thought we were out of our minds.

At ten past nine, the officer patrols who were to cover our advance left the trench. Since the two positions were perhaps half a mile apart, we had to move forward during the artillery preparation, and lie ready in no man's land, to be able to leap into the first enemy line as soon as nine-forty came. A few minutes later, then, Sprenger and I climbed up on to the top, followed by the rest of the company.

'Now let's show them what the 7th are made of!' 'I'm past caring what happens to me!' 'Revenge for the 7th Company!' 'Revenge for Captain von Brixen!' We drew our pistols and climbed over the wires, through which the first of the wounded were already dragging themselves back.

I looked left and right. The moment before the engagement was an unforgettable picture. In shell craters against the enemy line, which was still being forked over and over by the fire-storm, lay the battalions of attackers, clumped together by company. At the sight of the dammed-up masses of men, the breakthrough appeared certain to me. But did we have the strength and the stamina to splinter also the enemy reserves and rend them apart? I was confident. The decisive battle, the last charge, was here. Here the fates of nations would be decided, what was at stake was the future of the world. I sensed the weight of the hour, and I think everyone felt the individual in them dissolve, and fear depart.

The mood was curious, brimming with tension and a kind of exaltation. Officers stood up and exchanged banter. I saw Solemacher standing there in a long coat in the midst of his little staff, a short pipe with a green bowl in his hand, like a huntsman on a cold day, waiting for the gillies to do their work. We exchanged a fraternal wave. Often a mortar would fall short, and a shower of earth as high as a steeple would cover the waiting men, and no one would even flinch. The noise of battle had become so terrific, that no one was at all clear-headed.

Three minutes before the attack, Vinke beckoned to me with a full water-bottle. I took a long pull, as though it were indeed only water I was drinking. Now just the cigar was missing. Three times the air pressure snuffed out my match.

The great moment was at hand. The wave of fire had trundled up to the first lines. We attacked.

Our rage broke like a storm. Thousands must have fallen already. That was clear; and even though the shelling continued, it felt quiet, as though it had lost its imperative thrust.

No man's land was packed tight with attackers, advancing singly, in little groups or great masses towards the curtain of fire. They didn't run or even take cover if the vast plume of an explosion rose between them. Ponderous, but unstoppable, they advanced on the enemy lines. It was as though nothing could hurt them any more.

In the midst of these masses that had risen up, one was still alone; the units were all mixed up. I had lost my men from sight; they had disappeared like a wave in the crashing surf. All I had with me were my Vinke and a one-year volunteer by the name of Haake. In my right hand, I gripped my pistol, in my left, a bamboo riding-crop. Even though I was feeling hot, I was still wearing my long coat, and, as per regulations, gloves. As we advanced, we were in the grip of a berserk rage. The overwhelming desire to kill lent wings to my stride. Rage squeezed bitter tears from my eyes.

The immense desire to destroy that overhung the battlefield precipitated a red mist in our brains. We called out sobbing and stammering fragments of sentences to one another, and an impartial observer might have concluded that we were all ecstatically happy.

The shredded wire entanglements provided no obstacle at all, and we cleared the first trench, barely recognizable as such, in a single bound. The wave of attackers danced like a row of ghosts through the white seething mists of the flattened dip. There was no one here to oppose us.

Quite unexpectedly, the clatter of machine-gun fire rattled at us from the second line. I and my companions jumped into a crater. Another second, and there was a fearsome crash, and I sprawled on my face. Vinke grabbed me by the collar, and twisted me round on to my back: 'Lieutenant, are you hurt?' There was no sign of anything. The one-year volunteer had a hole in his upper arm, and assured us in groans that the bullet had lodged in his back. We tore the tunic off him and bandaged him up. A smooth furrow showed that a shrapnel shell had struck the lip of the crater on a level with our faces. It was a miracle we were still alive. It seemed the enemy were more obdurate than we'd given them credit for.

Others by now had overtaken us. We plunged after them, leaving our wounded man to his fate, having put up a piece of wood with a white strip of gauze hanging from it as a sign for the wave of stretcher-bearers that would follow. Half left of us the great railway embankment of the Ecoust–Croisilles line loomed up out of the haze; we had to get across that. From built-in loopholes and dugout windows, the rifle and machine-gun fire was pattering at us so thickly it was like having a sack of dried peas emptied over you. They could see what they were doing too.

Vinke had disappeared somewhere. I followed a defile, from whose sides flattened dugouts gaped. I strode along furiously, across the black opened ground that the acrid fumes of our shells seemed to cling to. I was quite alone.

Then I saw my first enemy. A figure in brown uniform, wounded apparently, crouched twenty paces away in the middle of the battered path, with his hands propped on the ground. I turned a corner, and we caught sight of each other. I saw him jump as I approached, and stare at me with gaping eyes, while I, with my face behind my pistol, stalked up to him slowly and coldly. A bloody scene with no witnesses was about to happen. It was a relief to me, finally, to have the foe in front of me and within reach. I set the mouth of the pistol at the man's temple – he was too frightened to move – while my other fist grabbed hold of his tunic, feeling medals and badges of rank. An officer; he must have held some command post in these trenches. With a plaintive sound, he reached into his pocket, not to pull out a weapon, but a photograph which he held up to me. I saw him on it, surrounded by numerous family, all standing on a terrace.

It was a plea from another world. Later, I thought it was blind chance that I let him go and plunged onward. That one man of all often appeared in my dreams. I hope that meant he got to see his homeland again.

Men from my company were jumping down into the defile from above. I was boiling hot. I tore off my coat, and threw it away. I remember shouting: 'Now Lieutenant Jünger's throwing off his coat!' several times, and the fusiliers laughing, as if it had been the funniest thing they'd ever heard. Everyone was pouring across the open terrain, careless of the machine-guns that can have been no more than four hundred yards away. I too ran blindly towards the fire-spitting embankment. In some crater, I landed on top of a pistol-potting figure in brown corduroy. It was Kius, who was in a similar mood to me, and who passed me a fistful of cartridges by way of greeting.

I concluded from that that our penetration into the cratered area in front of the railway embankment must have hit upon some resistance, because I had taken a good supply of pistol bullets with me before we set out. Probably it was the rest of the troops who had been dislodged from the trenches and had settled here, popping up in various places in among the attackers. But as far as this part of the story goes, I have no recollection. All I know is I must have got through it, and unhurt, even though there was firing from craters on all sides, not to mention the bullets fizzing down from the embankment on friend and foe alike. They must have had an inexhaustible supply of ammunition in there.

Our attention now shifted to that obstacle, which loomed up in front of us like a menacing wall. The scarred field that separated us from it was still held by hundreds of scattered British. Some were trying to scramble back, others were already engaged in hand-to-hand fighting with our forward troops.

Kius later told me things that I took in with the same sort of feeling as when some eyewitness tells you of amazing japes or stunts that you performed while drunk. For instance, he had been chasing a British soldier through a section of trench with hand-grenades. When he ran out of missiles, to keep his opponent on the run, he continued the chase with lumps of earth, while I stood up above, splitting my sides with laughter.

Amid such scenes, we had come up to the embankment, barely realizing it. It was still spewing fire like a great machine. Here my recollection begins again, with the registration of an extremely advantageous position. We hadn't been hit, and now that we were right up against it, the embankment changed from being an obstacle to being cover for us. As though waking from a deep dream, I saw German steel helmets approaching through the craters. They seemed to sprout from the fire-harrowed soil like some iron harvest. At the same time, I noticed that right by my foot there was the barrel of a heavy machine-gun, stuck through a dugout window covered over with sacking. The noise was such that it was only the vibration of the barrel that told us that it was firing. The defender was only an arm's length away from us then. It was that degree of proximity that kept us safe. And that spelled his doom. Hot haze rose from the weapon. It must have hit a great many men, and it was still mowing. The barrel moved little; its fire was aimed.

I fixed the hot, shaking piece of steel that was sowing death, and that I could almost brush with my foot. Then I shot through the sacking. A man who turned up next to me ripped it clean away, and dropped a hand-grenade in the hole. A shock and the issue of a whitish cloud told the rest of the story. The means were rough, but satisfactory. The muzzle no longer moved, the weapon had stopped firing. We ran along the embankment to treat the next holes in similar fashion, and so we must have broken a few vertebrae out of the spine of the defence. I raised my hand to let my troops, whose shots were ringing round our ears, know who we were and what we were about. They waved happily back. Then we and a hundred others scaled the embankment. For the first time in the war, I saw masses of men collide. The British were defending a couple of terraced trenches the other side of the embankment. Shots were exchanged at point-blank range, hand-grenades looped down.

I leaped into the nearest trench; plunging round the traverse, I ran into an English officer in an open jacket and loose tie; I grabbed him and hurled him against a pile of sandbags. An old white-haired major behind me shouted: 'Kill the swine!'

There was no point. I turned to the lower trench, which was seething with British soldiers. It was like a shipwreck. A few tossed duck's eggs, others fired Colt revolvers, most were trying to run. We had the upper hand now. I kept firing off my pistol as in a dream, although I was out of ammunition long ago. A man next to me lobbed hand-grenades at the British as they ran. A steel helmet took off into the air like a spinning plate.

It was all over in a minute. The British leaped out of their trenches, and fled away across the field. From up on the embankment, a wild pursuing fire set in. They were brought down in full flight, and, within seconds, the ground was littered with corpses. That was the disadvantage of the embankment.

German troops were also down among them. An NCO stood next to me watching the fighting open-mouthed. I seized his rifle and shot an Englishman who was tangling with a couple of Germans. They stopped in bafflement at the invisible assistance, and then ran on.

Our success had a magical effect. There was no question of leadership, or even of separate units, but there was only one direction: forwards! Every man ran forward for himself.

For my objective I selected a low rise, on which I could see the ruins of a house, a cross, and the wreckage of an aeroplane. Others were with me; we formed a pack, and in our eagerness ran into the wall of flame laid down by our own artillery. We had to throw ourselves in a crater and wait while the shelling moved forward. Next to me there was a young officer from another regiment, who, like me, was delighted with the success of this first charge. In a few minutes, the intensity of our mutual enthusiasm gave us the feeling we'd known each other for years. Then we leaped up, and never saw each other again.

Even in these frightful moments, something droll could happen. A man next to me pulled his rifle to his cheek and pretended to shoot at a rabbit that suddenly came bounding through our lines. It all happened so abruptly, I had to laugh. Nothing is ever so terrible that some bold and amusing fellow can't trump it.

Beside the ruined cottage lay a piece of trench that was being swept with machine-gun fire from beyond. I jumped into it, and found it untenanted. Immediately afterwards, I was joined by Oskar Kius and von Wedelstädt. An orderly of Wedelstädt's, the last man in, collapsed in mid-leap, and was dead, shot through one eye. When Wedelstädt saw this last member of his company fall, he leaned his head against the wall of the trench and cried. He wouldn't get through the day either.

Below us was a strongly fortified position across a defile, with a couple of machine-gun nests on the slopes in front of it, one either side. Our artillery had already steamrollered past; the enemy seemed to have recovered, and was shooting for all he was worth. We were perhaps five hundred yards away, and the spurts of fire buzzed across it like swarms of bees. _machine guns_

After a short pause for breath, not many of us headed over the top towards the enemy. It was all or nothing. After a few paces, there was just me and one other man facing the left-hand machine-gun. I could clearly see the head under a flat helmet behind the earthworks, next to a fine spout of steam. I approached in very short steps, to leave him no time to aim, and ran in a zigzag, to elude rifle bullets. Each time I hit the deck, my man offered me another clip of ammunition with which to carry the fight. 'Cartridges! Cartridges!' I turned round, and saw him lying on his side, twitching.

From the left, where the resistance seemed to be weaker, some men came running up and were almost within hand-grenade range of the defenders. I covered the final yards and tumbled over some wire right into the trench. The British, under fire from all sides, abandoned their position and the machine-gun, and fled across to the other position. The machine-gun was half buried under an enormous pile of brass cartridges. It was steaming and red-hot. Stretched out in front of it lay my adversary, an athletic-looking Englishman with one eye put out by a shot to the head. The colossus with the big white eyeball against his smoke-charred skull looked gruesome. As I was almost fainting with thirst, I didn't hang around but went looking for water. A dugout entrance looked promising. I put my head round the corner, and saw a man sitting at the bottom, fitting bullets into a belt over his knee. He seemed to have no idea that the situation had been transformed. I calmly levelled my pistol at him, but instead of squeezing the trigger, as common sense dictated, I called out: 'Come here, hands up!' He jumped up, looked at me wildly, and scampered into the back of the dugout. I threw a grenade after him. The dugout probably had a further entrance, because a soldier came round a traverse and observed laconically: 'He won't be doing no more shooting.'

At last, I managed to find a canister of cooling-water. I gulped down the oily liquid, slushed some more into an English canteen, and handed it to comrades who suddenly filled the trench.

As a curious footnote, I should like to mention that my first thought on forcing my way into this machine-gun nest concerned the cold from which I was suffering. All my life, I've had a tendency to throat inflammation; therefore, when I pressed my thumbs under my jaw, I was pleased to note that the vigorous exercise I'd taken had – like a sauna – helped me sweat off this latest bout.

Meanwhile, the right-hand machine-gun nest and the defenders of the defile sixty yards in front of us were still putting up a grim fight. The fellows really were giving it everything. We tried to aim their own machine-gun at them, but didn't manage that; instead, as I was trying that, a bullet whizzed past my head, brushed the Jager lieutenant who was standing behind me, and finished up giving a private a very nasty-looking wound in the thigh. A light machine-gun crew had better luck setting up their weapon on the edge of our little semi-circle and began raking the British from the flank.

The troops attacking on the right took advantage of the distraction we provided and attacked the defile head-on, led by our still-intact 9th Company under the command of Lieutenant Gipkens. And now from every shell-hole figures poured forth, swinging rifles and chasing with a fearsome hurrah towards the enemy position, from where defenders emerged in great numbers. They started running away with their arms aloft, to escape the initial fury of the first wave of shock troops, in particular that of Lieutenant Gipkens's orderly, who was rampaging like a berserker. I observed the confrontation, which took place just beyond our little earthworks, with rapt attention. Here I saw that any defender who continued to empty his pistol into the bodies of the attackers four or five paces away could not expect any mercy when they were upon him. The fighter, who sees a bloody mist in front of his eyes as he attacks, doesn't want prisoners; he wants to kill.

The captured defile was lined with weapons, uniforms and supplies. Dotted all about were dead men in grey and brown uniforms, and groaning wounded. Soldiers from all different regiments were standing together in a thick knot, all shouting and chattering at once. Officers pointed out to them the continuation of the dip, and the heap of fighters, gradually, with surprising indifference, started moving forward again.

The dip ran up into higher ground, where enemy columns appeared. Occasionally stopping to shoot, we advanced until we were stopped by fierce fire. It was a sobering feeling, having the bullets smash into the ground round our heads. Kius, who had turned up again, picked up a flattened bullet that had stopped inches from his nose. At that instant, a man far to the left of us was hit on the helmet, and the ringing echoed throughout the dip. We took advantage of a momentary lull in the firing to scoot into one of the not very many shell-holes there were hereabouts. There I met up with the other surviving officers of our battalion again, which was now being commanded by Lieutenant Lindenberg, since Lieutenant von Solemacher had been fatally shot in the stomach during the storming of the embankment. On the right edge of the little valley, to the general amusement, Lieutenant Breyer – who had been seconded to us from the 10th Jagers – was strolling about seemingly oblivious of the flying bullets, walking-stick in hand, and long huntsman's pipe in mouth, rifle slung over his shoulder, every bit as though out shooting rabbits.

We told each other quickly what we'd been through, and handed round canteens and bars of chocolate, then, 'by popular demand', we resumed our advance. The machine-guns, apparently under threat from the flank, had been withdrawn. We had probably taken two or three miles back already. The dip was now swarming with attackers. As far back as the eye could see, they were advancing in open order, ranks and columns. It was unfortunate that we were so densely packed; how many we left behind on the attack we luckily had no way of knowing.

Without meeting any resistance, we climbed to the top. To our right, khaki-clad figures were spilling out of a trench. We followed the example given us by Breyer, who, without taking the pipe out of his mouth, briefly stood still to loose off a round or two, and then marched on.

The heights were fortified by an unevenly distributed series of dugouts. They were not defended; probably our approach had gone unnoticed by the men in them. In some cases, clouds of smoke showed that they had already been flushed out, elsewhere

it was the men themselves that emerged, pale and with their hands in the air. They were made to hand over canteens and cigarettes, then they were pointed to our rear, in which direction they vanished with some alacrity. One young British soldier had already surrendered to me when he suddenly turned round and disappeared back in his dugout. Then, as he stayed there, apparently ignoring my call to come out, we put an end to his dithering with a few hand-grenades, and went on. A narrow footpath disappeared over the crest of the hill. A signpost said it led to Vraucourt. While the others were still busy looking over the dugouts, I passed the crest of the hill, with Heins.

Down below lay the ruins of Vraucourt. In front of it we could see the flashing muzzles of an artillery battery whose men took flight as our first wave approached and they came under fire. The occupants of a row of dugouts along the side of the path also ran away. I encountered one such as he was just about to leave the last one.*

Along with a couple of men from my company who had hooked up with me, I proceeded down the path. To the right of it was a fortified line, from where we came under heavy fire. We retreated to the first of the dugouts, over which the bullets of both sides were soon flying back and forth. It looked as though it had been a base for messengers and bicyclists attached to the artillery. Outside it lay my British soldier, little more than a boy, who had been hit in the temple. He lay there, looking quite relaxed. I forced myself to look closely at him. It wasn't a case of 'you or me' any more. I often thought back on him; and more with the passing of the years. The state, which relieves us of our responsibility, cannot take away our remorse; and we must exercise it. Sorrow, regret, pursued me deep into my dreams.

---

* A little gnomic, but I think we are to understand EJ shoots him. Hence, below, 'my British soldier'. Earlier editions were much more explicit on this point and others similar.

Ignoring the crescendo of firing, we settled into the dugout, and helped ourselves to the supplies left behind, since our stomachs reminded us that we hadn't eaten anything since the beginning of the attack. We found ham, white bread, jam and a stone jar of ginger beer. After I had fortified myself, I sat down on an empty biscuit case, and browsed in some English newspapers, all of them full of invective against 'the Huns'. After a while, we got bored, and scampered back to the beginning of the path, where a large number of men had by now assembled. From up there, we could see a battalion of the 164th already up alongside Vraucourt to the left. We decided to storm the village, and hurried back down the path. Just outside the village, we were stopped by our own artillery, which was pounding the same spot over and over again. A heavy shell landed plumb on the path, and killed four of our men. The others ran back.

As I found out later, the artillery had been given orders to carry on firing at the furthest extent of their range. This incomprehensible order snatched the fruits of victory from our hands. Grinding our teeth with fury, we had to make a halt before the wall of fire.

To look for a chink, we moved right, where a company commander of the 76th Hanseatic Regiment was just giving orders for an attack on Vraucourt. We joined in with gusto, but no sooner had we got into the village than we once more found ourselves under fire from our own artillery. Three times we charged in, and three times we were forced back. Cursing, we set up in a few craters, where a grass fire that the shelling had started, and that took off many wounded men, was extraordinarily unpleasant. Also, English rifle bullets accounted for a few men, among them Corporal Grützmacher from my own company.

Gradually, it got dark. Except for occasional flare-ups, the rifle fire gradually died down. The tired fighters looked for somewhere to lie down. Officers yelled their own names till they were hoarse, in an attempt to reassemble their companies.

In the course of the last hour, a dozen men of the 7th Company had grouped themselves round me. As it was starting to get cold, I led them back to the little dugout outside which my Englishman lay, and sent them out to find coats and blankets from the fallen. Once I had settled them all, I surrendered to my curiosity, and had a shufti at the artillery in the valley below. It was a bit of free enterprise, so I only took Fusilier Haller with me, who was adventurously inclined. Rifles at the ready, we strode down to the valley, which was still taking a pounding from our artillery, and began by inspecting a dugout that had apparently only recently been abandoned by British officers. On a table sat a huge gramophone, which Haller straight away set going. The cheery melody that purred off the roll had a ghostly effect on both of us. I threw the box on the ground where it scraped on a little longer, and then fell silent. The dugout was the height of luxury, even down to a little open fireplace with a mantelpiece with pipes and tobacco on it, and armchairs pulled round in a circle. *Merry old England!* Of course we didn't stint ourselves, but helped ourselves to whatever we fancied. I took a haversack, undergarments, a little flask full of whisky, a map case and some exquisite little items from Roger & Gallet, no doubt keepsakes from some romantic leave in Paris. We could see that the inhabitants had left here in a hurry.

looting

An adjacent space harboured the kitchen, whose supplies we stared at in wonder. There was a whole crate of eggs, which we sucked on the spot, as eggs were little more than a word to us at this stage. On shelves along the walls were stacks of canned meat, tins of delicious English jam, and bottles of Camp coffee, tomatoes and onions; everything to delight an epicure's heart.

It was a scene I often came back to later, when we lay for weeks in trenches, on meagre bread rations, watery soup and thin nondescript jam.

After that peek into the enviable circumstances of our foes, we left the dugout and investigated the valley, where we found two spanking-new artillery pieces. Great piles of gleaming, freshly fired shell-casings indicated that they had had a thing or two to say in the course of our attack. I picked up a piece of chalk, and chalked up the number of my company. I hadn't yet learned that the victor's rights were accorded scant respect by the following units; each one wiped away the mark of their predecessor, and wrote up their own, till the last one was that of some digging outfit.

Then, with our artillery still slinging iron about our ears, we went back to the others. Our front line, formed now from reserve troops, was a couple of hundred yards behind us. I posted two men outside the dugout, and told the others to keep their rifles handy. Then, after arranging the reliefs, having a little more to eat, and jotting down the day's happenings, I went to sleep.

At one o'clock in the morning, we were roused by hurrahs and brisk fire from our right. We grabbed our rifles, plunged out of the dugout, and took up positions in a large shell-hole. From ahead of us came a few scattered German soldiers, who received fire from our ranks. Two of them remained on the path. Alerted by this incident, we waited for the initial excitement behind us to die down, shouted out who we were, and returned to our own line. There we found the commander of the 2nd Company, Lieutenant Kosik, with a wound in the arm and such a heavy cold he couldn't speak, with roughly sixty men of the 73rd. Since he had to go back to the dressing-station, I took over the command of his detachment, which included three officers. Apart from them there were also the similarly thrown-together companies under Gipkens and Vorbeck.

The rest of the night I spent with some NCOs of the 2nd, in a little dugout where we all but froze to death. In the morning, I breakfasted off looted supplies, and dispatched runners to Quéant, to fetch coffee and food from the kitchens. Our own artillery started its bloody cannonade again, its first good-morning to us being a direct hit in a crater that was housing four men from a

machine-gun company. At first light, our group was reinforced
by Vice-Sergeant-Major Kumpart and some men under him.

No sooner had we managed to stamp the cold out of our chilly
bones than I received orders to band together with what was left
of the 76th and storm the Vraucourt positions – which we had
already begun to take – to the right of where we presently were.
In thick morning fog, we moved off to the jumping-off position,
a plateau south of Ecoust, where many lay dead from the previous
day. There was, as generally happens when orders are unclear,
some argy-bargy among the officers, which was only settled when
a machine-gun sent a spray of bullets whistling round our legs.
Everyone dived into the nearest crater, except for Vice-Sergeant-
Major Kumpart, who was left lying on the ground, groaning. I
hurried across to him with a medical orderly, to get him bandaged
up. He had a bad wound in the knee. With a bent pair of tongs,
we pulled out several fragments of bone from the wound. He
died a few days later. I was more than usually upset, because
Kumpart had been my drill instructor three years previously, in
Recouvrence.

In discussion with Captain von Ledebur, who was now in
overall command of our assorted units, I spoke of the futility of
a frontal attack, arguing that with part of the Vraucourt position
already in our hands, we could roll it up from the left with far
fewer casualties. We decided to spare our men the ordeal, and
the events were to prove us right.

For the time being, we made ourselves comfortable in some
craters on the plateau. By and by, the sun broke through, and
British aeroplanes appeared, dusting our holes with machine-gun
bullets, but they were driven away by our own planes. In the
Ecoust Valley, we saw a battery drive up, a rare sight for an old
front soldier; it was pretty promptly demolished too. A horse
broke loose and galloped over the landscape; a pale roan, looking
ghostly as it flew over the wide, lonely plains under the shifting

and variable clouds of explosive. The enemy aeroplanes were not long gone before we came under fire. First, there were a few shrapnels, then lots of shells, big and small. They had us on a plate. Timorous natures multiplied the effect of the fire by running mindlessly here and there, instead of getting their heads down in a crater somewhere and taking their punishment. You have to be a fatalist in such situations. I confirmed my adherence to that creed by sampling the delicious contents of a can of gooseberry jam I'd picked up from the British stores. And I pulled on a pair of Scottish woollen socks I'd found in the dugout. Gradually, the sun climbed higher.

For some time, we'd been able to observe activity on the left of the Vraucourt position. Now we could see the arc and the white puffs of German stick-bombs. That was our cue.

I gave the order to advance – or, rather, I raised my right arm, and set off towards the enemy position. We got into their trench without encountering much in the way of fire, and jumped in, getting a joyous welcome from a storm troop of the 76th. We made slow progress, rolling up the line with hand-grenades, as we'd done at Cambrai. Unfortunately, it soon dawned on the enemy artillery that we were making remorseless progress along their line. A sharp bombardment with shrapnels and light shells just caught the back of those of us who were in the van, and did worse to reserve troops who were just running up towards the trench. We noticed the artillerymen could see what they were firing at. That gave us the gee-up we needed to finish off the job as soon as we could, and slip in under the fire.

It appeared that the Vraucourt position was still being built, because some stretches of trench were merely indicated by the removal of the turf. Each time we came across a piece like that, we drew fire on us from several sides. We repaid the enemy in kind when it was their turn to dash across these death-strips, so that these undug places were before long thickly sown with the injured and dead. There was a wild hunt under clouds of shrapnel.

We raced past stout figures, still warm, with strong knees under their short kilts, or we crawled past them. They were Highlanders, and their way of fighting showed us that we were dealing with real men.

When we had made a few hundred yards in this fashion, the ever-thicker hail of rifle- and hand-grenades forced us to pause. It seemed the tide was about to turn. There was some fear in the air; I heard agitated voices.

'Tommy's counter-attacking!'

'Hold your ground!'

'I want to check that we're in touch!'

'More hand-grenades to the front; hand-grenades, for Christ's sake, hand-grenades!'

'Watch out, Lieutenant!'

Small reverses can be a serious matter in trench-fighting. A little troop makes its way to the van, shooting and throwing. As the grenade-throwers leap backwards and forwards to get out of the way of the lethal projectiles, they encounter the men coming up behind, who have got too near. The result is confusion. Maybe some men will jump over the top, and get themselves picked off by snipers, which encourages the rest of the enemy like nobody's business.

I managed to summon up a handful of men with whom I formed a focus of resistance behind a wide traverse. There was an open stretch of trench between the Highlanders and ourselves. At a distance of only a few yards, we exchanged shots with our invisible opponents. It took pluck to hold your head up when the bullets were pinging around, and the sand was being sprayed out of the traverse. One man beside me from the 76th, a huge Herculean dockworker from Hamburg, fired off one shot after another, with a wild look on his face, not even thinking of cover, until he collapsed in a bloody heap. With the sound of a plank crashing down, a bullet had drilled through his forehead. He crumpled into a corner of the trench, half upright, with his head

247

pressed against the trench wall. His blood poured on to the floor of the trench, as if tipped out of a bucket. His snore-like death-rattle resounded in lengthening intervals, and finally stopped altogether. I seized his rifle, and went on firing. At last there was a pause. Two men who had been just ahead of us tried to make it back over the top. One toppled into the trench with a shot in the head, the other, shot in the belly, could only crawl into it.

We hunkered down on the floor to wait, and smoked English cigarettes. From time to time, well-aimed rifle-grenades came flying over. We were able to see them, and take evasive action. The man with the wound in the belly, a very young lad, lay in amongst us, stretched out like a cat in the warm rays of the setting sun. He slipped into death with an almost childlike smile on his face. It was a sight that didn't oppress me, but left me with a fraternal feeling for the dying man. Even the groaning of his comrade gradually fell silent. He died in our midst, shuddering.

We made several attempts to work our way forward at the undug places, by crawling in among the bodies of the Highlanders, but were driven back each time by sniper fire and rifle-grenades. Almost every hit I saw was deadly. And so, the fore part of the trench was gradually filling up with the dead and wounded; but all the time reinforcements were arriving at the back. Before long, every traverse had a light or heavy machine-gun behind it. With the help of these, we held the British end of the trench in check. I took my turn behind one of the lead-spitters, and fired till my index finger was black with smoke. It might have been here that I hit the Scotsman who wrote me a nice letter from Glasgow afterwards, with an exact description of the location where he got his wound. Each time the cooling-water had evaporated, the canisters were passed around and topped up by a natural procedure that occasioned some crude humour. Before long the weapons were red-hot.

The sun was low over the horizon. It seemed as though the

second day of battle was over. For the first time, I took a close look at my whereabouts, and sent back a report and sketch. Five hundred paces from where we were, our trench intersected the Vraucourt–Mory road, which was camouflaged by lengths of cloth. On a slope behind it, enemy troops were hurrying across the field, with shells bursting all around them. The cloudless evening sky was crossed by a squadron of planes marked with our black, red and white. The last rays of the sun, which had already gone down, daubed them a shade of delicate pink, so they looked like flamingoes. We opened out our maps, and turned them face down, indicating to those above how far we had already pushed into the enemy line.

A cool breeze gave promise of a bitter night. Wrapped in my warm English coat, I leaned against the trench wall, chatting with little Schultz, who had accompanied me on the patrol against the Indians, and had turned up, in the timeless way of comrades, just where things were looking tough, toting four heavy machine-guns. Men of all companies sat on the fire-steps, the young, keen faces under the steel helmets, eyeing the enemy lines. I saw them looming stock-still out of the dim of the trench, as though on turrets. Their officers had fallen; it was by their own instincts that they were standing in exactly the right place now.

We were already settling in for a night of what we have we hold. I laid my pistol and a dozen British duck's egg grenades next to me, and felt myself a match for all comers, even the most obdurate Scotsman.

Then there came the sound of more hand-grenades from the right, while on the left German flares went up. Out of the gloaming rose a faint distant cheer. It caught on. 'We've got round the back of them! We've got round the back of them!' In one of those moments of enthusiasm that precede great actions, all reached for their rifles, and stormed forward along the trench. A brief exchange of hand-grenades, and a bunch of Highlanders were seen running for the road. Now there was no stopping us. In spite of warning cries: 'Watch out, the machine-gun on the left is still shooting!' we leaped out of the trench, and in no time had reached the road, which was swarming with disorientated Highlanders. They were fleeing, but their own entanglement was in the way. Briefly they paused, then they started running parallel to it. To our tumultuous shouts, they had to run the gauntlet. And that was the moment little Schultz turned up with his machine-guns.

The road presented an apocalyptic scene. Death was reaping great swathes. The echoing cry of war, the intense fire of handguns, the dull force of bombs, all exhilarated the attackers and lamed the defenders. All that long day the battle had been smouldering away; now it caught and burned. Our superiority grew with every second, because the narrow wedge of shock troops, now fanning out, was followed by broad sections of reinforcements.

When I reached the road, I looked down on to it from a steep embankment. The Scottish position was in a deepened ditch on the other side, it was some way below where we were. In those first few seconds, though, we were distracted from it; the vision of the Highlanders charging along the wire entanglement was all we had eyes for. We threw ourselves down along the top of the embankment, and fired. It was one of those very rare moments when the opposition have been driven into an impasse, and you feel the burning desire to be everywhere at once.

Swearing and trying desperately to fix my jammed pistol, I felt someone striking me hard on the shoulder. I spun round and looked into the contorted face of little Schultz. 'The bloody bastards are still firing!' I followed the direction he was pointing in, and finally spotted a line of figures in the little warren of trenches barely the other side of the road from us, some loading, some with their rifles to their cheeks, feverishly busy. From the right came the first hand-grenades, one tossing the body of a Scotsman high up into the air.

Common sense advised staying where we were and disabling

the enemy from there. He was an easy target. Instead, I threw away my rifle and plunged between the lines with my bare fists. Unluckily, I was still in my English coat, and my red-trimmed forage cap. There I was already, on the other side, and in enemy clothes! In the midst of the rush of victory, I felt a sharp jolt on the left side of my breast. Night descended on me! I was finished.

I supposed I'd been hit in the heart, but the prospect of death neither hurt nor frightened me. As I fell, I saw the smooth, white pebbles in the muddy road; their arrangement made sense, it was as necessary as that of the stars, and certainly great wisdom was hidden in it. That concerned me, and mattered more than the slaughter that was going on all round me. I fell to the ground, but, to my astonishment, I got to my feet again straight away. As I could see no hole in my tunic, I turned to the enemy once more. A soldier from my company ran up to me: 'Lieutenant, sir, take your coat off!' and he ripped the dangerous garment from my shoulders.

A new cheer rent the air. From the right, where all afternoon they had been working with hand-grenades, a number of Germans now ran across the road in support, headed by a young officer in brown corduroy. It was Kius. He was lucky enough to have been sent flying by a trip-wire in the very instant that an English machine-gun was about to fire its last rounds. The spray of bullets flew past him – so close, admittedly, that a bullet ripped open a wallet he carried in his trouser pocket. The Scots were now dealt with in moments. The area around the road was covered with the dead, while the few survivors were pursued by bullets.

In the brief seconds of my unconsciousness, little Schultz had also met his fate. As I was to hear later on, in that raving of his with which he had infected me, he had leaped into the trench to carry on rampaging there. When a Scot, who had already taken off his belt to surrender, saw him charging towards him in that condition, he picked up a rifle off the ground, and brought him down with a mortal bullet.

I stood, talking to Kius, in the conquered stretch of trench, heavy with the fog of hand-grenades. We were talking about how we should take the field guns that must be very near by. Suddenly he interrupted me: 'Are you wounded? There's blood coming out under your tunic!' Indeed, I could feel a curious lightness and a sensation of damp on my chest. We tore open my shirt, and saw that a bullet had passed through my chest directly under my Iron Cross, and diagonally over my heart. There was a little round entry wound on the right, and a slightly larger exit wound on the left. Since I had been leaping from left to right across the road, at a sharp angle, there was no doubt but that one of our troops had taken me for a Britisher, and shot at me from very close range. I strongly suspected it might be the man who had torn off my coat, and yet he had meant well by me, so to speak, and I had myself to blame.

Kius wrapped a bandage round me and with some difficulty prevailed upon me to leave the battlefield. We parted with a: 'See you in Hanover!'

I chose a fellow to accompany me, and returned to the fire-swept road, to pick up my map case, which my unknown helper had pulled off me along with the English coat. It contained my diary. Then we walked back, through the trench we had fought so hard to take.

Our battle cries had been so loud that the enemy artillery had woken up. The area beyond the road and the trench itself was under an extraordinarily thick barrage. Since the wound I had was quite sufficient for me, I made my way back cautiously, dodging from traverse to traverse.

Suddenly there was a deafening crash on the edge of the trench. I got a blow on the skull, and fell forward unconscious. When I came round, I was dangling head down over the breech of a heavy machine-gun, staring down at a pool of blood that was growing alarmingly fast on the floor of the trench. The blood was running down so unstoppably that I lost all hope. As my escort assured me he could see no brains, I took courage, picked myself up, and trotted on. That was what I got for being so foolish as to go into battle without a steel helmet.

In spite of my twofold haemorrhage, I was terribly excited, and told everyone I passed in the trench that they should hurry to the line, and join the battle. Before long, we were out of range of the light artillery, and could slow down, as the isolated heavy shells would only strike you if your number was up.

In the sunken road leading from Noreuil, I passed the brigade headquarters, had myself announced to Major-General Höbel, reported to him on our triumph, and asked him to send reinforcements to help the storm troops. The general told me I'd been reported dead the day before. It wasn't the first time that had happened in this war. Perhaps someone had seen me collapse in the assault on the first trench where the shrapnel wounded Haake.

I learned further that our progress had been slower than had been hoped. Evidently, we had been up against some elite troops of the British; our advance had gone through a series of strongpoints. The railway embankment had barely been grazed by our heavy artillery; we had simply charged it, in defiance of all the rules of warfare. We had not managed to reach Mory. Perhaps we could have done, had our artillery not got in our way. The opposition had been reinforced overnight. Everything that could be achieved by will-power had been, and perhaps more; the general conceded that.

In Noreuil, we passed a great stack of grenade boxes well ablaze. We hurried past with very mixed feelings. Just after the village, a driver gave me a ride on his empty munitions lorry. I had a sharp difference of opinion with the officer in charge of the munitions column, who wanted to have two wounded Britishers who had supported me for the latter part of the journey thrown off the lorry.

The traffic on the Noreuil–Quéant road was quite indescribable. No one who has not seen such a thing for himself can have any idea of the endless columns of vehicles and men that go towards making an offensive. Beyond Quéant, the crush became mythical. I felt a momentary pang when passing little Jeanne's house, which was reduced to its foundations.

I sought help from one of the traffic officers, distinguished by white armbands, who gave me a place in a private car to the field hospital at Sauchy-Cauchy. We were regularly made to wait for up to half an hour while wagons and lorries got disentangled on the road. Even though the doctors in the field hospital were feverishly busy, the surgeon found time to be surprised at the luck I'd had with my injuries. The wound to my head also had entry and exit wounds, and the skull had not been fractured. Far more painful than the wounds, which to me had felt like dull blows, was the treatment I received from a hospital assistant, once the doctor had stylishly pushed a probe through both wounds. That treatment consisted of scraping the edges of the wound to my head with a blunt blade and no soap.

After an excellent night's sleep, I was driven the following morning to the casualty clearing-station at Cantin, where I was delighted to see Sprenger, whom I hadn't seen since the beginning of the offensive. He had a bullet wound to the thigh. I also found my baggage waiting for me – further proof, if proof were needed, of Vinke's dependability. He had, once we had lost sight of one another, been wounded in the attack on the railway embankment. Before taking himself to the field hospital, and thence back to his farm in Westphalia, he would not rest until he knew that the things of mine that were in his care were safely in my possession. That was him all over; not so much a servant as my older comrade. Often enough, when rations were meagre, I would find a piece of butter waiting at my place at table, 'from a member of the company who wishes to remain nameless', though it was never hard to guess who. He was no adventurer, like Haller, but he followed me into battle like the squires of yore, and he thought his responsibility lay in nothing less than the care of my person. Long after the war was over, he wrote to me for a photograph 'so that I can tell the grandchildren about my lieutenant'. It is to him that I owe an insight into the stolidity and decency of the common people, of the character of the territorial soldier.

After a brief stay in the Bavarian field hospital at Montigny, I was put on a hospital train in Douai and taken to Berlin. There, this sixth double-wound of mine healed in a fortnight, just as well as all its predecessors had. The only unpleasant after-effect was an incessant ringing in my ears. As the weeks passed, it grew fainter and finally went away altogether.

It wasn't until I was back in Hanover that I heard that, along with many other friends and acquaintances, little Schultz had fallen in the fighting. Kius had got away with a harmless abdominal wound. At the same time, his camera had been broken, and a number of photographs of our attack on the railway embankment were lost.

Anyone who witnessed the celebration of our reunion in a little bar in Hanover, at which my brother with his stiff arm and Bachmann with a stiff knee also attended, would hardly have thought that barely a fortnight previously we had all been listening to other music than the merry popping of champagne corks.

Even so, there was a shadow over those days, because before long we understood from the news reports that the offensive had bogged down, and that, in strategic terms, it had failed. This was confirmed for me by the French and British newspapers I read in cafés in Berlin.

The Great Battle was a turning-point for me, and not merely because from then on I thought it possible that we might actually lose the war.

The incredible massing of forces in the hour of destiny, to fight for a distant future, and the violence it so surprisingly, stunningly unleashed, had taken me for the first time into the depths of something that was more than mere personal experience. That was what distinguished it from what I had been through before; it was an initiation that had not only opened the red-hot chambers of dread but had also led me through them.

British Gains

On 4 June 1918, I rejoined the regiment on rest near Vraucourt, which was now a long way behind the front line. The new commander, Major von Lüttichau, gave me the command of my old 7th Company.

As I drew near my quarters, the men rushed out to meet me, carried my bags for me, and gave me a hero's welcome. It was like returning to the bosom of a family.

We were staying in a group of corrugated-tin huts in the middle of neglected grass fields, amidst whose green innumerable yellow flowers glowed. The wild terrain, which we dubbed 'Wallachia', was grazed by herds of horses. If you stepped outside the door of your hut, you felt the intimidating sense of emptiness that oftentimes comes over the cowboy, the bedouin, and other inhabitants of wild, desert spaces. In the evenings, we would go for long walks around the barracks, looking for partridges, or for weapons half buried in the grass, souvenirs of the Great Battle. One afternoon, I rode up to the defile at Vraucourt that had been so dearly fought over two months before, whose edges were now rimmed with graves, on which I recognized quite a few names.

Before long, the regiment received orders to enter the line just ahead of the village of Puisieux-au-Mont. We rode on lorries overnight as far as Achiet-le-Grand, often compelled to pull over when the light from parachute flares dropped by bombers picked out the white ribbon of road from the surrounding darkness. The various whinings of the heavy bombs were engulfed by the rolling blasts of their detonation. Then searchlights probed the skies for the treacherous night birds, shrapnels exploded like toys, and tracer shells loped after one another in long chains like fiery wolves.

A persistent smell of carrion hung over the conquered territory, sometimes unbearable, sometimes not so bad, but always nettling the senses like an embassy from another country.

'Eau d'offensive,' I heard the voice of an old veteran next to me, as we seemed to have been going down an avenue lined with mass graves for the past several minutes.

From Achiet-le-Grand, we marched along the railway line leading to Bapaume, and then went cross-country to our position. The shelling was pretty lively. When we paused to rest once, a couple of medium shells landed very close. The memory of that unforgettable night of terror on 19 March assailed us. We were approaching the front line when we marched past a rowdy company that had obviously just been relieved, and was standing by; a few dozen shrapnels soon shut them up. With a hail of obscenities, my men dived into the nearest trench. A couple weren't so lucky, and needed to go back to the field dressing-station to get themselves patched up.

At three o'clock, completely exhausted, I pitched up at my dugout, whose cramped dimensions promised a rather uncomfortable stay.

The reddish light of a candle was burning in a thick fug. I tripped over a tangled mass of legs, and the magic word 'Relief!' brought some animation to the place. From an oven-shaped hole came a series of oaths, and then by and by there appeared an unshaven face, a pair of tarnished shoulder-pieces, an ancient uniform, and two clumps of clay, which presumably contained boots. We sat down at the rickety table and sorted out the hand-over, each trying to do the other out of a dozen iron rations

offensive

and a couple of flare pistols. Then my predecessor was disgorged through the narrow entryway, predicting that the rotten hole wouldn't last another three days. I remained behind, the newly promoted captain of A Sector.

The position, when I came to inspect it the following morning, was not a gladsome sight. No sooner had I left the dugout than I saw two bloodied coffee-carriers coming towards me, who had been hit by shrapnel in the communication trench. A few steps along, and Fusilier Ahrens reported himself hit by a ricochet and unfit to continue.

We had the village of Bucquoy ahead of us and Puisieux-au-Mont at our backs. The company was without support in a shallow position, separated from our neighbours on the right, the 76th infantry, by a wide untenanted gap. The left edge of our sector was formed by a piece of splintered woodland, known as Copse 125. In compliance with orders, no deep dugouts had been excavated. We were not to dig in, but remain on the offensive. We didn't even have any wire entanglements in front of the line. The men sheltered by twos in little holes in the ground with so-called tin Siegfrieds in front of them – curved ovals of corrugated metal about three feet high, which we put in front of the tight oven-shaped hide-outs.

Since my own dugout was behind another sector, I started by looking for new accommodation. A hut-like construction in a collapsed bit of trench looked like just the thing to me, once I had made it into a defensible proposition by hauling together various murderous weapons. There, with my orderlies, I led a hermit's life in the open, only occasionally bothered by runners or messengers who brought their pieces of bumf even into this secluded spot. I would shake my head as I read, between the explosions of shells, of how, among other less-than-earth-shattering items, the local commandant of X had lost his black-and-brown terrier who answered to the name of Zippi; that is, if I didn't happen to be reading about a suit for maintenance brought by a serving girl, Makeben, against one Corporal Meyer. Sketches and frequent announcements kept us continually on the hop.

But to get back to my refuge, which I named 'Casa Wahnfried'. My only worry was its relative porosity; though it was secure enough, so long as nothing landed on top of it. At any rate, I was comforted by the thought that I was no better off than my men. At lunchtime, Haller would lay a blanket in a huge crater, which we had made a path to, for me to use as a suntrap. There, I would work on my tan, disturbed, on occasion, by shells or whizzing fragments of metal coming too near.

The nights brought heavy bombardments like swift, devastating summer thunderstorms. I would lie on my bunk on a mattress of fresh grass, and listen, with a strange and quite unjustified feeling of security, to the explosions all around that sent the sand trickling out of the walls. Or I would walk out to the fire-step to take in the mournful nocturnal scene, and the strange contrast between its heaviness and the fiery spectacle whose dance-floor it was.

At such moments, there crept over me a mood I hadn't known before. A profound reorientation, a reaction to so much time spent so intensely, on the edge. The seasons followed one another, it was winter and then it was summer again, but it was still war. I felt I had got tired, and used to the aspect of war, but it was from this familiarity that I observed what was in front of me in a new and subdued light. Things were less dazzlingly distinct. And I felt that the purpose with which I had gone out to fight had been used up, and no longer held. The war posed new, deeper puzzles. It was a strange time altogether.

The front line had relatively little to suffer from the enemy bombardment, which was just as well, because it could not have held if it had. It was principally Puisieux and the hollows around that were targets for the bombardments that in the evenings worked themselves up into extraordinary ferocity. Bringing food and relieving other units were both greatly complicated. Now here, now there, a chance hit would knock out a link of our chain.

On 14 June, I was relieved at two in the morning by Kius, who like me had come back and was now commanding the 2nd Company. We spent our rest period at the railway embankment at Achiet-le-Grand, in barracks and shelters in the lee of its protective bulk. The British often sent heavy low-trajectory shells our way. Rackebrand, a sergeant with the 3rd Company, fell victim to one such. He was killed by a shard that drilled through the wall of the flimsy hut that he had set up as a company office on top of the embankment. A few days before that, there had been a real catastrophe. A bomber pilot had dropped a bomb right on top of the 76th regimental band as it was playing, surrounded by listeners. Among its victims were many men from our regiment.

In the vicinity of the embankment, looking like stranded hulls, were many shot-up tanks, which I would inspect closely in the course of my peregrinations. Also, I would have my company cluster round them to study methods of combating them, their tactics and their weak points – these ever-more commonly seen elephants of the technical war. They carried names and emblems and designs that were variously ironic, menacing or lucky; there was the clover leaf and the pig (for luck), and the white death's head. One was distinguished by a gallows with a noose dangling from it; that one was called 'Judge Jeffries'. All of them were in a bad way. To be in the narrow turret of such a tank, going forward, with its tangle of rods and wires and poles, must have been extremely unpleasant as these colossuses, in efforts to out-manœuvre the artillery, were forced to zigzag over the country like huge helpless beetles. I felt keen sympathy for the men in those fiery furnaces. Also, the countryside was dotted about with the skeletal wreckage of downed aeroplanes, an indication that machines were playing an ever greater part on the battlefield.

One afternoon, not far from us, the huge white bell of a parachute came down, as a pilot leaped from his burning aeroplane.

On the morning of 18 June, on account of the volatile situation, the 7th was obliged to go back to Puisieux ahead of time, to be at the disposal of the commanding officer of the line troops for carrying parties and other purposes. We moved into shelters and basements facing out towards Bucquoy. Just as we arrived there, a group of heavy shells came down in the surrounding gardens. Even so, I wasn't deterred from taking my breakfast in a little gazebo in front of my shelter. After a while there was another one came whistling across. I dropped flat on the ground. Flames spurted beside me. An ambulanceman in my company by the name of Kenziora, who was just bringing several cooking pans full of water, fell, hit in the stomach. I ran over to him, and with the help of a signalman, dragged him into the dressing-station, whose entrance, as luck would have it, was just opposite the place where the shell burst.

'Well, did you at least have a proper breakfast inside you?' asked Doctor Köppen, a real old sawbones, who had had me under him once or twice in his time, as he bandaged up the big wound in his belly.

'Yes, I did, a big dixie full of noodles!' whimpered the unhappy fellow, perhaps catching a ray of hope.

'Well, there you are then,' Köppen said reassuringly, before turning aside to me and nodding at me with a grave expression on his face.

But gravely wounded men have very acute instincts. Suddenly the man groaned, and large beads of sweat stood out on his forehead: 'That shell's done for me, I can feel it.' But in spite of his prediction, I was able to shake his hand six months later, when the regiment returned to Hanover.

In the afternoon, I took a solitary walk through the devastated village of Puisieux. It had already received a hammering in the course of the battles of the Somme. The craters and ruins had

Ruined villages

been overgrown with thick grass, dotted about here and there with the gleaming white plates of elderflower, which loves ruins. Numerous fresh explosions had ripped holes in the cover, and exposed the soil all over again.

The main village street was lined with the debris of our recent stalled advance. Shot-up wagons, discarded munitions, rusty pistols and the outlines of half-decomposed horses, seen through fizzing clouds of dazzling flies, commented on the nullity of everything in battle. All that was left of the church standing on the highest spot of the village was a wretched heap of stones. While I picked a bunch of half-wild roses, landing shells reminded me to be careful in this place where Death danced.

A few days later, we relieved the 9th Company in the line of resistance, some five hundred yards behind the front. In the process, we of the 7th suffered three men wounded. The following morning, just by my dugout, Captain von Ledebur was wounded in the foot by a shrapnel ball. Even though he had galloping consumption, he felt the war was his vocation. It was his fate to succumb to that slight wound. He died soon after, in hospital. On the 28th, the commander of my ration party, Sergeant Gruner, was hit by a shell splinter. That was our ninth casualty in a short space of time.

FLU

Following a week on the front line, we were again moved back to the resistance line, since the battalion which was to relieve us was almost wiped out by Spanish influenza. Several men a day reported sick in our company as well. In the division next to ours, the epidemic raged to such an extent that an enemy airman dropped leaflets promising that the British would come and relieve them, if the unit weren't withdrawn. But we learned that the sickness was also spreading among the enemy; even though we, with our poor rations, were more prone to it. Young men in particular sometimes died overnight. And all the time we were to be battle-ready, as there was a continuous cloud of black smoke hanging over Copse 125 at all times, as over a witches' cauldron.

The shelling was so intense there, that on days of no wind the explosive vapours were strong enough to poison part of the 6th Company. We had to go down into the shelters, like divers with oxygen masks, to drag the unconscious men back to the surface. Their faces were cherry-red, and their breath came in nightmarish gasps.

One afternoon, stepping out of my sector, I came upon several half-buried boxes of British munitions. To study the construction of a rifle-grenade, I unscrewed one, and took out the detonator. Something was left behind, which I took to be the percussion cap. However, when I tried to unpick it with my nail, it turned out to be a second detonator, which exploded with a loud bang, took off the tip of my left index finger, and gave me several bleeding wounds in the face.

That same evening, as I was standing talking to Lieutenant Sprenger on top of my dugout, a heavy shell hit near us. We disagreed about the distance, Sprenger reckoning it was about ten paces off, I nearer thirty. To see how trustworthy my estimates might be in this respect, I stepped it out, and found the crater – of a size to accord with an unpleasant manufacture – to be twenty-five yards away.

The 20th of July found us back in Puisieux. I spent all afternoon standing on a piece of crumbling wall, and watched the condition of the line, which looked rather ominous to me. Occasional details I wrote down in my notebook.

Copse 125 was regularly sheeted in thick smoke rising from the massive explosions, under red and green flares that rose and fell. If the artillery was silent for any time, you could hear the tactactac of machine-guns, and the dull crack of hand-grenades going off in the distance. From where I stood, the whole thing looked almost like a game. It lacked the brutish scale of a big battle, but one could feel the tenacious wrestling for all that.

The copse was like a festering wound that both sides nagged and worried at. Both sets of artillery toyed with it, like a couple of beasts of prey, wrangling over a victim; they shredded its trees and flicked them into the air. It never had very large numbers of men in it, but it could be defended, and, as it was so conspicuous in that wasteland all around, it was always available as an instance of the way that even the most gigantic confrontation of forces is nothing but a mechanism by which today, as in every era throughout history, a man's weight is taken.

Towards evening, I was summoned to the commander of the troops in reserve, where I was told that the enemy had managed to penetrate the trench network on our left flank. In order to clear a little space in front of us again, the instructions were that Lieutenant Petersen with the storm company was to clear the hedge trench, while I with my men cleared the communication trench that ran in a hollow parallel to it.

We set out at daybreak, but immediately came under such strong infantry fire that we postponed our mission. I ordered Elbinger Alley to be occupied, and caught up on some sleep in a huge cavern of a dugout. At eleven in the morning I was woken up by cracks of hand-grenades coming from our left, where we had put up a barricade. I hurried over, and found the usual scene of close-quarters fighting. White hand-grenade clouds whirling over the barricade, machine-guns on either side set back a few traverses clattering away at each other. And in between men, leaping forward and darting back. The minor essay by the British had already been repulsed, but it had cost us a man lying behind the barricade, shredded by hand-grenade splinters.

In the evening I received orders to lead the company back to Puisieux, and when I arrived there I found I had instructions to go on a small-scale initiative with two sections of men the next morning. The purpose was to roll up the so-called Valley Trench from red point K to red point Z, and this was to happen at three-forty in the morning, following a five-minute artillery and mortar barrage. Unfortunately, this enterprise, for which Lieutenant Voigt would lead a storm troop, and I a couple of platoons,

Bad orders

had clearly been dreamed up from the map, because the Valley Trench, as its name suggested, followed the lowest line, and could be seen into from many vantage-points from top to bottom. I wasn't at all happy with the whole thing, or at least I wrote in my diary, after the order: 'Well, with luck I'll be able to describe it tomorrow. On account of pressure of time, I must reserve my opinion of the order – I'm sitting in the bunker in F Sector, it's midnight, and I'm being woken at 3.'

Still, orders are orders, and so three-forty found Voigt and me with our men all ready in the breaking light at the jumping-off point by Elbinger Alley. We were in a knee-deep trench from which we could look down into the valley, which began to fill at the agreed hour with smoke and flames. A large splinter that flew up from this seething mass to our position hurt Fusilier Klaves in the hand. I had the same spectacle before me that I had had so often already before attacks: the image of a group of men waiting in poor light, inclining their heads each time the guns fall short, or else prostrating themselves on the ground, all the while excitement steadily mounts – a scene that grips the spirit like some terrible silent ceremonial that portends human sacrifice.

We jumped off precisely on time, and were favoured by the dense pall of smoke that the bombardment had cast over the Valley Trench. Shortly before Z, we encountered resistance, and forced our way through with hand-grenades. As we had reached our objective, and were not keen to continue fighting, we erected a barricade and left behind a platoon with a machine-gun.

The only satisfaction I took from the whole event was from the way the storm troops comported themselves – they strongly reminded me of old Simplicissimus. They were a new breed of fighter so far as I was concerned, the volunteers of 1918: still raw, but instinctively brave. Those young dashers with long hair and puttees would start quarrelling among themselves twenty yards in front of the enemy because one had called the other a scaredy-cat, and yet they all swore like troopers and threw their

weight around no end. 'Christ, we're not all such funks as you
are!' yelled one, and rolled up another fifty yards of trench
single-handed.

The platoon I'd left at the barricade came back in the afternoon.
They had taken casualties, and not been able to hang on any
longer. I must confess, I'd already given them up for lost, and
was amazed that anyone could make it back alive down the long
line of the Valley Trench in daylight.

In spite of that, and various other counter-punches, the enemy
was well entrenched in the left flank of our front line, and in the
barricaded communications trenches, and threatening our line of
resistance. This kind of semi-detached arrangement, with no no
man's land dividing us, felt distinctly uncomfortable in the long
run; we had a clear sense of not being safe even in our own lines.

On 24 July, I went off to reconnoitre the new C section of the
line of resistance, which I was to take over on the following day.
I had the company commander, Lieutenant Gipkens, show me
the barricade along the Hedge Trench, which was unusual inasmuch as on the British side it comprised a disabled tank, which
had been integrated into the fortifications like a strongpoint. To
take in the details, we sat down on a little seat cut into the
traverse. As we were talking away, I was suddenly grabbed and
pulled down. The next second, a bullet struck the sand where I
had been sitting. By a lucky chance, Gipkens had noticed a rifle
barrel slowly being poked through a loophole in the block only
forty paces away. His sharp painter's eyes had saved my life,
because at that range I was a sitting duck. We had happened to
sit down in the short stretch between the lines, and were as visible
to the British sentry as if we'd been facing him across a table.
Gipkens had acted promptly and sensibly. When I came to analyse
the scene later, I wondered whether I might not have frozen at
the sight of the rifle. I was told that this harmless-looking place
had seen three men of the 9th Company shot in the head; it was
a bad place.

In the afternoon, a not especially heavy burst of shelling lured me out of my coal-hole, where I had just been sitting and reading comfortably over a cup of coffee. In front of us, the signals for a barrage were going up in monotonous succession. Wounded men hobbling back told us that the British had entered the resistance line in B and C Sectors, and were approaching it in A Sector. Straight afterwards, we had the bad news that Lieutenants Vorbeck and Grieshaber had been killed. They had fallen in defence of their sectors, and Lieutenant Kastner was badly wounded. He had had a near miss only a few days previously, when his right nipple had been sheared off by a bullet. It was as neatly done as if by a scalpel, and he suffered no other injury. At eight o'clock Sprenger, who was in temporary command of the 5th, came into my dugout with a splinter in his back, took a pull at a bottle to 'steady his nerves', and exited with the words: 'Go back, go back, Don Rodrigo.' His friend Domeyer followed shortly afterwards with a bleeding hand. His parting words were a little less literary.

The following morning, we reoccupied C Sector, which had once more been cleared of the enemy. We had pioneers there, Boje and Kius with part of the 2nd, and Gipkens with what was left of the 9th. There were eight dead Germans in the trench, and two British, with the badge on their caps reading 'South Africa – Otago Rifles'. Hand-grenades had made a mess of all of them. Their contorted faces were horribly mutilated.

I gave instructions for the block to be manned and the trench to be tidied up. At a quarter to twelve, our artillery opened fire rather wildly on the positions in front of us, doing more damage to us than they did to the British. Shortly afterwards tragedy struck. The cry 'Stretcher-bearers!' was passed along the line from the left. Hurrying to the spot, I found the scattered remnants of my best platoon sergeant at the barricade in the Hedge Trench. He had taken a direct hit from our own shell amidships. Tatters of his uniform and underwear, ripped away by the force of the explosion, were spread out across the ragged branches of the hawthorn hedge that gave the trench its name. I had a tarpaulin draped over him, to spare us the sight. Immediately afterwards, on the same spot, three more men were hurt. Lance-Corporal Ehlers, deafened by the air pressure, writhed on the ground. Another man had both hands severed at the wrist. He tottered back, his arms laid across the shoulders of a stretcher-bearer. The little procession reminded me of a heroic relief, the helper was walking stooped, while the wounded man struggled to remain upright – a young fellow, with black hair and a fine, determined, and now marmoreally pale face.

I sent one runner after another to headquarters, demanding that the shelling either stop forthwith, or else that artillery officers present themselves in the line. Instead of any form of reply, we had a still-heavier mortar, which turned the line into a complete shambles.

At seven-fifteen, I received very belated orders, from which I understood that at seven-thirty a strong bombardment would commence, and that at eight o'clock two sections of the storm company under Lieutenant Voigt were to break out across the barricade in the Hedge Trench. They were to roll up the trench as far as point A, and meet up with a shock troop that would proceed along a parallel line to the right of them. Two sections of my company were to follow on behind and occupy the trench.

I quickly issued the necessary commands – the artillery barrage was already beginning – picked out the two sections, and had a brief discussion with Voigt, who set out a few minutes afterwards, as per the instructions I'd received. As I thought of the whole business as a kind of glorified evening constitutional, with no further consequences, I strolled behind my two sections, in a cap, and with a stick-bomb under my arm. At the moment of the attack, announced by clouds of explosions, every rifle anywhere near was directed at the Hedge Trench. We darted forward from traverse to traverse, and made good headway. The British retreated to a line behind, leaving one casualty.

To explain what happened next, I must remind the reader that we were not following the line of a trench, but one of many communication lines, where the British, or rather the New Zealanders, had established a foothold. (We were fighting, as I learned after the war, from letters addressed to me from the Antipodes, against a contingent from New Zealand.) This communications line, the so-called Hedge Trench, led along a ridge; on the left and below was the Valley Trench. The Valley Trench, which I had rolled up with Voigt on 22 July, had been abandoned, as described, by the section we had left there; it was now once more occupied, or at least controlled, by the New Zealanders. The two lines were connected by various cross trenches; from the lower parts of the Hedge Trench, we were not able to see down into the Valley Trench.

I was following the section as it worked its way forward, feeling quite chipper, for as yet all I had seen of the enemy had been several figures fleeing over the top. Ahead of me, NCO Meier was bringing up the rear of the section, and, ahead of him, I could sometimes see, depending on the twists and turns of the trench, little Wilzek from my own company. And so we passed a narrow sap, which, climbing up out of the valley, connected with the Hedge Trench, like a kind of tributary. In between its two separate entrances, there was a sort of delta, a mound of earth perhaps five paces long, which had been left to stand. I had just passed the first juncture, Meier was approaching the second.

In trench-fighting, with forks of this kind, one usually posts two men as a sentry to guard the rear. This Voigt had either forgotten to do, or in his haste he had overlooked the sap altogether. In any case, I now heard the NCO ahead of me shout out in alarm, and saw him raise his rifle and fire just past my head into the second fork of the sap.

Since the block of earth meant I couldn't see into it, I was mystified by this, but all it took was a step back for me to be able to look down the first fork. What I saw was enough to freeze my blood, for there was a strongly built New Zealander practically near enough to touch. At the same time I heard the shouts of still-unseen attackers running up from the valley to cut us off. The New Zealander who had, as if by magic, appeared at our rear, and whom I stood gawping at helplessly, was unhappily for him unaware of my being there. All his attention was on the NCO, to whose shot he replied with a hand-grenade. I watched him detach one of his lemon-shaped bombs to throw at Meier, who tried to escape his death by charging forward. At the same time, I took out the stick-bomb, which was the only weapon I had on me, and didn't so much throw it as lob it at the feet of the New Zealander in a short arc. I wasn't there to see him go up, because it was the last possible moment in which I had any chance of being able to make it back. So I dashed back, and just caught a glimpse of little Wilzek, who had been sharp and calm enough to duck under the New Zealander's grenade, dash past Meier and follow me. One steel egg that was hurled in his direction ripped his belt and the seat of his trousers, but did no further damage. That was how tight the noose was that had been drawn around us, leaving Voigt and the other forty attackers surrounded and doomed. Without guessing anything of the strange event I had witnessed, they felt pressure behind them pushing them to their deaths. Shouts and numerous explosions suggested that they were selling their lives dearly.

To come to their aid, I led cadet Mohrmann's section forward along Hedge Trench. We were forced to pause by a rain of Stokes bombs. One splinter struck me in the chest, but was stopped by the clasp of my braces.

A vehement artillery bombardment now began. All around geysers of earth spouted up out of various-coloured steam, and the dull thump of shells bursting deep in the earth mingled with a high-pitched metallic yowl that sounded like a circular saw. Blocks of iron burst with incredible vehemence, interspersed with the singing and flickering of clouds of splinters. As there was every prospect of facing an attack, I put on one of the steel helmets I saw lying around, and hurried back to the firing trench with a few companions.

Figures surfaced in front of us. We laid ourselves on the mangled trench walls and fired away. Next to me, a very young soldier was fumbling with the trigger of his machine-gun, and not getting off a single shot, so I tore the thing from him. I fired some shots, but then as in a nightmare the thing failed again; luckily, though, the attackers vanished into trenches and craters as the artillery heated up. As for our own – it seemed to be directed equally against both sides.

As I went into my bunker, followed by an orderly, something struck the trench wall between us, ripping the helmet from my head and hurling it away into the distance. I thought I had caught a whole load of shrapnel, and lay half numbed in my foxhole, whose rim a moment later was struck by a shell. The little space was filled with thick smoke and a long splinter shattered a jar of gherkins at my feet. So as not to be crushed to death, I crawled back out into the trench, and from below urged the two orderlies and my batman to be alert.

It was a grim half-hour; the already reduced company was further mangled. After the artillery fire had abated, I walked the line, inspected the damage, and established that we were down to fifteen men. The long sector could not be held by so few. Therefore I assigned Mohrmann and three men to defend the barricade, and with the rest formed a hedgehog in a deep crater behind the back wall. From there, we could take a hand in the fight for the barricade, or, if the enemy succeeded in breaking into our line, attack him with hand-grenades from above. In the event, further action was limited to a few light mortars and rifle-grenades.

On 27 July, we were relieved by a company of the 164th. We were utterly exhausted. The commander of the relieving company was badly wounded on the way out; a few days later, my bunker was hit, and his successor buried. We all sighed with relief when we finally turned our backs on Puisieux and the storm of steel of the finale.

Their advances showed how much the enemy's strength was increasing, supplemented by drafts from every corner of the earth. We had fewer men to set against them, many were little more than boys, and we were short of equipment and training. It was all we could do to plug gaps with our bodies as the tide flooded in. There wasn't the wherewithal for great counter-attacks like Cambrai any more.

Later on, when I thought of the way the New Zealanders triumphantly ran up and forced our sections into that deadly bottleneck, it struck me that that was exactly what had happened on 2 December 1917 at Cambrai, but with roles reversed. We had looked into a mirror.

My Last Assault

On 30 July 1918, we moved into rest quarters in Sauchy-Léstrée, a delightful spot in the Artois, surrounded by water. A few days later, we marched further back to Escaudœuvres, a quiet working-class suburb, cast out, as it were, by the rather fancier Cambrai.

I occupied the best bedroom of a Northern French working-class family, on the Rue-des-Bouchers. The usual massive bed was the principal item of furniture, a hearth with red and blue glass vases on the mantelpiece, a round table, chairs, and a few colour prints on the walls: such things as 'vive la classe' and 'souvenir de première communion'. A few postcards completed the décor. The view out of the window was of a graveyard.

The bright full-moon nights favoured the visitations of enemy aircraft, which gave us an appreciation of the growing superiority they enjoyed in terms of weaponry. Every night, several squadrons of bombers floated up and dropped bombs of extraordinary destructiveness on Cambrai and its suburbs. What bothered me throughout was less the mosquito-like drone of the engines and the clumps of echoing explosions than the timorous scuttling downstairs of my hosts. The day before my arrival, admittedly, a bomb had gone off just outside the window, which had hurled the master of the house, who had been sleeping in my bed, clear across the room, broken off one bedpost, and riddled the walls. It was, perversely, this circumstance that gave me a feeling of security, because I did at least partly subscribe to the old warrior's superstition that the safest place to be is in a new crater.

After one day of rest, the old training regimen set in again. Drill, lessons, roll-calls, discussions and inspections filled a great part of the day. We took up an entire morning agreeing on a verdict in a court of honour. For a while we were given nothing to eat in the evenings except cucumbers, which the men dubbed 'vegetarian sausages'.

Most of all, I was busy with the training of a small shock troop, since I had come to understand in the course of the last few engagements that there was an increasing rearrangement of our fighting strength in progress. To make an actual breach or advance, there was now only a very limited number of men on whom one might rely, who had developed into a particularly resilient body of fighters, whereas the bulk of the men were at best fit to lend support. Given these circumstances, it might be better to be at the head of a small and determined group than the commander of an uncertain company.

I spent my free time reading, swimming, shooting and riding. Some afternoons, I would fire over a hundred bullets in target-practice at tin cans and bottles. When I rode out, I would come upon propaganda leaflets which the enemy had taken to dropping in ever greater numbers as morale bombs. They were made up of political and military whisperings, and glowing accounts of the wonderful life to be had in British prisoner-of-war camps. 'And just remember,' one of them said, 'it's not that hard to lose your way at night, on your way back from getting food, or a digging detail!' Another reproduced the text of Schiller's poem, 'Free Britannia'. These leaflets were sent up on hot-air balloons, and were carried by favourable winds across the lines; they were bundled up with thread, and set adrift by a timed fuse after floating for a certain period of time. A reward of thirty pfennigs apiece showed that the high command did not underestimate the threat they posed. The costs were levied on the population of the occupied territory.

One afternoon, I got on a bicycle and pedalled into Cambrai. The dear old place was in a dire state. The shops and cafés were closed down; the streets seemed dead, in spite of the field-grey waves that kept washing through them. I found M. and Mme Plancot, who had entertained me so kindly a year ago, delighted to see me again. They told me that things in the town had got worse in every respect. Most of all, they complained about the frequent air attacks, which compelled them to rush up and down stairs, often several times a night, arguing whether it was better to be killed outright by a bomb in their first basement, or buried alive in the second. I felt very sorry for these old people with their worried expressions. A few weeks later, when the guns began to speak, they were finally forced to leave the house they had spent their lives in.

At eleven o'clock on 23 August, I had just dropped off to sleep when I was woken by loud knocking on the door. An orderly had come with marching orders. All day, the rolling and stamping of unusually heavy artillery fire had blown across from the front, and had reminded us on the exercise grounds, over our lunch and over games of cards, not to be too hopeful as far as the further duration of this rest period was concerned. We had coined an onomatopoeic front-line expression for this distant sound of cannons: 'It's whumping.'

We hurriedly got packed up and were on the road to Cambrai during a cloudburst. We arrived at our destination of Marquion a little before five in the morning. The company was placed in a large yard enclosed by the ruins of farm outbuildings, and told to take shelter wherever we could. With my one company officer, Lieutenant Schrader, I crept into a little brick building, which as its acrid aroma indicated, must have served as a goat-shed in peacetime, though our immediate predecessors were several large rats.

In the afternoon there was an officers' meeting, at which we were told that the following night we were to take up a position of readiness to the right of the main Cambrai–Bapaume road, not far from Beugny. We were warned of the danger from a new breed of rapid, agile tanks.

I paraded my company in battle order in a small apple orchard. Standing under an apple tree, I addressed a few words to the men, who were drawn up in front of me in a horseshoe arrangement. They looked serious and manly. There wasn't much to say. In the course of the last few days, and with a kind of sweepingness that is only to be explained by the fact that an army is not only men under arms, but also men fused with a sense of a common purpose, probably every one of them had come to understand that we were on our uppers. With every attack, the enemy came forward with more powerful means; his blows were swifter and more devastating. Everyone knew we could no longer win. But we would stand firm.

On a table improvised from a wheelbarrow and a door, Schrader and I ate our supper and shared a bottle of wine in the open. Then we bedded down in our goat-shed until two in the morning, when the sentry announced that the trucks were waiting in the market-place.

In spectral light, we clattered through the war-torn country of last year's Cambrai battles, wending our way through eerily devastated villages, along roads lined with walls of rubble. Just before Beugny, we were unloaded and led to our position. The battalion occupied a hollow on the Beugny–Vaux road. In the morning, an orderly brought instructions for the company to advance to the Frémicourt–Vaux road. This pattern of small advances afforded me the certainty that we were in for some action before nightfall.

I led my three platoons strung out in file across the terrain, with circling aeroplanes bombing and strafing overhead. When we reached our objective, we dispersed into shell-holes and dug-outs, as occasional shells came lobbing over the road.

I felt so bad that day that I lay down in a little piece of trench and fell asleep right away. When I woke up, I read a few pages of *Tristram Shandy*, which I had with me in my map case, and so, apathetically, like an invalid, I spent the sunny afternoon.

At six-fifteen, a dispatch-rider summoned the company commanders to Captain von Weyhe.

'I have some serious news for you. We are going on the offensive. After half an hour's artillery preparation, the battalion will advance at seven o'clock tonight from the western edge of Favreuil, and storm the enemy lines. You are to march on the church tower at Sapignies.'

After a little further discussion, and handshakes all round, we raced back to our companies, as the bombardment was to start in barely ten minutes' time, and we still had quite a stretch ahead of us. I informed my platoon commanders, and had the men fall in.

'By sections in single file twenty yards apart. Direction half-left, treetops of Favreuil!'

Testimony to the good morale we still enjoyed was that I had to nominate the man to stay behind to inform the cookers where to go. No one volunteered.

I marched along in the van with my company staff and Sergeant-Major Reinicke, who knew the area very well. Our artillery fire was landing behind hedges and ruins. It sounded more like furious yapping than anything seriously destructive. Behind us, I saw my sections advancing in perfect order. Alongside them, shots from aeroplanes sent up puffs of dust, bullets, empty shells and driving bands from shrapnels whizzed with fiendish hissing in between the files of the thin human line. Away on the right lay Beugnâtre, heavily attacked, from where jagged lumps of iron buzzed across and stamped themselves on the clayey soil.

The march got a little more uncomfortable still once we were over the Beugnâtre–Bapaume road. All of a sudden, a spate of high-explosive shells landed in front of, behind and in the midst of us. We scattered aside, and hurled ourselves into craters. I landed with my knee on something a frightened predecessor had left behind, and had my batman scrape off the worst of it with a knife.

Around the edge of Favreuil, the clouds from numerous shell-bursts congregated, and up and down in between them in rapid alternation went the geysers of soil. To find a position for the company, I went on ahead to the first ruins, and then with my cane gave a signal to follow.

The village was fringed with badly shelled huts, behind which parts of the 1st and 2nd Battalions gradually came together. During the last part of the march, a machine-gun had taken its toll. I watched from my vantage-point the little string of puffs of dust, in which one or other of the new arrivals would sometimes find himself caught as in a net. Among others, Vice-Sergeant-Major Balg of my company got a bullet through the leg.

A figure in brown corduroy strode with equanimity across this fire-swept piece of terrain, and shook me by the hand. Kius and Boje, Captain Junker and Schaper, Schrader, Schläger, Heins, Findeisen, Höhlemann and Hoppenrath stood behind a hedge raked with lead and iron and talked through the attack. On many a day of wrath we had fought on one and the same battlefield, and today once more the sun, now low in the Western sky, was to gild the blood of all or nearly all.

Elements of the 1st Battalion moved into the castle grounds. Of the 2nd, only my company and the 5th had got through the flaming curtain unscathed, or nearly so. We made our way forward through craters and debris to a sunken road on the western edge of the village. On the way I picked up a steel helmet off the floor and put it on – something I only ever did in very dicey situations. To my amazement, Favreuil seemed to be completely dead. It appeared as though the defensive line had been abandoned, because the ruins had the oddly tense feeling of a place that is unoccupied, and that spurs the eye to utmost vigilance.

Captain von Weyhe – who, though we didn't know this at the time, was lying all alone and badly hurt in a shell-hole in the village – had ordered the 5th and 8th Companies to form the first attacking line, the 6th the second, and the 7th the third. As there was no sign of the 6th or 8th anywhere yet, I decided to go on the attack without worrying too much about the plan of battle.

By now it was seven o'clock. I saw, against a backdrop of ruined houses and tree stumps, a line of men advancing across the field under moderate rifle fire. It must be the 5th.

I drew up my men in the sunken road, and gave orders to advance in two waves. 'Hundred yards apart. I myself shall be between the first wave and the second.'

It was our last storm. How many times over the last few years we had advanced into the setting sun in a similar frame of mind! Les Eparges, Guillemont, St-Pierre-Vaast, Langemarck, Passchendaele, Mœuvres, Vraucourt, Mory! Another gory carnival beckoned.

We left the sunken road as if it had been the exercise ground, except for the fact that 'I myself', as I had expressed it just now, suddenly found myself walking alongside Lieutenant Schrader on open ground way ahead.

I felt a little better, but there were still butterflies. Haller told me later, as he said goodbye to me before leaving for South America, that the man next to him had said: 'You know something, I don't think our lieutenant is going to come out of this show alive!' That strange man, whose wild and destructive spirit I so loved, told me things on that occasion which made me realize that the simple soldier weighs the heart of his commanding officer as in a goldsmith's scales. I felt pretty weary, and I had thought all along that this attack was a mistake. Even so, this is the one I most often recall. It didn't have the mighty impetus of the Great

Battle, its bubbling exuberance; on the other hand, I had a very impartial feeling, as if I were able to view myself through binoculars. For the first time in the entire war, I heard the hissing of individual bullets, as if they were whistling past some target. The landscape was utterly pellucid.

Isolated rifle shots rang out in front of us; perhaps the village walls in the background kept us from being too clearly seen. With my cane in my left hand, and my pistol in my right, I tramped on ahead, not quite realizing I was leaving the line of the 5th Company behind me and to my right. As I marched, I noticed that my Iron Cross had become detached and fallen on the ground somewhere. Schrader, my servant and I started looking for it, even though concealed snipers were shooting at us. At last, Schrader picked it up out of a tuft of grass, and I pinned it back on.

We were coming downhill. Indistinct figures moved against a background of red-brown clay. A machine-gun spat out its gouts of bullets. The feeling of hopelessness increased. Even so, we broke into a run, while the gunners were finding their range.

We jumped over several snipers' nests and hurriedly excavated trenches. In mid-jump over a slightly better-made trench, I felt a piercing jolt in the chest – as though I had been hit like a game-bird. With a sharp cry that seemed to cost me all the air I had, I spun on my axis and crashed to the ground.

It had got me at last. At the same time as feeling I had been hit, I felt the bullet taking away my life. I had felt Death's hand once before, on the road at Mory – but this time his grip was firmer and more determined. As I came down heavily on the bottom of the trench, I was convinced it was all over. Strangely, that moment is one of very few in my life of which I am able to say they were utterly happy. I understood, as in a flash of lightning, the true inner purpose and form of my life. I felt surprise and disbelief that it was to end there and then, but this surprise had something untroubled and almost merry about it. Then I heard the firing grow less, as if I were a stone sinking under the surface of some turbulent water. Where I was going, there was neither war nor enmity.

We Fight Our Way Through

Often enough I have seen wounded men dreaming in a world of their own, taking no further part in the noise of battle, the summit of human passions all around them; and I may say I know something of how they must have felt.

The time I lay completely unconscious can't have been that long in terms of chronometry – it probably corresponded to the time it took our first wave to reach the line where I fell. I awoke with a feeling of distress, jammed in between narrow clay walls, while the call: 'Stretcher-bearers! The company commander's been hurt!' slipped along a cowering line of men.

An older man from another company bent over me with a kindly expression, undid my belt and opened my tunic. He saw two round bloody stains – one in the right of my chest, the other in my back. I felt as though I were nailed to the earth, and the burning air of the narrow trench bathed me in tormenting sweat. My kindly helper gave me air by fanning me with my map case. I struggled to breathe, and hoped for darkness to fall soon.

Suddenly a fire-storm broke loose from the direction of Sapignies. No question, this smooth rumbling, this incessant roaring and stamping signified more than merely the turning back of our ill-conceived little attack. Over me I saw the granite face of Lieutenant Schrader under his steel helmet, loading and firing like a machine. There was a conversation between us that was a little like the tower scene in *St Joan*. Albeit, I didn't feel amused, because I had the clear sense I was done for.

Schrader rarely had time to toss me a few words, because I didn't really figure any more. Feeling my own feebleness, I tried to glean from his expression how things stood for us up there. It appeared that the attackers were gaining ground, because I heard him call out more frequently and with greater alarm to his neighbours, pointing out targets that must be very close at hand.

Suddenly, as when a dam breaks under the pressure of flood water, the cry went up: 'They've broken through on the left! They're round the back of us!' going from mouth to mouth. At that terrible instant, I felt my life force beginning to glimmer again like a spark. I was able to push two fingers into a mouse- or mole-hole level with my arm. Slowly I pulled myself up, while the blood that was bogging my lungs trickled out of my wounds. As it drained away, I felt relief. With bare head and open tunic, I stared out at the battle.

A line of men with packs plunged straight ahead through whitish swathes of smoke. A few stopped and lay where they fell, others performed somersets like rabbits do. A hundred yards in front of us, the last of them were drawn into the cratered landscape. They must have belonged to a very new outfit that hadn't been tested under fire, because they showed the courage of inexperience.

Four tanks crawled over a ridge, as though pulled along on a string. In a matter of minutes, the artillery had smashed them to the ground. One broke in half, like a child's toy car. On the right, the valiant cadet Mohrmann collapsed with a death shout. He was as brave as a young lion; I had seen that at Cambrai already. He was felled by a bullet square in the middle of his forehead, better aimed than the one that he had once bandaged up for me.

The affair didn't seem to be irrevocably lost. I whispered to Corporal Wilsky to creep a little left, and enfilade the gap in the line with his machine-gun. He came back straight away and reported that twenty yards beyond everyone had surrendered. That was part of another regiment. So far I had been clutching a tuft of grass with my left hand like a steering column. Now I succeeded in turning round, and a strange sight met my eyes. The British had begun to penetrate sectors of the line to the left of us, and were sweeping them with fixed bayonets. Before I could grasp the proximity of the danger, I was distracted by another, more startling development: at our backs were other attackers, coming towards us, escorting prisoners with their hands raised! It seemed that the enemy must have broken into the abandoned village only moments after we had left it to make our attack. At that instant, they tightened the noose round our necks; we had completely lost contact.

The scene was getting more and more animated. A ring of British and Germans surrounded us and called on us to drop our weapons. It was pandemonium, as on a sinking ship. In my feeble voice, I called upon the men near me to fight on. They shot at friend and foe. A ring of silent or yelling bodies circled our little band. To the left of me, two colossal British soldiers plunged their bayonets into a piece of trench, from where I could see beseeching hands thrust out.

Among us, too, there were now loud yells: 'It's no use! Put your guns down! Don't shoot, comrades!'

I looked at the two officers who were standing in the trench with me. They smiled back, shrugged, and dropped their belts on the ground.

There was only the choice between captivity and a bullet. I crept out of the trench, and reeled towards Favreuil. It was as in a bad dream, where you can't pick your feet off the floor. The only thing in my favour was perhaps the utter confusion, in which some were already exchanging cigarettes, while others were still butchering each other. Two Englishmen, who were leading back a troop of prisoners from the 99th, confronted me. I aimed my pistol at the nearer of the two, and pulled the trigger. The other blazed his rifle at me and missed. My hurried movements pushed the blood from my lungs in bright spurts. I could breathe more easily, and started running along the trench. Behind a traverse crouched Lieutenant Schläger in the middle of a group of blazing rifles. They fell in with me. A few British, who were making their way over the field, stopped, set down a Lewis gun on the ground, and fired at us. Except for Schläger and me and a couple of others, everyone went down. Schläger, who was extremely shortsighted, told me later that all he had been able to see was my map case flying up and down. That was his signal. The loss of blood gave me the lightness and airiness of intoxication, the only thing that worried me was that I might break down too soon.

Finally, we reached a semi-circular earthworks to the right of Favreuil, from where half a dozen heavy machine-guns were spitting lead at friend and foe alike. Either the noose hadn't been completely drawn tight, or else this was one last pocket of resistance; we had been lucky to find it. Enemy bullets shattered on sandbags, officers yelled, excited men leaped here and there. A medical officer from the 6th Company ripped my tunic off, and told me to lie down immediately, otherwise I might bleed to death in a matter of minutes.

I was rolled in a tarpaulin and dragged to the entrance of Favreuil, accompanied by some of my soldiers, and some from the 6th. The village was already heaving with British, so it was inevitable that we soon came under fire from very short range. The medical officer of the 6th, who was holding the back end of my tarpaulin, went down, shot in the head; I fell with him.

The little group had thrown themselves flat on the ground, and, lashed by bullets, were trying to creep to the nearest dip in the ground.

I stayed behind on the field, bundled up in my tarpaulin, almost apathetically waiting for the shot that would put an end to this Odyssey.

But even in my hopeless plight I was not forsaken; my companions were keeping an eye on me, and soon fresh efforts were made to rescue me. At my ear I heard the voice of Corporal Hengstmann, a tall blond Lower Saxon: 'I'll take you on my back, sir, either we'll get through or we won't!'

Unfortunately, we didn't get through; there were too many rifles waiting at the edge of the village. Hengstmann started running, while I wrapped my arms around his neck. Straight away they started banging away, as if it were a prize-shoot at a funfair. After a few bounds, a soft metallic buzz indicated that Hengstmann had stopped one. He collapsed gently under me, making no sound, but I could feel that Death had claimed him even before we touched the ground. I freed myself from his arms, which were still securing me, and saw that a bullet had drilled through his steel helmet and his temple. The brave fellow was the son of a teacher in Letter near Hanover. As soon as I was able to walk, I called on his parents, and gave them my report on their son.

This discouraging example didn't deter the next volunteer from making a bid to rescue me. This was Sergeant Strichalsky of the Medical Corps. He put me on his shoulders, and, while a second shower of bullets whistled around us, he carried me safely to the shelter of a little hump of ground.

It was getting dark. My comrades took the tarpaulin off a body and carried me across a deserted stretch of ground, under the jagged flash of ordnance, near or far. I got to know what a terrible thing it is to have to struggle for breath. Smoke from a cigarette that someone ten steps ahead of me was smoking almost choked me.

At last we got to a dressing-station, where my friend Dr Key was in charge. He mixed me some delicious lemonade, and gave me a morphine injection that put me to revivifying sleep.

The wild drive to the hospital the next day was the last difficult challenge to my powers of survival. Then I was in the hands of the sisters, and was able to carry on reading *Tristram Shandy* from where I had had to put it down for the order to attack.

Friendly solicitude got me safely through a period of setbacks – something that seems to be typical of lung shots. Men and officers from the division came to visit. Those who had taken part in the storm at Sapignies, admittedly, were no more, or else, like Kius, they were in British captivity. With the first shells landing in Cambrai as the enemy slowly gained the upper hand, M. and Mme Plancot sent me a kind letter, a tin of condensed milk they could ill afford to spare, and the only melon their garden had produced. There were bitter times ahead for them. My last batman was in the tradition established by his many predecessors; he stopped with me, even though he wasn't entitled to hospital rations, and had to go begging down in the kitchen.

During the endless hours flat on your back, you try to distract yourself to pass the time; once, I reckoned up my wounds. Leaving out trifles such as ricochets and grazes, I was hit at least fourteen times, these being five bullets, two shell splinters, one shrapnel ball, four hand-grenade splinters and two bullet splinters, which, with entry and exit wounds, left me an even twenty scars. In the course of this war, where so much of the firing was done blindly into empty space, I still managed to get myself targeted no fewer than eleven times. I felt every justification, therefore, in donning the gold wound-stripes, which arrived for me one day.

A fortnight later, I was lying on the rumbling bed of a hospital train. The German landscape was already bathed in the lustre of early autumn. I was fortunate enough to be taken off the train at Hanover, and was put up in the Clementine infirmary. Among the visitors who soon arrived, I was particularly glad to see my brother; he had continued to grow since his wounding, although his right side, which was where he was hurt, hadn't.

I shared my room with a young fighter pilot from Richthofen's squadron, a man named Wenzel, one of the tall and fearless types our nation still produces. He lived up to the motto of his squadron, 'Hard – and crazy with it!' and had already brought down a dozen opponents in single combat, although the last had splintered his upper arm with a bullet first.

The first time I went out, I went with him, my brother, and a few comrades who were awaiting their transport, to the rooms of the old Hanoverian Gibraltar Regiment. Since our war-worthiness was being put into question, we felt the urgent need to prove ourselves by vaulting an enormous armchair. We didn't do too well; Wenzel broke his arm all over again, and the following day I was back in bed with a temperature of forty – yes, my chart even threatened the red line beyond which the doctors are powerless to help. At such high temperatures, you lose your sense of time; while the sisters were fighting for my life, I was in those fever dreams that are often very amusing.

On one of those days, it was 22 September 1918, I received the following telegram from General von Busse:

'His Majesty the Kaiser has bestowed on you the order *pour le Mérite*. In the name of the whole division, I congratulate you.'